What Practitioners are Saying about this Book

This book unpacks the tools for practicing peace in crystal form. Theory and practice effectively interweave through stories of the years of community work. I am pleased to have a book that virtually instructs and grounds me through these stories. I have followed the instructions and see it work! Indeed, peace building takes constancy in practice. I have seen this in my life and in many of the scenes in the book, as I accompanied Nadine on several of her visits in Indonesia. ~ **ALMA APARECE**, human rights and environmental attorney and Dean of Planning, Bohol University, **Tagbilaran City, Philippines**

This training reconnects us with our own inherent goodness. We create the space to find and strengthen the unlimited intelligence of our hearts in this good work with these good humans. ~ **MEGAN CALLAHAN**, Founder, Parkside Yoga, Buffalo, **New York, USA**

Creating Cultures of Peace engages us with insightful and compassionate analysis, stories, activities and practices to overcome the rigidity of reactive and isolating habits; engage our consciences with increased awareness, presence and empathy; expand our vocabulary of emotions and abilities to release them; and invite the regenerative power of play. The human heart hungers for this transformation to love. Let us feast ~ **LAURIE CHILDERS**, former National Council Chair, Fellowship of Reconciliation-USA, artist and peace activist, Corvallis, **Oregon, USA**

As cycles of oppression, injustice, trauma and environmental disaster appear to be increasing in the world today rather than abating, this book is very timely. Balance in our lives, societies and our eco-systems needs to be restored with urgency if we are to avoid irreparable damage and even extinction. *Creating Cultures of Peace* draws upon decades of experience from the peace movement, faith communities and the author's own personal transformation to provide clear steps and strategies to bring transformational power into situations of violence, enabling peaceful change. Developing and utilising these clear and practical skills to overcome trauma and violence creates room within our hearts for forgiveness, replacing severity and harshness with kindness and compassion. Let this book serve as a guide and multiplier to enable many more of us to successfully embody the path of love and conscience. ~ **CHRIS HUNTER,** Programmes Coordinator, Peacebuilding UK, **Bude, United Kingdom**

This book brings a message of crucial importance: Peace is possible! Violence is not inherent to human nature! We each need to contribute to forming a peaceful global society. Peace must no longer refer to silence achieved through oppression and violence. True peace only flows from mutually enriching dialogue among citizens who respect each other as equal in dignity, who practice loving unity in enriching diversity, and who jointly care for all life on our home planet. Nadine's book will be an indispensable guiding light for everyone embarking on this path. ~ **EVELIN LINDNER**, Medical Doctor, Psychologist, PhD in Medicine, PhD in Psychology, founding President Human Dignity and Humiliation Studies, **Oslo, Norway**

Meeting Nadine and doing this workshop truly changed my life. It transformed my daily life as well as my teaching. I hope many will read and use it as a tool for creating a better, more peaceful life. ~ **TERESE LONGVA,** artist and art teacher, **Longva, Norway**

Creating Cultures of Peace provides a guidebook for facilitating local action that can have broad and powerful implications. As Hoover puts it, 'cultures of peace require the hard work of public and vigilant resistance to the dynamics of oppression' (234). Speaking up and taking action, bearing witness publicly against oppression, taxes us emotionally, physically, socially, economically, etc. Oppression causes us to treat one another solely as either oppressed or oppressor, polarizing and polluting the relational capacities necessary for liberation. In response, Hoover compassionately outlines step by step relational strategies for fostering individual and cultural habits that help to heal the harms done by oppression. Through a focus on love, conscience, and disparities of power, Hoover guides us to a key step in liberatory organizing for peace: the work to cease looking for the sources of oppression in one another and, instead, learning to cultivate relationships from which we have power to abolish oppressive forces. ~ **CHRISTIAN MATHEIS**, Ph.D., faculty in Justice and Policy Studies at Guilford College, Greensboro, **North Carolina, USA**

I began this training in Indonesia in 2005. It reconnected us to our ability to take right actions in our lives based on our conscience and reconnected our souls to our sense of value and capacity. This training emboldened my family and friends to start a peace movement in Pati. Thank you, Nadine for your dedicated efforts for peaceful society on the earth and willingness to document the work for us to use. ~ **PETRUS**, social activist and founder of Peace Place school and training center, Pati, **Central Java, Indonesia**

This training gave the courage and perspective to live ruthlessly aligned with integrity and peace. I notice the life and beauty inside everyone and everything, stay in my core self, and when listening, expect to be changed. The truth has its own power, let it go through us, but no matter how much we know, the first step is to love. ~ **ROSIE REMMERSWAAL**, Filmmaker, student of Te Reo Māori and peace activist, **Auckland, Aotearoa/New Zealand**

These activities create a safe atmosphere of trust and acceptance through structured interactions forming a solid base and resource for any group to do traumatic or stressful work without specialists. The appeal to the core self and focus on integrity supports self-reflection and stabilization. Participants explore topics to prevent trauma, violence and oppression ourselves. The Ukraine needs this, especially now, because we are in war with a huge number of wounded and displaced people. Teenagers particularly need opportunities to analyze and express themselves without violence. They are sensitive and want justice. These activities help them express themselves while staying peaceful inside. I am grateful to Nadine for such a gift, the tools and the good push to be more active peacemakers. ~ **ALLA SOROKA,** Program Manager, This Child Here, **Odessa, Ukraine**

Creating Cultures of Peace understands that each and every being is valuable, capable, and worthy. It asks questions about why we as humans make enemies and rely on systems that oppress, kill and incarcerate people as political strategy. The material offers tools to personally address the ways individual actions impact the world around us, and how we can collectively work towards the future we want to see. This material has laid the foundation for how I work to create my life, supported me in finding the value in every person I meet, and held me accountable for honoring the global community I am a part of. ~ **AUTUMN STAR,** Youth Advocate, Oasis Youth Center, **WA, USA**

This book holds a bounty of wisdom that will resonate deeply with people from every faith tradition, as well as the unaffiliated. The tools for building peace in one's heart, home, neighborhood, city and nation are here waiting to be shared that we might build a peaceful world together. Anyone who has taken a training with Nadine will be delighted to find every gem she shared throughout the time together, and so much more. For those who haven't had that blessing, here is your opportunity to begin the journey. ~ **JAYE STARR,** Muslim Chaplain, Ann Arbor **Michigan, USA**

Creating
Cultures of Peace

A MOVEMENT OF
LOVE AND CONSCIENCE

Nadine Clare Hoover

To love those called enemies and become friends,
so begins the work of peace.

Permissions:
- "A Very Old, New Story" (2010), printed by permission of Dean Hoover.
- "Dance upon This Earth," Marie and Sheila Burns (Philo, 1997) used by permission of the Burns Sisters Music.
- "If I Had a Hammer," Lee Hays and Pete Seeger (Ludlow Music, Inc., 1949) used by permission of TRO Inc., 266 W 37th St. # 1700, NY, NY 10018.
- "Step by Step," Waldemar Hille and Pete Seeger (Folkways Records, 1964) archived at the Smithsonian Center for Folklife and Cultural Heritage.
- "Two Wolves: A Cherokee Legend" (www.firstpeople.us, 2013) used by permission of First People, a child-friendly website about Native Americans and members of the First Nations.
- "Pledge of Nonviolence" (Metta Center, 2013) abbreviated and used by permission of Metta Center, mettacenter.org.
- "Vow of Wealth" (2009) used by permission of Jean-François Noubel.

Hoover, Nadine
        Creating cultures of peace: A movement of love and conscience
ISBN 978-0-9828492-2-4
1. Peace Studies GTJ
2. Development Studies GTF
3. Learned Societies GTN
4. Social Interaction JFFP

Cover Design: Amanda Micek
Technical Support: Devin Henry

Creating Cultures of Peace

A MOVEMENT OF LOVE AND CONSCIENCE

Nadine Clare Hoover

To love those called enemies and become friends,
so begins the work of peace.

Dedicated to:

Gay Howard

*She saw the world
and loved the world.
She saw me and loved me.
She called out the best in the world and in me.*

I am eternally grateful for her grace and attention.

Table of Contents

Acknowledgements   7

Foreword   9

Preface   13

Who Will Find This Book Useful?   17

Introduction   23

Part I: GET STARTED
Orienting Ourselves in Community

1. Preserve the Peace Intrinsic in Life   33

    Experience Love and Conscience Inwardly   34

    Commit to Transforming Private and Public Life 40

2. Create a Context for Peaceful Society   47

    Organize Supportive Community   49

    Establish a Reliable Foundation   52

    Introduce a Transformative Culture   57

3. Invest in Principled Friendships   63

    Treat Everyone as a Friend   64

    Adhere to Agreements to Practice   72

    "I'm Gonna Dance"   80

Part II: LOVE LIFE
Living Peaceful Private Lives

4. Love Life, Oneself and Others   85

    Talk Openly about Violence   88

    Rely on Life's Transforming Power   95

    Commit to Practicing Peace   101

5. Visit with Oneself   **109**

Care for and Get to Know Oneself   109

Meet Regularly with Companions   113

Value the Exchange of Attention   118

6. Practice Peace in Daily Life   **121**

Affirm the Good in Oneself and Others   121

Listen and Speak with Empathy   123

Appreciate Cooperation and Noncooperation   135

7. Tend to Emotional Well-being   **141**

Discharge Distress Physically   143

Build Resilience to Emotional Trauma   148

Reintegrate the Parts of One's Life   155

8. Learn through Play   **161**

Play to Recover from Violence   164

Organize Play for Adults and Children   167

Play to Invest in Development and Justice   177

"Be Like a Bird"   181

Part III: ACT ON CONSCIENCE
Living Peaceful Public Lives

9. Be Aware and Available   **185**

Become Confident   186

Discover Conviction   190

Transform Private and Public Life   192

10. Visit with Others   **199**

Live with Integrity in Community   201

Stay Open to Change   203

Respect the Ecology of Practices   205

11. Act in Community   **207**

Experiment with Conscience   211

Experience the Liberty of Conscience   218

Exercise Sovereignty as a Natural People   221

12. Liberate from Oppression   **225**

Overcome Prejudice with Equality   227

Illuminate the Dynamics of Oppression   231

Overcome Privilege with Simplicity   235

Bear Witness Publicly   239

13. Practice Discernment   **243**

Form Collective Stories   246

Test Discernment   250

Record Community Discernment   257

Attend to Individuals, Communities, and Society   263

"Step by Step"   265

Part IV: CREATE CULTURE
Engaging Peaceful Society

14. Create Cultures of Peace   **269**

Speak Up for Peace   270

Care for and Get to Know Strangers   273

Invest in Living Wealth   276

Express Love and Conscience   281

"If I Had a Hammer"   286

15. Step Up   **289**

Historic Steps   290

Simple Steps   294

Appendices

I. Volunteer Opportunities   298

II. Glossary   299

III. Learning Activities   305

IV. Cooperative Games   307

V. Personal Practices and Group Activities   315

VI. References   318

VII. Quotes   323

VIII. About the Author   325

Displays

Essential Structures for a Community of Practice   50

Session Agenda   53

Introductory Empowerment Training   56

Expectations for a Culture of Peace   58

Road Map for a Culture of Peace   60

Agreements to Practice   68

Good Companions   90

Emotional Discharge   91

Storytelling Protocol   93

Guides to Transforming Power   96

Transforming Power Mandala   97

Journal Topics   102

Self-Care: Zone of Adaptation   111

Companion Group Questions   115

Conversational Questions   125

I-Message   130

Broken Squares   135

Subjective Units of Distress (SUD) Scale   149

Definitions of Trauma   149

Five Sentences   150

Speak Up   154

River of Life   156

Dissociative Parts as Protectors   159

Hundred Languages of Play   163

Play Stations   169

Agreements for Play   170

Characteristics   171

Stay Aware: Order Daily Life   185

Gathering for Silence   188

Gathering for Sharing   189

Available and Prepared   194

Allow Conscience: Act on Conscience   212

Inward Dynamics of Oppression   232-233

Discernment: Things to Notice   247

Guides to Discernment   248

Tests of Discernment   249

Gathering for Discernment   259

A New Old Story of One Glass of Water   277

Vow of Wealth   280

Call on Each Other: Cultivate Expression   282

Pledge of Love and Conscience   295

Pledge of Nonviolence   296

~

I expect to pass through this world but once;

any good thing therefore I can do,

or any kindness that I can show

to any fellow creature, let me do it now;

let me not defer or neglect it,

for I shall not pass this way again.

~ Stephen Grellet, Quaker c. 1800

~

Acknowledgements

A rural community of Quaker farmers and professors in western New York State raised me, guided with the ideas and practices described in this book. They lived peaceful, loving, conscientious lives for the joy of it, without ulterior motives. They did not talk of how they did it. It simply felt like the most natural thing in the world.

They organized their lives around their experience of the Living Spirit. Then they focused on expressing that inward experience outwardly in family life, work endeavors, community service and civic involvement. From a young age I remember these adults visiting Attica Prison, migrant work camps, university laboratories and offices of Congress. In fact, they simplified their lives so that they may have full relationships with everything around them. They were available to whatever arose in the community or the world. They used what they needed, shared the rest, settled their debts and disputes promptly and cared for the young, the sick and the elderly. The *Swarthmore College Bulletin* noted (1973): "Quakerism, as a way of life, emphasizes hard work, simple living, and generous giving; personal integrity, social justice, and the peaceful settlement of disputes." I experienced their example as a joyful, connected, secure and generous life.

This book took shape through decades of generous attention from Vicky Cooley, Pamela Haines and Gay Howard. In addition, Chuck Esser and Diantha Horton offered their unwavering faith in me and support to this work over many years. Thank you to my father, Dean Hoover, for treating life as trustworthy, and to my mother, Sharon Hoover, for challenging prejudices with a deep commitment to justice.

Particular gratitude goes to Kim and Mark Tsocanos and the OBey Foundation. Without their generous, persistent faith and support I could not have dedicated the years required to develop this ecology of practices and articulate it in this book.

Thank you to Margot Silk Forrest for her direction; to Pamela Haines, Diane Leung, and Sarah Mandolang for their content review and feedback that made the text clearer, richer and more accessible; and to Trish Carn for proofreading. This book describes work "in progress," which is constantly developing and changing. Persisting errors are entirely my own.

And thank you to the dedicated people over my lifetime and before, who developed insights and tools for peace, civil rights, trauma healing, human development, social justice, overcoming oppression, the liberty of conscience and discerning a consensus of conscience. Specific gratitude goes to members of the Alternatives to Violence Project, Re-evaluation Counseling and the education and social justice movements.

Finally, thank you to the people in Aceh, North Sumatra, Central Java and West Papua who survived colonization, U.S.-backed militarism and corporate exploitation and still opened their hearts to strangers to work together towards a more peaceful, sustainable, prosperous society. Their forgiveness, generosity and humanity brought this work to fruition. I am grateful to the many people in the Philippines, Nepal, Korea, Palestine, Ukraine, Chechnya, England, Ireland, Norway, Australia, Aotearoa/ NZ, and the U.S. who take the time to work together to practice deep and lasting transformations to create cultures of peace, and thank you to Friends Peace Teams for making these connections possible. Together we can create a movement of love and conscience that allows peace to prosper and humanity to survive on this beautiful, glorious planet, Earth.

Foreword

by Sophia Roberts
A mother, performer and organizer,
Sophia supports people with developmental disabilities
to speak up for themselves individually and collectively.

How do we create peace?

After I had a child, I wanted a happy, healthy, peaceful home where she could thrive. I needed to reach out and not to become isolated in my parenting. We formed a childcare cooperative with shared hopes for connection, community and peaceful interaction. Grateful for one another, we set down a path to do something different from our parents, not to recreate the violence, addiction and dysfunction in our homes.

I lived with my partner and our toddler, as well as a friend, who was a single mom, and her toddler. We did our best to co-parent the children, but things went terribly. Patterns of trauma and dysfunctional communication made our home a miserable place to live. Despite our best intentions, we still recreated the violence and dysfunction we grew up with in our own homes and our childcare cooperative.

The closest thing to peace that I knew how to create was order, often achieved through violent means. I knew about fighting for peace, conscientious objection to war and organizing to protest the Gulf War. I knew nice talk and behavior that never addressed the inequities or violence I faced.

Every holiday we wished peace on earth for our friends and families. The desire for peace was visible everywhere, but the practice was not.

I reached out to my friend Fenna. For her 30th birthday, she hosted a presentation by her mother, Nadine Hoover. Fenna, who had facilitated nonviolence workshops since she was young, wanted a community to practice peace where we lived in Buffalo, New York. I did not fully grasp the depth and breadth of Conscience Studio's peace work, but I knew I needed help and others did too!

Conscience Studio did not just give me a set of words, it gave me a whole set of tools, practices and understandings to incorporate into the fabric of my everyday life at home and work. These workshops do best in communities where participants apply the practices and ideas to their unique settings and challenges.

We set up workshops to accommodate working parents. Instead of three- to ten-day intensives, we split sessions over months and held shorter three-hour sessions on Sunday afternoons with food and childcare. The Peace Education Fund of Buffalo awarded a grant to cover childcare for the first few months. A new world opened to us. We learned concepts and practices which had been developed through trial and error over decades of inquiry and practice. It has established a common understanding and language.

Visiting each other's homes for potluck meals and gatherings, we interwove changes into our intimate relationships. I saw Fenna interact with my child in peaceful ways exemplifying another way to parent. Practicing co-counseling and exchanging check-ins with attentive partners taught me that each of us has trauma to recover from before we are ready and available to peace.

From a birthday party, to a childcare co-op, to reaching out in our communities, the work rippled out. One parent in the Childcare Cooperative, Megan Callahan, opened a yoga studio. She committed to building a meaningful community through a holistic practice for peace both "on and off the yoga mat." She established Yoga Parkside in a church and offered space to Conscience Studio. Megan integrated these practices into her business influencing the lives of the workers and students through the culture of the studio.

Nadine's friend Jamuna, a facilitator from Nepal, visited the U.S. to host workshops in Hindi for Nepalese-speaking Bhutanese refugees resettled in Buffalo. They recognized the statues of Shiva and the Hindu gods in the Yoga Studio and felt at home. One participant, Ghana, began teaching yoga classes at Yoga Parkside and organizing Bhutanese community gatherings and children's language and culture classes to share knowledge and resources. With Jamuna interpreting, we visited one of the Bhutanese participants who turned out to be my neighbor. We developed new neighborly relationships. Congolese refugees heard and joined our workshops saying, "This is what I've been looking for in my life. This can save my life." The ripples continued to expand.

As we continued practicing, we connected with more people who wanted peace at home and in society. Chanda Ramirez-O'Donnell, a local activist for racial justice, introduced Conscience Studio to the Buffalo Anti-Racism Coalition (BARC). Michael Tritto, a board member, introduced it to the inter-faith grassroots social justice organization, VOICE Buffalo. VOICE addresses local issues such as prison reform, restorative justice practices with young people in city schools and political asylum for refugees. Conscience Studio draws together people from across social, economic and racial divides in the highly segregated city of Buffalo.

I incorporated the practices at work into the disability rights movement and the Self Advocacy Association of New York State. The insights and practices for liberation from oppression helped me with struggles in my life and in the movement. I went from burned out with the fighting at work to creating powerful, life-giving ways to work. As plant manager of Buffalo Recycling, Fenna gained more insight and skills to deal with conflicts that arose, and feels the strength of this diverse community around her.

Megan writes that the work of Conscience Studio "reconnects us with our own inherent goodness. We create the space to find and strengthen the unlimited intelligence of our hearts in this good work with these good humans."

How do we create peace?

We weave the wisdom and practice from lifetimes of people asking this question, with the ideas and practices in this book, into the stuff of our everyday lives. Then we learn and practice with one another and add our own discoveries.

The ideas and practices in this book drastically changed my home, work, relationships and life from the misery that led me to reach out for help to the hope and support I feel now.

Along the way, I came to believe peace is not only something worth fighting for, but also peace is truly possible and worth living.

∼

War is an unnecessary evil.

We know how to create cultures of peace.

∼

Preface

My daughter, Fenna Mandolang, booked a hall in Buffalo, New York, for her 30th birthday, August 2, 2012 and asked me to speak on "the way you think." I felt honored. What a blessing to be asked to share how I think. Her invitation was a gift as much for me as for herself. Afterwards, many of her friends remarked to her, "I understand you so much better now!"

Fenna holds perspectives and uses language differently from those around her. This makes communication difficult, both understanding others and being understood. She rarely has the luxury of listening and adding, "Oh yeah," or, "Me too." People who see things differently must invest time and attention to figuring out what others mean and helping others understand them. Otherwise, they must either conform or withdraw.

I invested months to organize "the way I think" into a presentation and years to turn that into a book. My intent has been to describe how to approach creating and preserving cultures of peace in the most unlikely places—from refugee to militant or professional communities.

I have worked with thousands of people, primarily in the U.S. and Asia, to recover from extreme violence and create peaceful, nonviolent communities. Over decades I saw them shift from despair, revenge and hatred to enthusiasm, confidence and genuine love for themselves and others. They even reached out to include people they considered enemies. Along the way, we identified tools that worked across diverse cultures, languages and religions. We witnessed astonishing transformations of violent, destructive communities into peaceful, productive ones.

Global cultures of peace rely on love and conscience as opposed to violence and war. We still face the challenges of law, order and protection. But war, the systematic, preemptive killing of people—children, adults and the elderly—as a political strategy to further our own interests does not create peaceful, healthy societies.

In 1975, men incarcerated in Greenhaven and Auburn prisons in New York State called on civil rights and peace activists. They asked for help to stem the violence within the prisons and their communities. The activists integrated the best activities from their nonviolence training with innovative, experiential, educational approaches of the time. Since they refused to allow prison staff to observe the workshops, the administration required they produce manuals. These manuals became known as the Alternatives to Violence Project workshops. Sadly, the manual did not include activities on civil disobedience and noncooperation because they were prohibited by the prisons.

Re-evaluation Counseling began in the 1950s among unemployed labor workers in Seattle to support one another during trying times. They developed effective tools for peer counseling. As those tools spread around the world, they united people to end racism and oppression. They mapped out how human beings internalize and reproduce cycles of oppression and how we can liberate ourselves from them.

In the 1980s, new literature on the causes and effects of trauma taught us how to recover from trauma and to increase our resilience to it. This research clarified the role of creative play in developing the minds of young children and adults. In fact, creative play reconstitutes adults' mental capacities eroded by violence and sustained stress. Playful interactions among adults and children play an essential role in preserving peaceful, nonviolent, healthy societies.

Just as human beings once had to understand germs and sanitation to survive in cities, we now need new knowledge to survive the growing pace of change. As we are bombarded by news and information, understanding power, trauma and play helps us live healthy lives. We are learning how to interrupt cycles of oppression, prejudice and privilege to live humane lives in accord with love and conscience. Organizing based on discerning a consensus of love and conscience promises to help us live ecologically sustainable lives on this fragile planet. New knowledge and tools exist to better equip us to create cultures of peace.

The pressures of social displacement, environmental devastation and war compel us either to insist on ethical public standards or to risk extinction. To apply this knowledge takes time. Still, to preserve a habitable planet we must, without hesitation. Cultures of peace include everyone and treat everyone with respect and dignity. As technology eases communication and travel, cultures dependent on enemy-making cannot survive.

In his book, *On Killing*, Dave Grossman (2001) reported that soldiers in World War II shot most of their bullets into the air or the ground, while only twenty percent were actually shot at someone. Afterward, the U.S. government invested in learning how to break the human conscience to increase "the efficiency of a bullet." This research led to sensory-deprivation torture, drive-by shooting of villagers[1] and other government-sponsored brutality.

Today we have the social, diplomatic and economic skills to resolve conflicts without violence. War has not achieved peace or democracy, but perpetuates an industry of wealth accumulation. The unjust and immoral use of economic oppression subverts everyone engaged in it, regardless of their intentions. Unnecessary harm to others, let alone harm for profits' sake, makes war immoral today. We need to hold our public officers accountable for treating every living thing with dignity and respect.

Wherever there is war, there are children. Killing and terrorizing innocent people creates generations of resentment and revenge. Today war threatens human survival on the planet. As Gar Smith (2017) argues in his seminal book, *The War and Environment Reader*, (a global anthology chronicling the environmental impacts of militarism), it is time to make war and preparations for war illegal and declare peace—with humanity and with nature.

This book offers practical guides to how to live in accord with love and conscience now and into the future. This book is licensed in the

---

1. *The US military learned that if they drove by "an enemy village" and shot people randomly, the territory became easier to control. Drive-by shootings began in the US after soldiers brought this training home with them from Vietnam.*

Creative Commons. We do not claim copyright. This allows you to use any of the contents as long as you attribute the source and agree to "share alike" in the Creative Commons. I chose this to encourage cultural evolution and creativity. So please send us feedback and publish your own insights and experiences for us to learn from you as well.

The Religious Society of Friends, the Quakers, received the Nobel Peace Prize in 1947 for "the silent assistance from the nameless to the nameless." I hope this book continues that tradition with you whom I may never meet. May life's transforming power open in ways you cannot yet imagine, bringing goodness, love, beauty and joy into our lives on this generous planet, Earth!

~

Love without truth deceives;
truth without love hurts.

Truth doesn't triumph,
truth guides and prospers.

Love doesn't win,
love persists and endures.

~

Who Will Find This Book Useful?

Citizen leaders developing peaceful homes, communities and societies will find an abundance of compelling ideas and tools in this book. Their sequence illuminates the operating dynamics of how to rely on life's transforming power, resist violence and create cultures of peace. Ideas should not be mistaken for the experience of them. To grasp their implications requires practice. So this book includes personal practices and group activities found essential for restoring and preserving peace.

Community leaders will find enough detail to apply the knowledge in private and public life as well as to adapt and innovate. While we seek to transform society, we do so by transforming ourselves.

So expect to experience dissonance between current perceptions or behaviors and new insights. Dissonance offers great opportunities for learning and change, but too much dissonance stimulates distress, overwhelming one's functioning and causing distraction, sleepiness, irritation, cynicism and more. When this occurs:

- Take a break but return to the reading. Love and conscience grow as you pay attention to them. So be observant, persistent and patient with yourself and your learning.

- Stay open to and trust reality. Notice what is regenerative and what is degenerative. Explore the source of your distraction, release and learn from it, then shift your attention back to the reading.

- Experiment with the ideas in your life. Test them by believing in and applying them. Ask yourself, "What if it were true?" Try the practices in daily life with confidence and curiosity to see what happens.

- Test the ideas with others. Read and practice with an existing or new group. Write in a journal. Express the ideas to others throughout your daily life. Discuss with friends.

We encourage you to try each practice and activity with a partner or a small group of four to six people. We practice peace the same way we practice any art, sport or musical instrument. So attend a Conscience Studio training or invite a team to offer a training in your community. Results come from practice and the invaluable guidance of a skilled practitioner.

Adapt the activities to suit you and your situation only after experiencing them. Give them a chance to change you before changing them. Then share your experiences, applications and adaptations.

Warning: Many of us, especially the most intelligent, gloss over or lose patience with the simplest elements. We focus on what we prefer and discount or ignore the rest. We revert to what we do best or fastest instead of trying something new. Habits empower but can obstruct learning and change, and so obstruct the power to implement new ideas.

These activities work as an interdependent ecology, not as a smorgasbord from which to pick the ones you prefer. The smallest acts may prove the most difficult in practice yet the most powerful in effect. They each demand a willingness to open and see anew.

- Slow down to respect simple ideas and practices.
- Make both tiny and huge changes for love and conscience' sake.
- Do what is needed, not just what comes readily, easily or fits well.
- Stay teachable. Let go of old ways and open to new possibilities.

We can transform our private and public lives when we welcome change as natural, a normal part of being alive.

Even as I write this advice, I realize how often I gloss over the simple elements. Because I *know* how to slow down, sometimes I do not think I have to *do* it! Busy writing this book or conducting training, I tell myself I will slow down later. I sometimes push for smarter and smarter responses and activities that give me a sense of competence. I miss the small or postpone the substantial. Then I remember. I know what to do *and* I actually have to *do* it! So I slow down—often. As easy as this advice sounds, it turns out to be more difficult in practice than I imagine. Ah, we seek that elusive balance between natural spontaneity and disciplined intentionality, yielding and self-control.

Capable, healthy adults learn self-control and restraint. We need our other side too: the inner fool, trickster or child. This allows us to open to the slow, simple, transforming truths gained through spirals of stopping, opening, releasing, receiving, experimenting, reflecting and expressing. Each part of this book introduces a vital area of practice, which together form an ecology of practice:

- *Part I. Get Started* with an orientation to prepare for this work.
- *Part II. Love Life* with practices for peaceful private lives.
- *Part III. Act on Conscience* with practices for peaceful public lives.
- *Part IV. Create Culture* with practices for peaceful societies.

I describe each Part in detail below for your easy reference. Together, these interdependent practices form self-referential cycles. Transformed individuals shape and transform communities, that shape and transform societies, that shape and transform individuals. Ecological systems that use their own outputs as inputs are regenerative.

Part I. Get Started: Orienting Ourselves in Community outlines the infrastructure for creating cultures of peace.

Chapter 1. Preserve the Peace Intrinsic in Life turns attention to the peace already present here and now in the unconditional gift of life intrinsically. This chapter describes the intrinsic power and gift of life that meets every human need, heals our pain and suffering and develops our security, capabilities and prosperity. To value life forms the ground on which a people of love and conscience can stand.

Chapter 2. Create a Context for Peaceful Society describes how to organize community groups to undertake these practices. It covers cultural expectations and agreements that shape group interactions in ways that make peace and nonviolence possible.

Chapter 3. Invest in Principled Friendships cultivates relationships with ourselves and others that enliven our hearts and minds while staying grounded in our cultural expectations. These practices are so simple we often ignore or skip them, but they create an essential and powerful foundation.

Part II. Love Life: Living Peaceful Private Lives describes how to transform our private lives to become loving people who practice peace and nonviolence in daily life.

Chapter 4. Love Life, Oneself and Others calls us to love ourselves, others and the natural world with our full human condition; stay grounded in our core selves while tending emotion and facing violence; and make a personal commitment to practice peace and nonviolence in our daily lives.

Chapter 5. Visit with Oneself challenges us to spend time with ourselves. It covers skills on how to get to know and care for oneself, organize companion pairs or small groups and ask for good attention. To love life and prepare oneself to meet life's challenges we get to know and learn how to care for ourselves and one another in small, immediate ways.

Chapter 6. Practice Peace in Daily Life attends to the precursors to violence: how to avert and reduce violence, reframe conflict with curiosity and rely on life's transforming power. This chapter covers specific skills to affirm the good in oneself and others, listen and speak plainly and notice when to cooperate and when to resist.

Chapter 7. Tend to Emotional Well-being describes ways to discharge emotion, reprocess memory and reintegrate internal parts to build resilience to emotional distress and trauma. We share a concern for each other's emotional well-being and recognize that our emotional condition affects others in ways that can limit or liberate them.

Chapter 8. Learn through Play invites us to let down our guard and explore the social and natural worlds with creativity. It describes the interdependence of peace and education. The way we play can reinforce or change patterns of social interaction formed over generations. Play allows us to discipline our thoughts and behaviors. As we play, we learn to protect ourselves and our work products while we practice connecting and interacting with others and the natural world.

Part III. Act on Conscience: Living Peaceful Public Lives describes how to transform our public lives to engage loving people in conscientious, discerning communities.

Chapter 9. Be Aware and Available broadens our awareness of transforming power in the good and hard times that builds confidence and conviction. This work makes us available and prepared to transform our public lives with clarity and strength.

Chapter 10. Visit with Others invites us to dedicate time to visit with others in our routine habits and schedules. These relationships give room for love and conscience to grow. We expect change because we ground our lives in living truths that are ever-growing, changing and maturing. This chapter describes the regenerative nature of the social ecology of these ideas and practices.

Chapter 11. Act in Community clarifies how conscience, while an inward awareness, only exists in relationships with others and the natural world. This chapter offers guides to listen to and experiment with love and conscience in daily life. It describes our need to shift from a perspective of guilt to one of joy and liberty—which we experience when we live in accord with our conscience. This chapter invites us to exercise our sovereignty as natural people and fulfill the responsibilities that bears.

Chapter 12. Liberate from Oppression challenges us to recognize and resist prejudice and privilege and to overcome intergenerational patterns of oppression. It illuminates the unnecessary, unfair, rigid patterns of prejudice and privilege and how they take root in childhood experiences. We see how recognizing the value of every life contradicts prejudice and attending to the simplicity of direct relationships contradicts privilege. It points out our obligation to bear public witness to peace with confidence and conviction.

Chapter 13. Practice Discernment describes how to organize based on the human capacity to discern a consensus of love and conscience. This chapter covers basic skills for forming collective stories, exchanging feedback and testing discernment. It describes cycles of discernment by individuals, communities and societies that lead to keen insight and judgment.

Part IV. Create Culture: Engaging Peaceful Society describes how to extend love and conscience to create cultures of peace and nonviolence.

Chapter 14. Create Cultures of Peace invites us to cultivate our unique collective intelligence, capabilities and creativity to respond to life's needs and challenges. It identifies four common concerns: speak up for peace, invest in living wealth, visit with strangers and express and record love and conscience in the many forms of public record to convey them into the future and around the world.

Chapter 15. Step Up calls us to follow transforming power through complete cycles of discernment to discover unique ways to express confidence and conviction for creating cultures of peace. This chapter notes a few historic steps forward in the progress of humanity. It challenges us to consider what steps we could take right now while realizing that historic action grows out of the simple steps we take in our daily lives.

Appendices include:

- *Volunteer Opportunities* lists organizations that have shaped our lives, since practitioners commit to volunteering at least twice a year to something that creates cultures of peace.
- *Glossary* defines the way terms are used in this work.
- *Learning Activities* lists many activities to consider preparing for in your home or community center for children when they arrive and for yourself as opportunities for play and recreation.
- *Cooperative Games* describes many cooperative, group games.
- *Personal Practices and Group Activities* lists the practices and activities with page number for easy reference.
- *References, Quotes, and About the Author* for your information.

For the many people working to preserve peace, we welcome your feedback on the ideas in this book and on ways you have created cultures of peace in your lives and communities.

Introduction

The practices described in this book have led to astonishing transformations: from violent and destructive to peaceful and productive communities. Transformations occurred in communities where people, both inside and outside the community, least expected change:

- Aceh, the north tip of Sumatra in Indonesia, where people survived a thirty-year civil war and widespread exploitation of natural resources.
- North Sumatra, home to thousands of people driven out of Aceh during the war where people lost everything and "thought of nothing but revenge."
- Central Java, the densest populated island of Indonesia, where religious violence rages between Christians and Muslims and adults migrate for labor into Asia and the Middle East.
- The United States, where oppression reinforcing many forms of prejudice permeates communities and the magnitude of resources and privilege obstructs solutions.

Despite long-standing patterns of violence, people everywhere crave love, healing, connection, justice and human development. People everywhere want to live more peaceful and ecologically sustainable lives and create new possibilities for a peaceful society.

During the 1965 U.S.-orchestrated *coup d'état* in Indonesia, the Indonesian military executed the leadership of Aceh and anyone accused of being a communist. The U.S. offered General Suharto financial backing if he would cut off both communist and Islamic political power in the region. This installed him as president under what was called a Guided Democracy for more than thirty years. By 1976, Aceh declared a war of independence from Indonesia in response to this deadly assault. The war reached a peak during the reign of terror in 1998–2000.

Even during the desperate months following the 2004 tsunami, this thirty-year war persisted in Aceh. During my adult lifetime, the world abandoned the Acehnese people many times as war decimated their society. Tsunami victims knew how futile it was to rebuild homes when soldiers would burn them to the ground again.

The Acehnese asked me why people cared so much about a tsunami. "They clearly do not care about us. The tsunami only hit one day. The war hits day after day! If they cared about us, they'd care about victims of the war, not just survivors of a tsunami."

So, I turned my attention to visiting every side: tsunami and war survivors; former combatants and victims (one person could have experienced both) and Acehnese and Javanese displaced by the war. I continued visiting until it was no longer necessary, not when the funds ran out or I got tired. I visited twice a year for a decade, from 2005 to 2015, and once a year since then.

The support of donations and traveling companions came through Friends Peace Teams' Asia West Pacific Initiative (see FriendsPeaceTeams. org). This Quaker organization develops long-term relationships with people who have experienced violent conflict who commit to peace and reconciliation. We worked as volunteers and lived on little to nothing. By avoiding costly expenses, we were unshackled from funding and program obligations and freed to use our best discernment to preserve peace. We then expanded our visits from Aceh and North Sumatra to Java, Nepal, the Philippines, South Korea and the Ukraine, among others.

We draw on many resources, which those familiar with them will recognize as U.S.-influenced: the Alternatives to Violence Project, Re-evaluation Counseling, trauma therapy, early childhood education, Quaker practice, conscientious objection to war and the peace and civil rights movements. Yet the Acehnese and Javanese saw their own histories, cultures and experiences in these activities, as did others, both indigenous and cosmopolitan. People of various backgrounds would say, "This is what our [family, tribe, or religion] teaches us," adding, "They just never expected us to *do* it!"

The tremendous diversity in Asia revealed the universality of particular activities. Antibiotics work the same everywhere. They are not dependent on culture. Regardless of their heritage, communities ravished by violence face distress and emotional disorder from the physiological effects of trauma. People not familiar with the well-documented aftereffects of trauma often blame the victims as weak or having poor character, of being deceitful, untrustworthy, cruel or selfish. But most people facing extreme violence for prolonged periods show these same behaviors, anywhere in the world.

Trauma affects people the same way everywhere. So does the work of love and conscience to recover honest, trustworthy, kind and peaceful lives. We invite you to practice doing what you consider right—as opposed to what you prefer, agree with or even understand. Experiment with things that ring true as loving and conscientious and see how they bear fruit, improve lives and help everyone flourish.

Peace requires a politics of no enemies. In a diversity of gender, race, ethnicity, class and faith, we discover our common humanity. When we realize our commonalities, we gain a tremendous sense of security, which opens us to curiosity in our differences. To their amazement, people who had thought of nothing but revenge for decades discovered they could befriend their enemies and form lasting relationships.

They experienced the transforming power of life, a palpable power that restores and regenerates.

In any moment, we choose the type of power we draw on: Violent, degenerative and deforming? Or peaceful, generative and transforming? (Halpern, 2009). People use peaceful, nonviolent approaches to solve conflicts every day. To increase our awareness, we look for turning points in events. We strive to recognize the inner nature or relationships of things to say "yes" to the regenerative and say "no" to the degenerative. When we rely on creative rather than destructive power in these turning points, this living power transforms us, others and events.

We identified activities that lead to a cascade of results for individuals and communities: a sense of security, confidence, conviction, liberty, joy, calmness, openness, curiosity and creativity. The transformations have been staggering.

The voluntary and personal nature of this work carries with it an authenticity and sincerity. Because of this, we get invited into the most unlikely places, even into closed, militant, extremist communities. Such communities do not accept or trust outsiders. But if we arrive as a guest of a respected insider, others may drive us out, but they will not harm us. Doing so would start an internal feud. The leaders of these communities test us for hidden agendas. I tell them the only promise I made to others is to use our best mutual discernment to do what ensures peace. Our authenticity and sincerity, along with our respectful engagement and realism, proves to have significant currency in brutalized, oppressed communities.

People in these communities, who have experienced generations of interpersonal violence and extreme abuse by authorities who should have protected and served them, then become the people who call for war. The dangerous people we fear. But we owe them a huge debt of gratitude. Their suffering created the crucible that refined most of the activities in this book, making significant contributions to our learning. Because they lived under the worst of circumstances with severe stress, they tested and identified what worked. Ironically and sadly, the level of distress they live with makes them the least able to sustain activities for themselves.

We then brought these practices and activities back to the U.S. in 2013. Participants appreciated extending the practices of empowerment and nonviolence to trauma recovery, resiliency and developmental play. They found them transforming. But the activities on conscience and discernment fell flat. At the Alternatives to Violence Project-USA preconference workshop in Miami, John Michaelis and I wondered why these activities felt so flat in the U.S. yet were so vital in Asia. We realized these groups' thinking avoided any reference to the dynamics of exploitation, humiliation or oppression. So we asked participants to share in pairs experiences of prejudice and oppression. We asked how oppression affects their lives and how their lives would be different if society were not oppressive. A third were relieved to speak the unspoken at last. A third were stunned to consider this entirely new question. And a third felt oppression had no affect on their lives whatsoever. This gave me my first clear glimpse into the blinders of privilege.

During the past five years we explored this issue in more depth. People in privileged communities specialize in occupations that bring in money to secure a place in the community, often choosing a job that brings in the most money possible. Privileged people may read and travel a great deal, but the time spent on one specialty plus the mediated nature of their endeavors limits embodied knowledge. People still face personal problems, but society foists nothing upon them—as long as they stick with the program. They get to choose what social issues to pay attention to or not. The speed and ease with which intelligence, cultivated over generations, finds solutions to immediate problems often makes one impatient with others and disinterested in larger, entangled social problems. Privileged people rarely notice that their solutions are not viable for everyone, while dismissing solutions that serve everyone—but need sacrifices on their part—as unrealistic, naïve or downright strange.

The more resources, education and intelligence, the more limited the breadth of perspective becomes. It should be no surprise then that group thinking and decision-making in privileged communities often produces elaborate, impractical and inconsequential results.

Brutalized, impoverished communities have their own blinders, but they often recognize elegant solutions that would have widespread effects. Oppressed people grasp the dynamics of oppression and show keen insight into social solutions. Yet they may suffer from internalized oppression, limited resources and skills or a driving aspiration to have oppressive power for themselves. This limits their ability to trust or to apply their insights and discernment.

We garner the greatest insight and direction when we work together. But crossing the class, geographic and ethnic divide can be rare, difficult and challenging. Explicitly addressing prejudice, equality, privilege and simplicity exposes the dynamics of oppression and offers the grounding needed for successful discernment. Just as learning to educate people with varied abilities improved education for everyone, learning to create peace within oppressed communities improved our ability to create peace anywhere. The reverse proved true as well. Learning to create cultures of peace in privileged communities benefits everyone. When privileged people grasp the dynamics of oppression, they show keen insight into creative as opposed to violent solutions and bring resources to this work.

To develop the work, we experimented with our own lives, in both Asia and the United States. Parents saw huge changes in their children and brought them to our schools, especially children with varied needs. Adults struggling to function recommended our training to one another. With affection, they nicknamed our school *bengkel manusia*, which means the "people's shop" in Indonesian, because our activities "fixed people." People who were suffering and seeing their children suffer from violence showed great interest and appreciation.

As the work matured, we identified as people of love and conscience. We rebuilt our trust in the power of love and conscience to order our lives. As we continued to seek a way forward, our experiences became examples and resources inspiring and informing others. Increasing numbers of people touched by this work agreed to practice living peaceful, nonviolent lives. Even though we are realistic about the flawed and inconsistent nature of human beings, we still expect the best from ourselves and others, celebrate life and commit to healing our distress. We examine our words, deeds and patterns to seek how to invest in wellness and develop conscientious relationships with one another and the natural world.

To the best of our ability we resist cooperating with or contributing to violence, recognizing that it oppresses and damages everyone and the natural world. We reduce consumption, simplify, resist prejudice and oppression, exercise our sovereignty as natural persons, purchase from conscientious sources and rely on those relationships with confidence, conviction and joy. We don't try to do everything, but focus on what arises during each day. Each effort to speak or act in accord with love and conscience ripples out far beyond what we can see. This audacious agreement—to practice doing what feels loving and conscientious—strengthens as we experience successes and reap its fruits.

We do not seek truths that are "just my size." Truths come in their own size, none too small or too large. We learn to trust the truth and act in accord with it. As long as we can stop and stay open to external feedback, we can trust our inner sense of right action. In this manner, both individuals and groups refine actions through experience, documentation and reflection. We do not need excessive control. We only need to cultivate our ability to identify, choose and act on the creative rather than the destructive to the best of our ability in each moment.

It sounds simple enough. Do the right thing. We often assume we already do it because most of us think of ourselves as good people. But when truths appear tiny or enormous and the social tide runs against them, we give up and violate them with ease, even as a matter of habit. "I know better, but," "Just this once," "Just for now" or "What choice do I have" become habitual refrains.

As people of love and conscience, we swim against the social tide, changing tiny and enormous things while soliciting the feedback and participation of others. As we do so, we meet fears, desires, egos and other obstacles, both within ourselves and within others. These can confuse, distract, distress or derail. It turns out that this work requires surprising levels of dedication, discipline and courage.

As we experience the fruits of acting despite our torments and temptations, we experience an increase in courage, confidence and conviction. A great sense of joy, liberty, pride and security accompanies this experiment with love and conscience in our lives.

∼

I warn you of two unruly aspects of this book.

First, it points to practices we can only know by experiencing and practicing, not by reading about them. Each unique person, situation and moment opens opportunities for unique responses of infinite variation. To understand requires practice, on one's own and with others, in both our private and public lives.

Second, each section grew out of years of trial, error and practice. The book offers guideposts for direction, but it requires ongoing practice and testing. The power described in this book is a living power, not a theoretical or strategic power. Its nonlinear, miraculous nature transforms people and situations and grows as we commit to life's transformative power, which often defies logic, theory or strategy.

As Angeles Arrien (1993) says, "Show up, pay attention, tell the truth and don't get attached to the outcome." I place the outcome of this book in your hands. I appreciate everyone who wants to live loving, conscientious, creative lives and hope you find *Creating Cultures of Peace* of value.

Part I

~

GET STARTED:

Orienting Ourselves in Community

~

Love was the first motion.

~ *John Woolman, 1720 - 1772*

~

Chapter 1

~

Preserve the Peace
Intrinsic in Life

Human beings rely on the Earth's unconditional love and generosity. With each sip of water, bite of food, breath of air and beat of our hearts we receive life freely. When we stop, let go of our distress and open to life's beauty and joy, we settle into the peace of being our whole selves, our perfect part of the perfect whole of life. Human beings do not make, build or create peace. Peace is already present as a pure gift of life. Human beings can reject violence, heal from our distress and organize in accord with the transforming power of life to preserve its intrinsic peace.

Peace. Loving, harmonious, relaxed, non-anxious relationships with a sense of tranquility, sincerity and well-being legally ordered free from intentional violence, hostility or war.

The Earth has natural predators. Even if we subsist on gathering plants and herbs without eating meat or plowing under fields, other life forms die for us to live. Many traditional peoples balance this perpetual sacrifice with gratitude and a sense of responsibility for life in return.

The more time I spend in war zones, the more I realize people need peace, just as we need to drink clean water, breath clean air or eat nutritious food.

We need safe haven. War and violence destroy and obstruct everything else. Safe haven should be considered the first basic human need and right.

Life endows human beings with innate faculties of love and conscience, predisposing us to peacefulness and compassion that lead to progressive improvements in social conditions. Love and conscience make us human and unite us for peace and nonviolence as the guiding assumption of public as well as private life.

At the same time, as human beings we have the fundamental agency of choice. In any moment we may choose destructive, degenerative options or constructive, regenerative ones. What we each think, believe, say and do affects the world. We are learning beings. People do what we are trained to do. We are creatures of habit. We cannot train for violence to exploit others and the natural world, then wonder why violence increases.

A. J. Muste said, "There is no way to peace, peace is the way." Practices and activities in this book don't ensure a culture of peace, but people who create cultures of peace find these practices helpful. This chapter describes inward experiences of love and conscience and how to form communities and friendships to bring a culture of peace alive.

Experience Love and Conscience Inwardly

Generations of people throughout time have experienced the creative, regenerative force of life—the universal source of love and conscience. We experience it in the tiny seed, tender sprout, gentle baby, laughter of family or friends, wafting smells of good cooking. Both glorious and ordinary moments exude the immense power of life with joy, ease and delight.

But after dropping the atomic bomb, human beings faced a new notion: that of nuclear winter, that human destructiveness could wipe out all life as we know it. This myth suggested that the destructive power of human beings is greater than the regenerative power of life. This misconception spread around the world. Commercial devastation of the environment amplifies the sense of the preeminence of human destructiveness.

Violence increases, not because it's our nature, but because we invest resources and train ourselves to perpetrate it. Research in breaking human conscience to increase the "kill rate" of ammunition entrenched violence even deeper. We reap what we sow. In the university class I taught, young American men said they would go to war and die if needed to protect their family's lifestyle. They described this as the right to own an SUV and a big screen TV. How tragic that young people believe their lifestyles need war and environmental devastation and that their families value electronic entertainment equipment more than the lives of their own children.

Cultures of peace stand up against state-sanctioned violence and invest in training people to think and act from love and conscience. We notice that, although tragic on a human scale, human destructiveness pales compared to the immense creative force of life. We experience love, an inward openness to life with a sense of its preciousness. We experience conscience, an inner knowledge of right and wrong with an inward drive to do what is right, true and loving.

Love. *An open, tender affection for and sense of the preciousness of another, while free to take leave without ill judgment or retribution.*

Conscience. *An inner knowledge of right and wrong with an inward drive to do what is right.*

We notice that love and conscience do not spring forth fully formed, they grow as we pay attention to them, rely on them. It takes time, attention and interest for an awareness of this inward landscape to permeate, shape and guide our interactions and relationships. Those who choose peace take an interest in one another's inward life. We seek a compassionate connection between our whole, true, core selves and the whole, true, core selves of others. Sustained attention to this inward life changes us and our society.

The tragedy of dropping the atomic bombs on Hiroshima and Nagasaki was not only in the death toll but also in the human suffering and environmental destruction that exceeded any sense of decency or humanity. These sorrows echo for generations. We cry over the lasting pains of the 125,000 people or more who died in the blast, firestorms and subsequent radiation poisoning. But still, new life bursts forth every day. Grass, trees, birds, people, all spring back. The city bustles. Life's transforming power continues to move on its powerful, regenerative path.

Transforming Power. *The palpable living, creative, regenerative, healing movement of life that changes individuals and situations for the better.*

Even as our current lifestyle drive species to extinction and threaten our own survival, humans cannot threaten life itself. Life may recede, but the source that formed life out of wind, rain and sun, that brought us from blue-green algae to the complexities of present day life, presses forward. That's its nature.

We choose the power we draw on in any moment: peaceful, generative and transforming or violent, degenerative and deforming. Human civilization does not require social or environmental destruction to advance or flourish. Threats to civilization arise from within, not from outside. The greatest threats to human survival stem from greed, deception and hypocrisy. The accumulation of money, the legalization of falsehoods and the devastation of wars drain our capacity to invest in living wealth.

Living Wealth. *Natural gifts of life such as time, health, talent, conscience, love, beauty, relationships, knowledge, skills, capabilities and natural materials that maintain our strength, promote our well-being and allow human beings to survive and flourish.*

Right use of these gifts bears even more wealth: joy, peace, honesty, maturity, integrity and sincerity. Natural systems regenerate living wealth in perpetuity. We can design the properties, performances, interrelationships and evolutionary capacities of social systems to regenerate living wealth rather than accumulate degenerative wealth (Brock, 2009).

Human destruction intimidates, making us a timid, fearful, broken people. It does not create, generate or protect. It robs and destroys. Financial wealth enables us to accumulate products, but it does not create or generate new life. Human survival depends on peace, which depends on us to notice, trust and rely on the creative, rejuvenating power of life in every moment to shape and guide our decision-making and actions. As we do so consistently, it becomes a habit.

Culture of Peace. *Unique ways we cultivate collective intelligence, capabilities and creativity to respond to the needs and challenges of life in friendly, harmonious, relaxed, nonanxious relationships legally ordered in ways that transmit around the world and into the future.*

We must not only know how to create peaceful cultures, we must put that knowledge into practice at home and in public. We must pay attention to life's transforming power and then embody that knowledge and power. Brian Swimme (1994) invites us to lie in a field without trees or buildings in sight. Then imagine yourself suspended over the vault of space. Imagine the Earth laying on your back with gravity alone pulling you back to earth. Words alone do not equate to experience. When we embody knowledge, we can engage with courage, vulnerability and conviction.

PERSONAL PRACTICE: Welcome Each New Day
"Take time each day to sit. Relax onto your skeleton. Stop in your body and mind. Feel your breath and heartbeat and where they come from. Notice the unconditional gift of life. Peace is already here. Let go of what you agree with, prefer or understand. You are alive and valuable. Nothing you say or do can make you any more valuable than you are right now. This is it; this is enough. So from now on trust where love and conscience lead. Speak and act for the pure joy of it. Throughout your day, practice this. Stop, let go, open and notice the value of life in and around you. Come from this place when you think, make decisions, act and speak. And invite others to do the same."

Human faculties of love and conscience guide us when we stop, let go and listen. At first, it may feel awkward or not like yourself. But practice prepares and changes us, similar to driving or learning a new language, art, sport or instrument. Personal practice shapes our awareness, habits and sense of normality.

Practice. To perform activities that exercise particular skills to gain or maintain proficiency. To learn from the contrast between experience and what was intended to adjust what we imagine, expect and believe.

Herein lies one of those simple ideas that proves challenging yet effective. Love and conscience need discipline, patience and persistence, but prove to be fruitful. To act from love and conscience structures our lives and unites us regardless of our differences. Yet even we who act in this way still can become distressed or paralyzed by pain and suffering.

Distress. Extreme physical or emotional strain that arises when current events restimulate painful memories, interrupting our usual functioning, flexibility and adaptability.

Trauma. A perceived threat that overwhelms usual functioning or adaptability with a sense of terror or helplessness, constricting attention to self-preservation. A mental state of collapse and disorganization that occurs when one cannot resist or flee a perceived threat instilling deep patterns of emotional distress.

Distress obscures our core selves. And it floods our minds with images and sensations, constricting our responses to reenacting rigid patterns for self-preservation. The brain responds the same to threats as it does to acts of violence, which makes threats effective. Physiological changes occur when one becomes overwhelmed and freezes. As fear rises, the brain cannot afford the time to stop and think. So the thinking part of the brain shuts down. We then function from the emotional brain without access to language, analytical capacity or sense of time. Because the emotional brain houses long-term memory, it stores memory in long strands of connected images and sensations. These memories replay the full story in flashbacks. With no ability to interrupt or redirect our reactions, we loop back and repeat them. With no sense of time, we feel as if the situation has always gone on and will always go on without end.

The first time trauma occurs, the danger comes from outside. As events replay, the danger occurs inside. This obscures our inward awareness of love and conscience. We may even come to dislike and distrust ourselves. We think if anyone knew, they would not like or trust us either. So, we often avoid intimacy. We may come to believe prejudices against us and self-sabotage. Or we may provoke others to at least control *when* attacks occur so we can brace ourselves for them. Or, we take the role of rescuer or perpetrator to save ourselves from becoming the victim. The more often we reenact the pattern, the more rigid, even addictive, it becomes. In this manner, victims become perpetrators.

But violence only begets violence, it does not create peace. Public cultures that glorify and glamorize violence as honor, duty or heroism fail to account for the day-to-day devastation of domestic violence, exploitation and deprivation it spreads.

Violence. *Intentional threat or act to hurt, humiliate, denigrate, exploit, damage or kill someone or something, often for personal or political gain.*

Nonviolence. *Removal of or resistance to a damaging force, humiliation or intimidation and redirection towards peaceful means, often for social benefit.*

Most people do not see ourselves as violent. We may not realize violence can exist in the way we think about or look at someone, raise our voice, use a tone or make dismissive remarks or gestures. We may not see the violence in paying taxes for war or purchasing products from abused labor or pillaged land. Many people use intimidation or threat, even in a brief glance, for personal advantage. Even if we manufacture the guns and bombs, we see the others as the violent ones and ourselves as defensive.

When we recognize violence in its smallest forms, we may recognize opportunities to resist and resolve it in ourselves and others before it permeates our lives. As John Woolman (1774) calls for in *A Plea for the Poor*, "May we look upon our treasures, and the furniture of our houses, and the garments in which we array ourselves, and try whether the seeds of war have nourishment in these our possessions, or not."

In a culture of peace we practice *choosing* peace in every moment of every day. Life's transforming power becomes available when we practice stopping and relaxing our bodies and minds and giving up the addiction to stress, despair or rage to fuel our work or life. When we touch the power of peace within and around us, we find a new fuel, a "clean energy," for creating culture and forming society.

How can we weed violence out of our daily lives? We learn how to stand up to violence in our private and public lives without reverting to violence ourselves. Then we can experience the regenerative power of life that teems through the ordinary, simple aspects of our lives. Trust builds.

Commit to Transforming Private and Public Life

We commit to staying aware of the unconditional gift of life to guide regenerative decisions that shape vibrant, peaceful society. We rely on experimenting with love and conscience. We say yes to peaceful power and no to violent power. Our outward lives come to manifest our inward sense of what rings true. But then, we still must learn to discharge emotion and hone creative capabilities and connections if we are to transform our personal lives and not revert to violence.

- *Rely on life's transforming power* in private and public life. Be loving but hold to community expectations and agreements. Speak in public on the power of peace and nonviolence. This leads to an amazing sense of empowerment and transformation—until distress intrudes. Then we realize we must learn to tend emotions …

- *Tend emotions* to discharge distress, heal past wounds and learn tools for resiliency. This leads to an amazing sense of vitality—until incompetence and disconnection obstruct. Then we realize we must hone our capabilities …

- *Hone capabilities* to create, connect, cooperate or resist and organize with others and natural materials. This leads to feeling capable, confident and delighted with life.

Together these tools form a three-legged stool that transforms private lives. These practices help us recover from violence and become well, capable and secure. Yet transformed private lives don't fit well in existing social structures. Family members and coworkers do not understand the changes. We no longer talk, joke, play or work the way we did. Our sense of purpose and goals change, and we question the integrity of what we—and others—think, say and do.

Integrity. Consistency among beliefs, words, actions and reality:
1) accurate and reliable, 2) authentic and genuine, 3) fruitful and valid.

Questioning integrity may make others feel judged, blamed or offended. They may dismiss us as arrogant or naïve.

We invite others to experiment with love and conscience in community to transform our public lives.

- ***Experiment with love and conscience*** in interactions with confidence and conviction. This leads to an amazing sense of community—until the dynamics of oppression intrude. Then we realize we must liberate ourselves from intergenerational oppression …

- ***Liberate each other from oppression*** through challenging prejudice with dignity, and countering privilege with simplicity. Invest in relationships without aspiring to unnecessary and unfair power over others. This leads to equality, liberty and justice—until we clash with vying opinions. Then we realize we must organize based on a discernment of conscience …

- ***Organize based on discerning a consensus of conscience*** in governmental, social and business organizations. Cultivate collective stories, test through discernment and document the consensus of conscience. This leads to simple, powerful, resilient organizations that pursue ecological and social justice and development.

Together these tools form a three-legged stool that transforms public lives. These practices help us stand up for and create a culture of peace. Yet even as we transform our public life, deceit, cruelty and brutality continue to intrude if we do not extend our understandings and practices to others and to the next generation.

- ***Create a culture of peace*** by learning to speak up for faith in the transforming power of life. Organize private and public lives to express love and conscience. Cultivate living wealth without exploitation and share this across the planet and with future generations through writing, art, music, education, law and court records. And value and act on behalf of humanity.

These practices have brought the work of creating vibrant, loving, conscientious communities full circle. Individuals create self-generative, peaceful societies in ways that reach around the world and into future generations to guide individuals. We can transform whole communities, even when only a few people commit. This powerful experience restores our faith in humanity and in the possibility of human survival.

After learning this full range of practices, Pak Sunhadi invited me to his village, Tondomulyo in Central Java, Indonesia.

The next day he apologized, "It's not the right time."

The following day he asked again, "Would you come visit my village?"

Then he called the fourth day, "I don't know what I was thinking! It won't work."

I almost asked him why, but decided against it. I replied, "That's okay. Hopefully I can come someday."

I hung up and looked at Petrus, the founder of Peace Place Training Center in Pati in Central Java. I started to explain but only got as far as, "That was Pak Sun. He asked me to visit his village ..." Petrus looked sick to his stomach and four devout Islamic women sitting on the floor leapt in front of me. "No! No! No! You can't go there! It's not safe. They don't consider *us* Muslim enough!" They insisted, even though they were practicing Muslims. They explained that the Tondomulyo teachers brought the preschool and elementary school children into the courtyard every morning to chant and act out cutting off the heads of "non-believers."

I called Pak Sunhadi and said, "It turns out I'm free on Friday morning, so I'll come by just after seven. Thanks so very much for the invitation. Bye." I hung up without waiting for a response.

I had grown up in a closed, rural community in western New York State. If a resident invited you to come, others might drive you out or ostracize your host but are unlikely to hurt you for fear of starting a family feud that could last for generations.

When I arrived in Tondomulyo the only people in sight were Pak Sunhadi and his family. They were standing in front of a large home on the courtyard beside the mosque in front of the school and the *pesantren*, an Islamic study center for unmarried adults. Pak Sunhadi's hand swung back and forth, hesitant, wondering how to greet me. I clasped my hands behind my back, ruling out the option of touch. He looked relieved. He motioned toward his house, "Come in, I guess."

"No." I replied. "We'll greet the Imam first." At his blank stare I continued, "Pak Sun, this is Indonesia. In Indonesia you always say hello to the oldest person first. Then you may go about your business."

"Ah, ah, yeah. I guess so," he stuttered.

Confused, the women of his family returned to the house as Pak Sun walked past me towards the *pesantren*. Dozens of men instantly appeared in front of me presumably to protect the Imam. They had never had visitors, so they didn't know how to receive them, let alone a white American Quaker woman! They were not sure what would happen if I touched the Imam, but imagined they would have to kill me and wash him for thirty days. There would be no touching here today!

I kept my hands clasped behind my back. The Imam appeared in a doorway as I approached. I launched into an extended, traditional Javanese greeting, including sentiments such as, "Thank you so much for receiving me. It's an honor to be here. Thank you for your gracious reception. I assure you my intentions are good. Please guide me if I behave in any way not consistent with good intentions. If I make any errors or do any wrong, from the cradle to the grave I beg your forgiveness. Please guide me and set me straight because I mean no offense. I wish only the best for everyone and to show my gratitude for your tremendous hospitality." And so forth, repeated three times.

When I finished, the men stood stunned. I realized no one knew what to do next. To avoid embarrassing anyone or forcing them to say something, I smiled and turned to go. As I walked away, my hope came true. Since Muslims go to the Mosque for prayers on Friday, the preschool children let out early that morning.

"Children!" I called out. Children poured out from the preschool door running about in the courtyard. I lit up and smiled. They were confused to understand me when I spoke to them in Indonesia. Some of the girls peeled off and ran around to the other side of the building. I asked some boys, "Can you do this?" I twisted my arms palms toward each other, clasp my fingers and brought my hands up in front of my chest. They looked confused and tried. I pointed to their fingers without touching them. "Can you move that finger?" They struggled to move the finger from the hand I was pointing towards, and laughed. The laughter attracted more children. The adults watched. None of them had never seen a Westerner under any circumstances, let alone imagined one playing with children in their courtyard.

I ended up inviting the teachers to go shopping at the household supply, hardware, gardening and cooking stores for six hours. I purchased supplies for ninety educational play stations. With over a hundred villagers crowded around watching, I explained to the teachers how to use ordinary household items to support the development of young children. Then I cleaned the classroom, scrubbed the floor, burnt the trash and set up ninety developmentally appropriate play stations, enough for thirty children to play. I stayed for three days training the teachers and parents. We learned how to help children understand violence, nonviolence and transforming power, recover from trauma and learn through creative, interactive play.

Since then, I have returned every six months. Over time, this training transformed many people and their transformations transformed others. At first the Imam revoked Sunhadi's right to speak in the mosque for consorting with outsiders. But eventually the Imam asked me and our community to pray for him when he was ill. The men looked confused, eyes bulging and eyebrows furrowed as the Imam added, "Tsk! Well, each according to their own faith." These word blasted his men, who literally stumbled backwards catching their breath.

I grabbed a chair, sat directly in front of the Imam and said, "Tell me about it." He told me about his illness. No one dared interrupt.

This community's transformation was unimaginable. People from other violent, militant communities around southeast Asia sometimes ask me, "Are you the one who went to Tondomulyo?" If I confirm, they look around to make sure no one's looking and add, "Can you come to my village?"

No one could have planned or expected such a massive transformation, but I have become used to watching miracles occur every day.

Mislan, a security officer in a resettlement camp in Indonesia, laughed, "You don't hear the word 'strange' often, because by definition it seldom occurs, unless Nadine's here. Then multiple times a day someone says, 'Strange, how strange, but true!'" People become kind and honest, they forget revenge and rage and we win justice in the most unlikely cases. "Strange, but true!"

Doing this work does not spare us from life's ordinary problems. People of love and conscience still experience success, failure, risk, reward, betrayal, love and heartache, just as we did before. We get distressed, depressed, discouraged and tired and sometimes feel like a fraud or a failure. But this level of personal and social development gives us real options in the ways we face these challenges.

We even become grateful for mistakes, failures and inadequacies because they create the cracks through which we see beyond our own egos. As we experience life's transforming power in newer, fuller ways with our whole selves, mistakes and failures become a source of connection, humility and conviction.

Humility. An experience of being brought down to one's core self, grounded in the absolute, incomparable, equal value of every life that leads to a wholehearted, authentic, unpretentious, unassuming manner.

Conviction. An experience of life's transforming power beyond our own ego, understanding or control accessible when we feel inadequate, fail or become the perpetrator.

Our weaknesses may connect us to others' strengths and our needs may fit with others' resources and vice versa. We can bring our full selves to the power of life so firmly we rely on it in the face of opposition and against all odds. Our failings and shortcomings do not diminish our goodness, resourcefulness or capabilities. As Marianne Williamson (1992, pp. 190–191) points out eloquently in *A Return to Love*:

"Our deepest fear is not that we are inadequate. Our deepest fear is that we are powerful beyond measure .... Your playing small does not serve the world .... As we are liberated from our own fear, our presence automatically liberates others."

We understand much more now than we did two thousand, two hundred or even twenty years ago. We can and need to be our full, authentic selves to be healthy and to create healthy social organizations in cultures of peace.

~

We preserve peace by living in accord

with life's transforming power.

~

Chapter 2

~

Create a Context
for Peaceful Society

We practice peace in community. We can practice with a local neighborhood, community or interfaith group, an Alternatives to Violence Project (AVP)[2] or other peace group, or start a new group. Invite people who are committed to acting in accord with love and integrity — be it in the home, community, or society.[3] Invite people who together seek to base their best discernment and consensus on love and conscience (Chapter 13).

Discernment. The human ability to comprehend the inner nature and relationships of things, especially when obscure, that leads to keen insight and judgment.

People have organized based on discernment for centuries. The truth offers its own structure that can direct thought, decision-making and work. It

---

2. *AVP drew on innovative education, civil rights and Quaker peace training to adapt the training for men incarcerated in prison in 1975. The prison required a written manual, which preserved details of this historic training. Sadly, many activities on noncooperation and civil disobedience, not allowed in the prison, were lost. AVP workshops have now spread to over sixty countries (see AVP.International).*
3. *The activities in this book draw on Re-evaluation Counseling (RC) and its initiative, United to End Racism. A local RC community can expand counseling and liberation supports to individuals to bring clear minds to creating cultures of peace.*

seems so natural, we often take it for granted. So organizations that rely on discernment seldom document how they do it.

Groups using discernment can be highly organized and productive with minimal roles and guidelines: scientists around a research topic, professionals around an occupation, players around a game or religious people around a faith. The topic, profession, game or faith can structure the group and their work, if the members seek insight and skill. From the beginning, many professions and associations grew in direct relationship to the power of their collective discernment.

Modern organizational development tools, both hierarchical and consensus-based, obfuscate the simple yet powerful organizing structure of discernment. Intelligent people find themselves trapped in a maze of laws, rules, regulations and procedures, cornered into unintelligent even unethical decisions and behaviors. Institutions explicitly create structures for some people to exert unnecessary and unfair power over others, or implicitly accommodate and compromise with those who do, for the sake of order. People in work places, schools, families and community groups use expedient forms of guilt, punishment, shame and coercion for control. Even organizations that profess to work for a culture of peace prefer students, staff or clients who are compliant and well-adjusted to unnecessary, unfair power and control over them.

A culture of peace turns out to require more change than most people want to risk, and insight into how violent their approaches have become. Even people who say they want change find it disturbing and annoying. Undoing habits as parents, teachers, organizers, managers, professionals or other roles proves one of the greatest obstacle to creating cultures of peace.

Change requires changing. Good intentions are not enough. So if you apply these practices in existing groups, be realistic about the challenges and pragmatic in your response. To transform an existing organization may require coaching beyond the scope of this book.

In this book, personal practices and group activities develop the tools to experiment with love and conscience in our private and public lives, something we *do* in community. The next two sections describe how to organize supportive communities and facilitate events to form a foundation for a culture of peace—whether formal training or informal community events. If you are not in such a group, or able to start a group, then you may encourage community events to follow these structures. Understanding expectations and the road map for a culture of peace expose the underlying assumptions of this work.

Organize Supportive Community

Communities of practice grow from one person experimenting with love and conscience reaching out to others in our own affinity groups—age cohort, family, social circles, neighborhood, occupation or religious group. And reaching out to people in groups outside our circles—different age groups, family structures or neighborhoods, people incarcerated, returning citizens, recovery groups, other social or religious groups, specialized homes, military, police, state troopers, political parties and so on.

We invite teenagers and young adults to attend our training. Sometimes those under 13 years old beg to join. We allow them to join, but make an agreement that they cannot come and go. If they need to leave a session to rest or play, they may return to any future event. Typically nine-year-old boys or eleven-year-old girls have begged to attend. When a young person wants to join, she or he often does well and stays to the end. They become amazing facilitators. Only once an eight-year-old boy participated. He stayed to the end and over thirty years later he still facilitates. Changing adult patterns of violence requires changing the way adults interact with children. So we reach out to parents of young children, offer childcare and food and include children when possible. Do not take on too much. Take your time, but do not dally. Reach out.

The sense of goodwill, mutual interest and loving care creates friendships that ironically can make us resistant to newcomers. So maintain practical ways to welcome newcomers on a regular basis while deepening the practice in a committed group.

Vital communities schedule introductory and ongoing training, companion groups, community gatherings, outreach opportunities and leadership support. Scheduling often becomes the greatest challenge. So experiment with shorter and longer events. Flexibility offers adaptability, but can cause confusion. Regularity matters more than duration or frequency. Notice the degree and pace of change that the group can follow and absorb.

Essential Structures for a Community of Practice

- *Training:* a nine-hour introductory training establishes a culture and basic skills of community building and transforming power. Three-hour sessions of group activities support ongoing practice of tools in the operating dynamics of a culture of peace.

- *Companions:* sessions in pairs or small groups to practice stopping, discharging emotion and experimenting with our lives.

- *Gatherings:* local gatherings for silence, sharing and discernment; and societal gatherings for mutual care and direction.

- *Outreach:* interactive talks, videos, websites, articles, pamphlets and Power of Goodness thematic workshops.

- *Leadership:* team building sessions to mentor apprentices and to nurture and recognize leadership.

Training. A nine-hour workshop in one or two days serves as a prerequisite for other events. It covers basic tools and activities described in Chapters 1–2: Expectations for a Culture of Peace, Road Map, Agreements to Practice, Affirmation in Pairs, Journal Writing, Core Self, Good Companions, Stories of Violence and Nonviolence, Transforming Power and Personal Commitment. Offer this at least every three to four months.

∼

Groups such as a classroom may schedule an hour a week, a couple hours every other week or three to four hours a month, bimonthly, weekly or daily. Community groups may do one to six three-hour sessions at a time. At a farmers' market or festival booth, a greeter may show pairs or small groups through preparative activities at tables, then host group activities in a tent with a schedule on a sandwich board. Groups work best with six to 24 people. If more, then form multiple groups. Announce an annual calendar so people can plan. Work to train one to three percent of your community members engaged in creating cultures of peace.

Companions. Two to five people meet every one to four weeks. They exchange attention to cultivate love and conscience, experiment with transforming power in daily life and test each other's discernment. When a sixth person asks to join, split the group into two groups of three people or have a strong member form a pair to start a new group.

Gatherings. Twelve to 35 but up to 75 people commit to experimenting with our lives. Communities gather weekly, bimonthly or monthly for silence, sharing and discernment. When the group exceeds 35 to 48 active members, consider splitting in two or have a strong member invite a few members to form a new community. Multiple communities meet at regional gatherings annually or semi-annually and continental or global gatherings meet annually or triennially. Regional societies work well with six to 24 member communities. When a society approaches 24 communities, consider splitting into two regions.

Outreach. Offer interactive talks or mini-workshops to orient the larger community and invite new people. Tell stories from the Power of Goodness story collection in schools, libraries and religious centers. Submit stories of nonviolence and reconciliation to www.Power-of-Goodness.info. Organize photographers, writers and administrators to document and archive your activities. Make a list of media outlets in your community and send announcements and news of these events. Raise the sympathies of forty percent or more of your citizens engaged in creating cultures of peace.

Leadership. Anyone who makes a personal commitment to practice love and conscience in their daily life may apprentice on facilitation teams, with the guidance and support of a mentor. Together, they and their mentor discern when the apprentice becomes a full-fledged facilitator, prepared and able to fly on their own facilitating this work in a community. When a facilitator schedules an event, they invite apprentices to join their team. Through team building and practicing activities before sessions, apprentices become familiar and facile with the work. Facilitators build their leadership as they apply the tools and aims of nonviolence and reconciliation in daily life and practice the tools in workshops for refinement and reinforcement. We lapse after one year and become inactive after two years. Leaders organize trainings, mentor new facilitators and document the movement. Good documentation shows attention, discipline and care for the community.[4]

Establish a Reliable Foundation

Life moves and changes; that's its nature. Simple, minimal structures can support a culture of regenerative, self-organizing interactions.

Agenda Format. The agenda format is a tool to create a familiar rhythm, order and flow in community life that distributes power and builds connection and trust. Facilitators prepare the space, keep the time and ensure smooth transitions between activities. Participants grasp instructions through facilitator modeling. Facilitators use the fewest words possible. Give simple instructions then model the length and nature of the response expected without elaboration or entertainment. Facilitators should give instructions and take part, not draw attention to themselves. Invite participants to take turns reading posted lists. Ask open questions after activities and wait for participants to respond. If a facilitator has a personal insight, wait for three participants to speak in the activity debriefing before you, then share your insight along with everyone else.

Facilitators sit in the circle three minutes before the appointed time. Cultures differ on timeliness. We do not punish people for arriving late, but try to start activities on time. If needed, start with optional activities until the group gathers. Negotiate time. The work requires an intact group that spends time together, so we often ask if the group would prefer to end as much later as we started or to cut activities. Even cultures with a flexible sense of time arrive promptly when they know something valuable will happen. People do not want to miss a thing!

---

4. *Leaders prepare and store records: 1) manuals, materials and training reports; 2) directory of inquirers, participants, apprentices and facilitators; 3) annual calendar of trainings, companion groups and community gatherings; 4) community and society discernment journals; 5) newsletter of news, social events, announcements and special topics; and 6) financial reports, annual reports and a history of each decade.*

Session Agenda

- Welcome
- Opening: Name and …
- Agenda Preview
  - Activity
  - Play
  } Repeat for a 3-hour session
- Reflection
- Next Steps
- Closing

The welcome gathers the group. Speak clearly and gently. "Welcome. To be inwardly guided by love and conscience, we must stop, not as a special meditation but as our state of mind. So keep your eyes open and mind alert as you sit comfortably. Feel your body relax onto your skeleton. Stop and let the tension go from your body. Your brain is a muscle. Stop and relax your mind. Feel your breath and your heartbeat. Feel where they come from, the unconditional gift of life. Let yourself fall away. Let what you prefer, understand or agree with fall away. Open to the transforming power of life. You are alive and valuable. Nothing you say or do can make you more valuable than you are right now. This is it. This is enough. From now on, do whatever you do for pure love, truth and joy."

Post the welcome at home or work and internalize it to convey from your own experience. Invite people to practice in every moment: stop, let go and open to the value of life within yourself and around you.

The opening invites everyone to speak at the start of each session. This shares attention and power evenly. People who tend not to speak get a chance to practice speaking. Those who tend not to listen get a chance to practice listening. A facilitator starts by saying, "Now we will do the Opening. Please say our name and [topic]. My name is Jay and …" Then gesture to the right or left for the next person to say their name and complete the same prompt. Go around the circle until everyone has spoken. The opening prompts a simple statement about ourselves or what has happened since the last meeting, an insight on the topic, or something orienting, light or humorous. Keep prompts concrete by asking about time, person, place or way or one word for something. Examples of concrete prompts include:

- What I had to leave to be present here.
- What I'm hoping for at this gathering.
- What brought me to this training.
- What I expect from this session.
- Something that describes me (my best, true self).
- A place I felt safe as a child.
- A power or gift I have for good.
- A person I respect and why.
- Three words for how I feel right now.
- One thing from the training that empowers me.
- How I feel, expressed as a weather report.
- One sentence on how I feel right now (in "cat language").
- One practice that helped me love more.
- One change I've made in my life that's gone well.
- One time I felt fully alive. My favorite color and why.
- A time I was scared of being left out.
- My favorite body part and why.
- A saying or quote that helps me do what's right.
- A person whose feedback I appreciate and why.
- One way I test whether something is true.
- Something I trust about my community.
- A practice that rejuvenates me. One thing I'm taking home.

The agenda preview orients people, assures preparation and provides a quick reference to how far the group has progressed in the allotted time. Participants help move activities along when they see more activities to come. Read the session agenda aloud. Each session has a theme which you may include in the session title. The opening prompt, central activities and choice of play coordinate with that theme. Read only the contents, not the name of the person who facilitates. Stand beside the agenda posted on the wall if that helps to draw attention to it. This can focus large groups or people with developmental challenges.

The activities connect ideas to experience, embody knowledge and create common references. They build skills while creating bonds and trust. Alternatives to Violence Project programs in schools, prisons or other self-contained groups explore a wide range of activities. I limited the activities in this book to ones we found essential to overcome violence, create cultures of peace and support direct action for peace. Most main activities take 45-50 minutes.

The activity debriefing provides time and questions for participants to reflect on a main activity in the whole group. It connects experience and insights to create "Ah ha! moments" to boost comprehension.

To keep it simple, ask, "What did you notice in this activity?" To draw out more details, ask, "What did that feel like? What did you learn? How will you change after this experience? How does this experience relate to transforming power in your private or public life?" For more depth, use these steps:

1. Invite people to take three to five minutes to write implications for changes in their lives. Note that sharing implications with others sometimes supplants action, so we keep personal implications to yourself until you have tested and applied them.
2. Ask groups of three to listen to each person for a couple of minutes on: "What did you learn from the content or format of this activity?"
3. Ask the whole group "What implications did you notice for us as a people or a culture?" Most people have not considered this question. So offer them adequate time to consider their responses. Responses improve as we continue to ask.

The play serves a vast number of purposes. It grounds us when overstimulated, interrupts and redirects repetitive thoughts, reminds us of our core selves, cleanses the palate of our hearts and minds, shifts attention between topics, energizes gross motor neurons stimulating the whole brain and more. Play brings down our guard and offers tremendous opportunities for learning (Appendix IV: Cooperative Games).

The reflection offers participants time to look back over the agenda and recall the activities, which improves retention. Ask participants, "What did you like, not like or any suggestions for the team?" Facilitators do not respond. If a criticism occurs say, "Thank you, the team will take that into account." Keep an attitude of gratitude and consider the feedback. Ask, "What if it were true?" Often kernels of truth come in unpleasant packages. Practice looking for kernels of what "rings true." Let go of the rest.

The closing brings the group together to acknowledge "us as a people." It helps us transition from our work together to our work apart. Keep it brief. Give a gift, affirmation or song to the group.

Use this simple agenda format for meetings, events or training sessions to orient newcomers and preserve a culture of peace at home, community or work.

The Introductory Empowerment Training reveals our core selves, sets cultural expectations and illuminates daily choices between violence and peace. The experiential, interactive format supports a wide range of learning styles to embody knowledge and practice skills. Use the agenda format above with the activities below for this nine-hour training (three three-hour sessions). Community members rotate facilitation. Three or more facilitators are preferred for each training. The team selects prompts for each session opening that are right for the group and circumstances.

Introductory Empowerment Training

ACTIVITY	PLAY
Session I: Community	
Opening Talk: History, Approach, Logistics	
Affirmation Names	Big Wind Blows
Agreements to Practice	Blanket Game
Affirmation in Pairs with Good Listening	
Session II: Nonviolence	
Good Companions with Core Self	Earthquake
Stories of Violence	Jail Break
Session III: Transforming Power	
Stories of Nonviolence	Sun & Umbrella
Transforming Power	Slo Mo Tag
Journal: Personal Commitment	

The opening talk covers history, approach and logistics. Keep it brief.

- *History.* This training builds on the Alternatives to Violence Project (AVP) begun in 1975 by Quakers, civil rights activists, educators and men incarcerated in New York State. We have added elements from Re-evaluation Counseling (RC) begun in the 1950s by laborers in Seattle. Both voluntary networks have expanded around the globe. Friends Peace Teams worked in former war zones and identified a set of practices essential to restoring and preserving peace.
- *Approach.* Present the Expectations and Road Map for a culture of peace (below). Invite participants to read each expectation and discuss them if needed. Explain that these assumptions underlie the training, so strengthening our awareness and confidence in them strengthens our work together.
- *Logistics.* Review the schedule of times for each session posted on the wall. Confirm that everyone agrees. Ask people to write unanswered questions as they arise on the Open Questions poster to discuss later. Invite volunteers to serve as a photographer. Ask if anyone does not want their picture shared. Ask everyone to be sure to pay. Then give information about bathrooms, drinking water, snacks, meals, child care, lodging and any other logistics.

Activities for Session I are described in this chapter, including a detailed description of each Agreement for Practice. Chapter 2 describes activities for Sessions II and III. The team adjusts the play as they see fit, except for Big Wind Blows, which we consider an essential activity (Appendix IV).

Introduce a Transformative Culture

As populations increase in size and mobility, we need to be able to articulate our cultural expectations explicitly. Communities of people create culture through the unique ways we respond to human needs and challenges in life, which have no universal solution. So introduce the *Expectations for a Culture of Peace* to your community. Then speak up for and hold public life accountable to these underlying assumptions.

Expectations for a Culture of Peace

- Everyone is good and capable.
- The Earth is beautiful and generous.
- Focus on learning, not religion or therapy.
- Act as a learner and a teacher.
- Everyone's journey is different; include all ages and backgrounds.
- Learn through experience, reflection and expression.
- Value commonality and diversity.
- Commit to personal change in private and public life.
- Discern decisions together.
- Participate voluntarily.
- Practice! Enjoy!

~ Expanded AVP Philosophy Statement (1975)

GROUP ACTIVITY: *Expectations for a Culture of Peace*

In the Opening Talk say, "Now we will read the Expectations for a Culture of Peace." Sitting in a circle, invite each person to read one point at a time. Only clarify points as needed. Ask for comments or questions at the end. Then refer to these cultural expectations when needed. Always post the expectations to help orient new people and to remind everyone.

Everyone is good and capable. Value life, including your own. Actions have consequences, but the value of life persists. Every one of us is alive and valuable. Nothing we say or do can make us any more or less valuable than we are right now. Greet each person with love and compassion.

The Earth is beautiful and generous. The Earth gives us everything freely without condition. Respect the fullness and beauty of the natural world. Allow love and truth to structure our decisions and choices. Make peace with the Earth, so we may make peace with each other.

Focus on learning, not religion or therapy. Learning unites us. Participants vary in language, tradition and religion, but have a common need for peace. Focus on learning what we need to create a peace.

Act as a learner and a teacher. Take turns leading and being led, depending on the talent, skill and experience needed for the task at hand. Practice fluidity with enormous humility and confidence in oneself and others.

Everyone's journey is different; include all ages and backgrounds. Reach out to diverse segments of society, from teens to the elderly. When we balance substance and play and modify as needed, we create a healthy environment for everyone. Adapt for individuals of any age as needed.

Learn through experience, reflection and expression. When we recall experiences and reflect on them, we create "Ah ha! moments" that crystallize insight. Embody those insights by experimenting with them in daily life and documenting their results to share across space and time. Others cannot make us learn, we must be open and teachable ourselves.

Value commonality and diversity. Acknowledge and value our common humanity and our differences. Peace requires all humanity across a diversity of age, ethnicity, religion, class and gender. Diversity illuminates what we have in common. From our common ground we can enjoy diversity.

Commit to personal change in private and public life. Changing ourselves changes how we relate to others, which changes others and society. Embody new knowledge to change your private and public relationships as you cultivate talents, gain insight and improve skills.

Discern decisions together. Discern decisions based on what rings true, affirmed by others in a consensus of love and conscience, not of opinion. We often do not prefer, understand or agree with reality, but we can comprehend the inner nature and relationship of things, even when obscure, that leads to keen insight and judgment.

Participate voluntarily. We cannot buy, require or coerce a culture of peace, we must choose peace. We may offer a stipend for administration or facilitation, but not a primary income.

Practice! Enjoy! Be joyful, playful, curious, awestruck, surprised, creative, hospitable and loving. Practice peace for the sheer joy of it!

After we have read the underlying expectations, we present the road map. It charts the way though the web of practices that restores and sustains a culture of peace. The upper section charts the way through personal transformation. The lower section charts the way through societal transformation. We view personal confidence and conviction in the transforming power of life as fundamental ingredients for societal transformation. A culture of peace relies on our ability to experience and articulate that confidence and conviction.

Increased population and mobility increases tensions. A road map guides our social interactions. Do not rush. We use skills developed at each step in subsequent steps. Invest time to develop skills through experience, reflection, practice and improvement at every step along the way.

Road Map for a Culture of Peace

Love Life: Transforming Ourselves

EMPOWERMENT	RESILIENCY
Friendship	Agreements
Affirmation	Safety
Communication	Remembering
Cooperation	Reconnection

Act on Conscience: Transforming Society

POWER	LIBERATION
Confidence	Equality
Conviction	Simplicity
Transformation	Discernment
Direction	Settlement

GROUP ACTIVITY: *Road Map for a Culture of Peace*
Say, "Now we will review the Road Map for a Culture of Peace." Each block is a sequence. If you cannot cooperate, stop and try to communicate. If you cannot communicate, stop and say something affirming. If you cannot say something affirming, stop and get to know each other, become

friends. Display the upper-left column in the Empowerment Training, the entire upper part in the Trauma Resiliency Training, and the whole Road Map in the Liberation and Discernment Trainings.

Transforming ourselves rests on the three-legged stool of empowerment, resiliency and play. We found that without skills in these three areas—personal power, facing tragedy and developing capabilities—people revert to violence. The upper left section on Empowerment through **Friendship, Affirmation, Communication and Cooperation** was recognized by AVP in 1975. By addressing the precursors to conflict, this sequence has proven rigorous in disarming violence. The upper right section on Resiliency through **Agreements, Safety, Remembering and Reconnection** was recognized in research as the primary stages of trauma recovery (Herman, 1983). This sequence extends our skills to face painful or difficult conditions. Empowerment skills help us make positive choices in our use of power. Resiliency skills help us face human tragedy, heal, and stay well. Play helps us develop capabilities for survival, creativity and joy. Transformed people need transformed societies in which to live, work and play, and help their societies transform into healthy places.

Transforming society rests on the three-legged stool of power, liberation and culture. We found that without skills in these three areas—transforming power, liberation from oppression, and the liberty of conscientious, creative culture—people cannot escape structural violence. The lower left section on Power through **Confidence, Conviction, Transformation and Direction** was recognized by the Quakers in the 1650s. This sequence attunes our attention to life's transforming power and reveals ways to allow it to shape and guide community and society. The lower right sequence on Liberation of **Equality, Simplicity, Discernment and Settlement** draws on new understandings of intergenerational cycles of oppression. This extends our skills to overcome prejudice, privilege and disputes. Transforming Power make peace possible. Liberation frees us from oppression. Culture helps meet life's needs and challenges as a people.

Following this road map enables us to lead friendly, harmonious, legally ordered lives in a manner we can transmit to other cultures and future generations. Post the Expectations and the Road Map in a visible place in your home, work, school or community center. Read them. Use language from them. Discuss them with family, friends, colleagues and coworkers. Pay attention to how you apply them in your life. Revise them, but be prudent. Include only what you find necessary as you create cultures of peace in your life and community.

∽

A full experience of life's transforming power

balances strength with kindness,

integrity with love and

justice with compassion.

∽

Chapter 3

~

Invest in Principled Friendships

Life's transforming power exists in the direct relationships among people and with the natural world. Friendships are direct relationships with shared loving attention, goodwill, trust and support. They include global, professional and cultural connections as well as close friends. Friendships weave the fabric of a peaceful society. The word "friend" comes from the root "free." Exchange of loving, honest attention among friends sets us free to act in accord with our conscience rather than under the control of others.

Yet loved ones, friends and neighbors perpetrate on each other some of the worst violence in the world. Peace flourishes when we hold one another to agreements on basic principles that form loving and conscientious friendships. We build friendships among people similar to and different from ourselves. This chapter describes how to cultivate relationships that enliven hearts and minds, relationships that are bound by peaceful, cultural expectations and agreements. Do not underestimate or skip the simple work of making friends and practicing basic agreements.

Treat Everyone as a Friend

I remember the day my three-year-old daughter came stomping home with a group of friends in tow. She came straight up to the front door and declared, "Tell them, Mom, there aren't really any monsters or strangers in Tallahassee are there?!"

A Stranger Danger program at preschool taught them to fear people they did not know. It must have made strangers sound like monsters. My mind raced. How to respond? We did not think of strangers that way. Even at her young age, Fenna had spent half her life in Indonesia and half in the U.S., so she had met lots of new and different people.

I replied, "Well, when you meet someone new, you ask their name, right?" Indonesians consider it impolite to use pronouns for people older than you, so children have to learn people's names to speak to them.

"Of course," she said.

"And you're friendly and kind to others, right?"

"Of course!" She looked shocked at the idea that anyone could treat another unkindly.

"Well then, I guess not," I said. "A stranger is someone you don't know. If you introduce yourself and get to know them, they're no longer a stranger." I figured it was my job to be street-smart and distinguish real from perceived threats. As a three-year-old, it was not her job to fear others.

In cultures of peace, we begin with a friendly attitude. We offer attention to others without an agenda except to get to know and care for one another and the natural world in which we live. Friendships form through visiting, communication and cooperation, which requires scheduling. Make plans to spend special time with people close and with people different from yourself. Make a special effort for people you fear, dislike or dismiss or who come from a different age cohort. Consider who you are least comfortable around, then visit someone from that group. Acknowledge irreconcilable differences with particular individuals, but resist applying those differences to entire groups of people. Peace increases through doing structured activities with diverse people, even enemies. Many traditions regard hospitality and visiting a fundamental part of spiritual life. Speak to people on the street and in stores. Invite neighbors over for tea or a meal. Spend time with others to enjoy each other's company, work on a common purpose or task and discuss concerns.

PERSONAL PRACTICE: Make Friends

Maintain friendships with people similar to and different from yourself, including those who disagree with you. Dismiss no one. Be friendly in your facial expression, body language and gestures towards everyone.

Greetings matter. No universal method exists for greetings, respect or friendship. The way people greet one another differs depending on the person, location, occasion and culture. When we greet, we may or may not smile, bow, hug, shake hands, pat shoulders, nod downward or upward, place hands together or to our sides, salute, touch noses or foreheads, touch foreheads to the others' hand, or raise a hand to one's heart.

PERSONAL PRACTICE: Greet People

Greet people when you meet them. Turn your body towards them, look at them, smile and say their name. Notice if you follow their way of greeting or they follow yours. If you do not remember their name, ask. To the degree practical, greet everyone you meet and try to name everyone in the room. Dismiss no one. Exchange names. Share one interesting thing about each of you. For example, speak for two or three minutes on what you are looking forward to, then ask, "What are you looking forward to?" Consider other engaging topics such as something I'm proud of, a life lesson I've learned or one good thing going on right now. I often say, "Tell me something about yourself." If they retort, "Like what?" I reply, "I don't know your life. Something that matters to you." They may take a while to think, so wait for the answer. Do not rescue them or press them to disclose more than they want. Respect your own and others' privacy.

People often feel awkward when they greet others, because greetings are cultural. There is no universal correct way to greet. Follow the other person's example, ask others how they do it or make it up yourself. In public, approach and greet others the way you want to be greeted or copy them. Notice and accommodate other's responses. Feel free to be creative.

Greeting initiates relationship and a culture of peace. In certain circumstances, using names and greeting may even avert imminent violence. Look at someone, then nod, bow or put your hand out to shake hands and say, "My name is ___. What's your name?" Surprisingly, children who grow up in the same class or on the same street often cannot name everyone in their group contrary to their own and others' assumptions.

Affirmation Names. Many people say they don't remember names and hate to ask, but repetition helps. Play with names, write names or say names often in conversation. Using names helps both yourself and others. It shows respect and interest and changes the atmosphere. When we use names and get to know one another, we reduce neglect and violence and increase goodwill and trust.

GROUP ACTIVITY: Affirmation Names

Say, "Now we will do Affirmation Names." Note that when violence or stress affects the brain, a person loses most of their vocabulary and the words left are negative. To assess the health of your brain, brainstorm positive words. If you have trouble, practice doing this every day.

Ask people to get in pairs. "With your partner, please brainstorm at least 3-5 positive adjectives that start with the sound of each of your names." Give them time to do this, then ask, "Have each of you thought of at least three positive words for each of your names? Was that easy or not?" Take a couple of comments, then say, "Okay, now each pick one affirming word to use with your name as an affirmation name. For example, my name is Nadine and I pick "neighborly," so I will be Neighborly Nadine." To learn everyone's name, go around the circle and have each person say their adjective and name clearly. Ask the whole group to repeat your affirmation name by saying, "Hello, ___." Invite them to find a different pair. See if you each can say everyone's name and go ask the person if you can't remember. Come back to the whole group. Ask them to use this affirmation name before speaking to help us learn names and hear positive words frequently. When tensions arise, think of three or more positive words and see if using them reduces the tension. Note: If needed, explain that an "adjective" means a describing word and that "affirming" means a word that identifies the goodness, gift or capability of a person.

Knowing each other's names sets a positive tone and creates the conditions for friendship. In a recent workshop, a participant said learning names is important, but this was the first group that actually did it! I learned how powerful names and affirmation were when people arrived late and could never catch up. So now when someone arrives late, I remember to stop, greet them, exchange names and affirmations before moving on.

Big Wind Blows. Big Wind Blows is one of those seemly trivial activities with powerful effects. This activity structures group norms.

GROUP ACTIVITY: Big Wind Blows

Say, "Now we will do Big Wind Blows." One person stands in the center with no empty chairs or spaces in the circle. "The person in the center says, 'The big wind blows for anyone who ...' and adds something true about yourself that introduces you to others or helps you get to know the others. If it's true for you too, stand up and find a new spot across the circle. Do not return to your own seat or shift one seat to your right or left. Give an example, "The big wind blows for everyone who ..." Others then follow your example. Use something meaningful to you or to the group, such as anyone who has ridden a horse, loves to sing, has cooked with their grandmother or likes to walk at sunset. After the group has done this for ten or twelve minutes, the facilitator stays in the middle and says, "Thank you. Please stay in your seat." The facilitator pulls up a chair to sit in the circle. Ask people to sit in different seats with different people around the circle whenever the group reconvenes and to call "hurricane" whenever you want everyone to move and change seats.

When we vary where we sit and with whom, we literally form a culture of peace. When we pick certain people to sit beside and talk to them alone and not to others, we create a culture of division, confusion and/or rigidity. (Sun & Umbrella in Appendix IV: Cooperative Games makes this point visible.)

Agreements to Practice. We practice applying and gently reminding one another of these agreements. We know that some of the worst violence in the world is among loved ones, friends and neighbors. Violence takes root in small seeds, detectable long before they grow. These agreements help us weed out violence in its smaller forms and plant seeds of peace.

GROUP ACTIVITY: *Agreements to Practice*

Say, "Now we will read the Agreements to Practice. In our experience, if we agree to practice these points, then we can create a peaceful, nonviolent culture. If problems arise, we can usually track them back to a breach of one of these agreements." Sit in a circle and post the agreements on the wall.

Agreements to Practice

- Affirm myself and others, no put downs or put ups.
- Stop, listen, don't interrupt.
- Speak simply and honestly without fear of mistakes.
- Speak from my experience, not other's without permission.
- Tend emotions, then speak directly to someone if in dispute.
- Ask for and offer hospitality, feedback and help.
- Make friends not enemies with people who are similar and different.
- Use what I need and share the rest fairly.
- Use my rights to pass and to consultation.
- Volunteer myself only, not others.
- Care for each person, the community and the natural world.
- Live in integrity with life's transforming power.

Expanded from the Alternatives to Violence Project • AVP.International

---

Invite someone to read one agreement and add one sentence on what it means to them or something important about it. If anyone asks for clarification, turn to the group to respond. Add a comment only if needed. Clarify and ask the group to agree to each one. Participants may challenge one or more. Keep the balance between respecting the individual's and the group's needs. Do not insist, persuade or push to finish. Let go of exercising unnecessary or unfair power over any participant or over the group. When someone asks to edit an agreement, promptly add their words to the poster unless you have an important reason not to do so. At the end, ask the group if they agree to practice and remind one another of these agreements. Then ask the group if they want to add any agreements. Write added ones on a poster. Keep the agreements posted to remind everyone.

The next section gives details on important aspects of each Agreement. In an outreach event or short program we may limit agreements to:

- Affirm myself and others, no put downs or put ups.
- Stop, listen, don't interrupt.
- Speak simply and honestly without fear of mistakes.
- Speak from my experience, not other's without permission.
- Use my right to pass.
- Volunteer myself only, not others.
- Care for each person, the community and the natural world.

Then post the full list of agreements at every other event. Trauma resiliency depends on tending emotions and asking for and offering help. Liberation from oppression depends on making friends not enemies, and on using what I need and sharing the rest fairly. Applying these agreements in daily life proves more challenging than one might expect, in part because they are so simple. The agreements shift over time and location, so adapt them as you see fit, but only after you apply them and give them a chance. Challenge yourself to record agreements that prove essential for you to create a peaceful, conscientious culture. Sometimes go back to the original agreements to look for elements you discarded, misunderstood or lost.

Good Listening. The next step in friendship is to share something about oneself and learn something about others. We do this best with good communication skills in listening and speaking.

GROUP ACTIVITY: Good Listening
Tell the group, "Now we will brainstorm Good Listening." As the group brainstorms elements of good listening, interject or put up a poster:

1. **Stop**—*stop in your body and mind, stop thinking of other things, fidgeting, fiddling, looking around or speaking.*
2. **Turn**—*turn your body and attention towards the person and make eye contact available as culturally appropriate.*
3. **Track**—*follow what the speaker is saying, don't get ahead.*
4. **Imagine**—*imagine life if what the speaker says is true.*

Listeners communicate nonverbally, through body language and facial expression. So you may say, "Right now, with your face and body show me what bad listening looks like. Okay stop, we don't want to practice that! Now show me what good listening looks like. Show me impatient listening, such as 'I really want to listen, but I'm late to work,'" or use other examples. "Notice how the muscles in your face, body and breathing communicate good or bad listening. You read others and they read you, even unconsciously."

A friend from my teenage years came to a workshop. Afterward she said, "You've known this all your life and didn't tell me?!" She thought she listened to her husband, but she didn't stop what she was doing and turn towards him when he was talking. This simple act made amazing changes. "This could save my marriage," she exclaimed. Since listening happens in our body through habit, it takes deliberate physical practice.

GROUP ACTIVITY: Read My Face
Notice "the language of the face." Child have genuine facial expressions. Adults' facial expressions have often gone flat or hide our feelings. What does your face convey to others? Ask everyone to find a partner. One person shows a specific facial expression and the other says what it conveys. Emphasize the reader is right. They tell you what your face conveys to them. Learn from what they say. Realize your face may give messages you did not intend.

Affirmations in Pairs. Good speaking requires knowing what we want to convey and putting it into words. Integrity aligns our words, actions, beliefs and thoughts with each other and with reality. It requires specific, concrete information about ourselves and others. Much parenting and schooling focuses on the negative, giving us extensive experience in identifying and articulating criticism of ourselves and others. Most of us need far more practice identifying and articulating specific, concrete positive things about ourselves and others.

GROUP ACTIVITY: *Affirmation in Pairs*

State, "Now we will do Affirmation in Pairs." Ask everyone to find a partner, turn your attention to your partner and decide who will speak first. Say, "Okay, one person will practice good listening. If the speaker stops, wait for them to think of more things to add. The other person will talk for three minutes on: 'Positive things I love and respect about myself are ....' I will tell you when to switch." After everyone has a turn, debrief this activity.

PERSONAL PRACTICE: *Affirm Self, Others and Life*

- *Greet people, use their names and use words that describe their gifts, talents and strengths.*
- *List words for positive feelings and use these words during the day.*
- *Point out what people say and do that makes the day go well. Tell them how it felt and the positive effects or consequences it had.*
- *Say one to three specific positive things before offering a criticism.*
- *Notice put downs or put ups in conversations or joking and ask the speaker to stop and offer three concrete affirmations, noting a person's gifts or strengths without inflating or ranking above others.*
- *List what makes you feel affirmed and ask others to list what they find affirming. Compare and discuss the similarities and differences.*
- *Notice how observing positive things changes you and others.*
- *Notice when you use or aspire to unnecessary or unfair power over others and let go of that power. Apologize. Affirm the other's inherent value and right to self-determination.*

Loving, affirming attention frees us to act in accord with our conscience. The basic skills of friendship prove more powerful than they appear. They create the solid ground for sustainable, effective action.

Adhere to Agreements to Practice

Earlier in the chapter, Agreements to Practice (p. 68) were presented as a key element of ***Treat Everyone as a Friend***. People around the world say these agreements describe a good person, friend, community member, parent or teacher. We post the Agreements in homes, schools, clinics, stores, workplaces and community settings. They seem so obvious and simple, but have far-reaching implications.

Each agreement is elaborated in this section to encourage you to discuss what they mean and how to apply them. Commit to practicing these agreements in every part of your life. This may seem impossible to many people. But the experience is so fruitful and offers such a sense of liberty and joy, you will wonder why you ever waited. In addition, introduce them to others and invite others to practice them. Even if people around you decline, it's worth asking.

These agreements are not a magic pill, however. We still have our trials from losses, pains, griefs, fears and injustices to endure. We make mistakes, hurt others and feel alone or insecure. Still, returning to these agreements provides an opportunity to rely on and learn from one another and to create new habits and patterns.

Affirm myself and others, no put downs or put ups, not even in joking. Craft concrete, specific, true statements that name the authentic goodness and capabilities of ourselves and others. Affirmations value, uplift, uphold, support, encourage, strengthen and defend one another's inherent goodness.

This poses challenges when we disagree with other's choices or behaviors. But begin by learning how to affirm ourselves and others. Once we become good at that, we discover ways to strengthen our ability to challenge destructive behaviors while respecting the dignity of the person.

Root out put downs in our thoughts, words, actions and gestures— whatever discounts, dismisses or devalues any person or group of people. Challenge dismissive or destructive words or behaviors while remembering the inherent goodness, capabilities and dignity of each person.

Root out put ups also, elevating one person or group over others. This both masks a self put down and lowers expectations of ourselves. At first people insist that elevating a person shows respect, but it denies equality, dehumanizes the other and distances us from them. It initiates a sense of superiority that can lead to supremacy. Ignoring weaknesses and mistakes closes off room for interaction, learning and mutual support. Before long we find ourselves knocking them off the pedestal we put them on!

Stop, listen, don't interrupt. Stop your body and your mind and relax. Let go of distress and tension. Turn towards the speaker. Follow their lead. Do not speak, share a similar story, give advice, pursue your own curiosity or take what they say personally. Don't cut them off by thinking of what you want to say, finishing their sentences for them or speaking before they finish. Open your mind to imagine what the person means and what life is like for them if it were true. Pay attention to how you listen. Keep your breathing relaxed and easy. If asked, repeat back to them the main points of what you heard using their words as much as possible. Ask them if you have it right. If not, they may need to work to articulate their meaning or you may need to work to hear their meaning. Repeat back without interpretation or judgment before offering a response. This practice works even among people who have lived as enemies for decades.

At the same time, do not take abuse. If someone speaks incessantly or abusively, immediately say, "When you're ready to talk with me let me know," and walk away. Let it go. Do not take it personally or discuss it with others. No one has the right to abuse you verbally or hold you captive.

Speak simply and honestly without fear of mistakes. Balance speaking with listening. Speak honestly and frankly while leaving time for others. If you speak easily, ask others what they think first then speak your mind without repeating or over-elaborating. Consider what you want to say and state that as simply as you can. Process your thoughts and emotions in personal meditation, writing or with a companion or small group. When speaking in a larger group, speak on ideas that may affect everyone.

If you speak reluctantly, risk sharing your thoughts and feelings in the group so everyone can get to know you. Group identity and sense of community depends on each of us sharing ourselves. Challenge yourself to find one relevant thing to say in the group. Speak up, but do not feel pressured to share anything you do not want to share. Many people avoid speaking for fear of misunderstandings or mistakes. Remember, mistakes offer opportunities to learn. We appreciate mistakes because they are a source of connection, humility and conviction. To do this, sometimes we must find physical ways to overcome our terror of making a mistake.

PERSONAL PRACTICE: Learn from Mistakes
Groups can create a culture of encourage learning from mistakes. In Indonesia, people decided to respond to mistakes by smiling, clapping and cheering. The Friendly Folk Dancers wrapped their arms around themselves and hugged three times, saying, "Oh [hug] no [hug], how terrible [hug]!" In both cases, everyone joins in, smiling and laughing. When we settle down, someone asks, "What was the mistake? What can we learn?" The instigator points out what words or actions (not which person) did not seem right to them. We discuss it in the spirit of learning: What did the person intend or mean? What seems wrong about it? What rings true?

We agree not to lie by falsehood or omission. When the telephone rings, do not say, "If it's for me, tell them I'm not here." When you hear someone say something false, speak up. Point out what is not true and state what is true. Ask people to tell the truth. Explain why telling the truth is important to you and to society. Lying, regardless of intent, trains the brain to disconnect words from reality. This stunts learning and erodes integrity and discernment. Our security rests on our honesty, integrity and sincerity.

Speak from my experience, not other's without permission. Honor and value your own experiences. Notice meaning in your own life. Just hearing another person's story does not give permission to repeat it. If a story is so meaningful you want to repeat it, ask for permission.

PERSONAL PRACTICE: Ask for Permission to Share Other's Stories
Notice when you want to use another person's story to make a point. Contact that person to tell them what you learned from their story and ask their permission to use or quote it.

The effort to ask for permission shows respect and draws attention to the insights gained. We recognize that if a friend allows me to try on their jacket that does not give me permission to take it home with me. If you want to use another person's story, whether you perceive it as negative or positive, ask for permission. Notice this does not agree to confidentiality or secret-keeping. If someone shares something that disturbs you, it becomes part of your story and you should react. This is not a religious or therapeutic environment. If something needs to stay secret, do not share it, no matter how respectful and safe the environment feels.

Tend emotions, then speak directly to someone if in dispute. Take care of emotions by discharging them with a companion or co-counselor. The Good Companions activity in Chapter 4 introduces skills to do this, which are elaborated in Chapter 5. We commit to tending our emotions by discharging them from the body through crying, shaking, pacing, wailing, laughing and conversation, and encourage others to do so.

We use the term discharge because it refers to letting go of and allowing emotion to move out of the body, not just reliving it. This takes the charge out of the emotion and heals, instead of revving up by yelling, raging or destroying things. Then we return to the here and now, afresh.

Cultural inhibitions of showing emotions may protect individuals from perseverating and communities from emotional dumping, which exacerbate distress. But cultural inhibitions also obstruct the natural healing process by preventing emotions from discharging through the body. We cannot keep our pain and get better too. Sometimes we are not ready to let go of our pain. The more we let go and heal, however, the more we realize how much our emotions stem from past hurts that continue to intrude on and affect us and others today. This makes our emotional condition a public as well as a private matter.

If a dispute persists after tending emotions, either let it go or speak to the person. Do not gossip with others. Meet the person to settle the matter so it does not linger or fester, unless doing so could cause harm. Consider whether and when to act. Settling a dispute requires both parties. When speaking together does not resolve the situation, you may bring a friend. If that does not resolve the situation, bring it before the community.

Ask for and offer hospitality, feedback and help. Agree to receive and offer hospitality, which requires imposing on one another in both reaching out to visit and accepting visits. Visit without an agenda to provide room for love and conscience to grow as you listen to one another, think things through, pool resources and seek solutions together.

We also agree to receive and offer feedback (Chapter 10). This requires paying attention to one another. The best feedback often begins by giving feedback to oneself in front of others. Afterwards, others may add specific, concrete things you did or said that helped them or the group. Finally they may note anything you did or said that caused difficulties and add an achievable suggestion that could improve the situation or results.

If we enjoy helping others but never want help ourselves or feel needy but do not feel capable of helping others, we should reexamine. Everyone has needs and resources. Maintaining a balance between receiving and offering encourages respectful, equal, healthy relationships.

Ironically, help often does not help. So, figuring out when and how to ask for or offer help becomes a major learning opportunity. Often, we help others to maintain a sense of control or avoid our own sense of worthlessness, even unconsciously. This type of help erodes the other's or our own sense of self-esteem and capability. We may need to wait for someone to ask for help. Even then, stay present and encourage him or her to talk, discharge emotion and wait for their mind to clear. Then they can see the way forward themselves. At the same time, be quick to lend a hand and lighten the load of someone's daily work, illness, brokenness or loss. The art of learning how and when to help or not takes practice and honesty.

Make friends not enemies with people similar to and different from me. We value the simple work of building friendships, then extend that work to more difficult relationships. We build friendships of generosity that share loving attention and goodwill. Love can operate powerfully when given time and attention. An open, tender affection for the other grows when free to take leave without ill judgment or retribution. Our sense of each others' preciousness then grows, along with mutual trust and support.

Building friendships with people similar to us may be easy or hard. When we internalize messages that are oppressive towards ourselves, we often turn on people similar to ourselves making friendships difficult. Building friendships with people different from us takes greatest effort in segregated societies. Such relationships can expand trust and support while challenging prejudices and assumptions. Based on experience, United to End Racism (RC.org) suggests we will not end conflicts among adults until we change the way adults interact with young people. So we also give special attention to building friendships across age cohorts.

∽

To love those called enemies and become friends,
so begins the work of peace.

∽

Use what I need and share the rest fairly. This agreement does not define "need" or "sharing." It commits to discussing them in public. We often reserve this agreement for advanced training. Adults assume young children should use what they need and share the rest fairly. But when applying it to ourselves we find it conflicts with societal pressures to accumulate personal resources and protect them as a private concern.

Cultures of peace lead to prosperity, which isolates, ironically. Thus, prosperity often reduces generosity, narrows experience and limits understanding while expanding financial wealth, opportunity and knowledge. In prosperity, individuals often attribute success to themselves, cling to their our own access to wealth and stop questioning the integrity of their decisions.

In daily life, however, we trade the gifts of nature freely given to us—time, talent, health, natural resources—for money. Therefore money is a proxy for the generosity of life's abundance. We have the responsibility to use these gifts, including money, to meet our needs. Then we have the obligation to share the rest in care of others and the planet that support us. We need to garner as much collective guidance on facing prosperity as we have on facing injustice and unearned suffering for conscience' sake.

PERSONAL PRACTICE: Ask, "Is it Needed? How Can I Share?"
Look for the opportunity to ask daily, "Is this needed?" If the answer is
no, then ask yourself, "How can I best share it?" Asking these questions

every day for six weeks forms a habit. Once you form the habit, find one to three other people to join you in asking these questions regularly to meet everyone's basic needs and care for the planet.

Use my rights to pass and to consultation. First, no one must speak or join an any activity. Everyone has the right to pass. Sometimes we need to rest, observe, absorb, build trust, get privacy or take a breath. We should choose deliberately when to cooperate and not cooperate. Second, anyone who loses track of what a group is doing may ask for consultation. Anyone may ask how much longer an activity will go, when the group will break or if the group can move on or go back to a subject. Answer their question or consult with the whole group on a decision. If a question persists, consider writing it on a posted sheet labeled Open Questions or ask if you can discuss it on the next break. Leaders encourage participants to exercise their rights while paying attention to the needs of the whole group.

Volunteer myself only, not others. This agreement reminds us to volunteer. We each need to do our own part to care for ourselves, others, the group and the natural world with joy and generosity. Habits form among family members, friends and coworkers. When we volunteer others, we rob them of their own decision-making and control. Notice when you volunteer others and the degree to which it masks self put downs, devalues others or reinforces prejudices or privilege. Notice how your relationship changes when you volunteer yourself only.

Care for each person, the community and the natural world. Take responsibility to care for yourself, others, the group and the natural world. The work of creating a culture of peace requires consistent strength and stamina. To do it well, we need to get enough sleep, water, nutrition, exercise and attention. We recognize that we are a part of interdependent social and ecological systems. To stay vibrant, we take into account the needs of others and the natural world. We stand up to crimes against nature as well as against humanity. We work to consume local resources and not use things that hurt or poison the land, air or water. Life becomes a win-win infinite upward spiral of regeneration, not a zero-sum finite downward spiral of degeneration. The health and well-being of others and the natural world, as well as ourselves, define the quality of our lives.

Live in integrity with life's transforming power. We work to stay aware of and open to transforming power. Allow it to shape and guide our lives and decision-making. Remember, integrity requires honesty, authenticity and alignment among our beliefs, words and actions. Agree to align your life choices with your best sense of the nature and relationship of things. Honesty and authenticity require we get to know ourselves as well as the real nature and ways of life.

PERSONAL PRACTICE: Adhere to Agreements

Notice when and where agreements apply in your private and public life. Explore resistance you feel in yourself or in others as you apply them. Carry them on a card in your wallet and post them in visible places at home, school or work. Read them often, use them and discuss them with others. Write about them in your journal. When you encounter problems creating a culture of peace, look for roots of those problems in ignoring, misunderstanding or violating one of these agreements.

The ordinary activities of greetings and making friends who practice these agreements enables us to form principled friendships that lead to extraordinary transformations. Love, trust, honesty and mutual support cultivate astonishingly powerful, vibrant, nonviolent, peaceful communities. To view this work as anything other than ordinary, however, places people or the practices on a pedestal. This distances and separates us from each other and the work. Yet as one friend said, "Okay, but this seriously upgrades my sense of the ordinary!"

Communities of practice can set aside a place and a time for experimenting with love and conscience — gathering tools, practices and materials to aid in listening and expression. Much like a wellness center, a Conscience Studio can offer a space to study, create, conduct training and host companion groups and community gatherings. Such a space can be dedicated in a retreat center, study center, religious building, school, home or community center. We gather with people of any age and background, those similar and different from ourselves—even those considered enemies—to learn, practice and invest in cultures of peace.

"I'm Gonna Dance"

In Aceh, Autumn Star taught me a song by Marie and Sheila Burns called *Dance upon This Earth* (Philo, 1997). With their permission, I am reprinting the chorus below, because it captures our sense of approaching the world, full of life, joy and liberty, dancing on the Earth:

> *I'm gonna dance upon this Earth.*
> *I'm gonna find the joy in all this madness.*
> *I'm gonna be the one that you see,*
> *Livin' here and now and feelin' free.*
> *Dancin' on this Earth,*
> *Dancin' on this Earth,*
> *Is part of me!*

Peace is present …

and possible …

when we … preserve the peace intrinsic in life,
knowing nothing we say or do can make the
transforming power of life any more or less valuable;
we have already arrived.

when we … love life, ourselves, each other and the natural world,
build long-term, principled friendships
with people similar to and different from ourselves,
discharge our distresses and cultivate our
goodness and capabilities.

when we … listen honestly to our consciences,
overcome prejudice and privilege,
make decisions based on what rings true
and express conscience through
cooperation, noncooperation and in public record
simply for the joy, liberty and future of it.

Part II

~

LOVE
LIFE:

Living Peaceful
Private Lives

Loving people practice peace and nonviolence.

~

To love those called enemies and become friends,

so begins the work of peace.

~

Chapter 4

⌒

Love Life,
Oneself and Others

Love is the first motion. Learn to love life, including yourself, others and the natural world. Stop and listen for what rings true, but let your words and actions flow from love.

Love's inward openness, tenderness and affection can define, arrange and organize our relationships to shape and guide our lives in reliable ways. Love calls us to sit still, settle into the silence and connect with the life teeming within and among us. When we connect from this place, we need no reassurance or proof of the transforming power of life. We can imagine no other condition. Love transmits the life within us as it flows forth through our heartbeat and our breath. It never stops as long as we live. Drink from those headwaters. Let go of distress. Feel compassion. Connect with yourself and with life. Allow yourself to feel loved, lovable and loving.

You are valuable. Nothing you can say or do can make you any more or less valuable than you are right now. This is it. This is enough. Love life here and now. This awareness colors everything we feel, think, say and do. We experience this love of life as the most natural thing in the world.

Although our lives are inseparable from the generative, transforming, creative, loving power of life, as human beings we may be tempted or broken, our survival threatened, our expectations disappointed or our egos crushed. Our hearts may be hardened from failure or pain. We become constricted by loss, threats, injustice or pain. We may lose our love for ourselves and for life.

We experience human tragedy as tragic, on a human scale. Yet on a larger scale everything enfolds back into the creative momentum of life itself. If humans beings make enough loving, conscientious decisions, then the planet may stay habitable. If not, we may make the planet uninhabitable—at least for ourselves. Humans do not have the power to "wipe out all life." Life goes on, with or without us. That's its nature.

Internalizing a love for life requires regular attention. It can take twenty minutes to let go and settle, but even a few seconds can calm us. We remind ourselves to approach life and work with love and conscience. When I began this practice, I noted the percentage of each day I kept my awareness alert to life's transforming power. At first, I wrote numbers in my journal such as +10% or +15%. Then I wondered if I could raise that percentage. When it hovered in the mid to high twenties, I tried to keep it stable at that level. As if on its own, the percentage jumped. To my surprise, as if on its own, it became a habit I found almost impossible to lose.

I saw each person as a whole person with history, emotions, hopes and gifts shaped by the water, nutrition, resources and relationships that sustained them. Ideas and traditions from so many others flowed through them, affecting still others. So many of these interconnections flowed through each person. Love flooded through every moment. I saw each person within a context and felt a part of that web of life. I see everything culminates from the natural materials and lives of the people who discovered, extracted, designed, crafted, transported, delivered, installed and used it. When I pick up an item, I sense the interconnections with the Earth and its inhabitants. Over centuries, so many people and materials made it possible to be here and now. Every person and item has a history, a story and consequences that set their tone.

I never imagined such a keen awareness was possible. But when the habit took hold through genuine attention and practice, I found it difficult not to sense every breath, heartbeat, light beam, element, heartache or moment as part of this tremendous teeming power of life. Each one was loved, appreciated and valued. At that juncture, even human frailties, mistakes and tragedies existed within the context of this greater movement of life. My heart grew in compassion. I no longer feel as if I could or need to control life around me. Instead, I sense the endless resource of love running through and around me. It gives me the strength to call people to its power and not to give in to the tragedies of human suffering. Now I frequently invite people to remember moments we felt fully alive, present and in touch with our core selves.

GROUP ACTIVITY: *Core Self*

Say, "Now we will draw our Core Self. Remember a time when you felt fully alive and totally yourself. Notice your true, authentic, core self that felt good, capable, compassionate, caring, calm, clear, courageous, curious, connected, creative and confident. Make a drawing to represent that with oil pastels or crayons. Begin with your non-dominant hand. We are not about drawing a picture, we're drawing a feeling. Start with your non-dominant hand then switch back and forth."

When a few people finish, say, "As you finish, please put your name and three words anywhere on the front of your drawing. You can draw more later, but we'll take another minute or two to finish up for now." When only a few people are still drawing, ask the others to please clean up the area while the last few people finish. Then ask everyone to read their name and three words and tape their drawing to the wall.

Now say, "Let's stand back and look at all the pictures together. Notice, what we each look like and what we look like all together as a group. Whenever we've lost touch with our core selves, we can ask for time to discharge emotion and return to our core selves before proceeding. We think, make decisions and take action best from our core selves."

The core self has its own flexible, connected structures of love and conscience that can direct our decisions and actions. Love occurs when our core self connects with compassion to the core self of another. Conscience awakens when the insight in our core self is reflected in another.

Core Self. An experience of one's whole, authentic being, which is good, capable, free of distress and constant, yet can mature with awareness, knowledge and experience.

We each experience life's transforming power within ourselves differently. Expression of this inward experience in outward form anchors us to this power. It allows us to get to know ourselves and one another in this infinite and eternal power. Try the Core Self activity with your family or friends, at work or in a community group. Post the drawings on the wall to refer to when needed. Get to know each person and the group through the drawings. This chapter offers tools to talk openly about violence, rely on life's transforming power and make a personal commitment to practice love and conscience in private and public life.

Talk Openly about Violence

Ironically, we must be willing and able to face the violence within and around us in order to live loving, peaceful lives. Our shortcomings, inadequacies and mistakes offer us a valuable source of humility, learning and compassion. As Jalaluddin Mevlana Rumi suggests, "The wound is the place where the Light enters you."

Opening to life's transforming power in good times instills tremendous confidence, while opening in hard times instills conviction. As suggested by the root "convict," we discover conviction in our shortcomings. Our human tragedies and failings create the cracks through which we see beyond our own egos. There we meet the source of the power within yet beyond ourselves teeming through an interconnected web of life.

A culture of peace requires we learn to talk openly about violence as well as nonviolence. Circumstances foist violence upon certain people. Others seldom experience violence except on the news or in therapy rooms. For the former, societal violence is inescapable. For the latter, society keeps violence in its place, not out here in public.

In a culture of peace, we learn to hear stories of violence to reduce its surprise, control and power over us and to become resilient in the face of it. We avoid telling stories of violence. We may fear getting lost in the memory. Or, we may not want to put ourselves or a listener through it again. To stay resilient, we learn to open and discharge emotional pain, then return to the here and now when we want to stop remembering, or to stay relaxed and nonanxious in the face of it. This matures our whole, true, loving and loved core selves.

PERSONAL PRACTICE: *Ground Oneself in the Present*

When we want come out of an emotional state or stay relaxed and nonanxious in the face of emotion, we learn to ground ourselves in the here and now. Use a memorable phrase such as, "Look around. Right now you are safe. Notice all the goodwill around you." Then ask a random, factual question such as: What color is your shirt? What is the capitol of Norway? How many colors can you see? Name three, two then one thing you can see, touch or hear. Pick up an object and describe its colors, textures, functions, writing and so forth. Walk, run or do physical work. Play a game or sport. Do anything to bring yourself back to this time and place. Say "We need to come back to the here and now. Are we all here?" When we repeat the same words, we create a "voice" that replays in our minds when we need it. Use a grounding technique whenever you want to reduce distress and come back to the present.

Practice staying in the here and now while offering attention to someone. Practice returning to the here and now after discharging a painful memory. Learn to ground yourself or others when tensions escalate. Help someone ground when they get so emotional that they lose language or become hysterical. Leave no one "out there," collapsing internally into distress. Practice visiting the past to heal, rather than to relive it. Then practice coming back to the present. Both require equal attention.

Successful experiences grounding and returning to the present builds confidence. The more we use these skills to return fully after we remember something distressing, the more courage and confidence we have to remember and reprocess our own memories. We recognize that distress does not come from personal failings, it comes from past hurts caused by a lack of attention or insight at a time when we needed it. Or it comes through others' or societies' unresolved hurts from abuse and oppression played out upon one another. The more skillfully and reliably we stay grounded, the more we can heal ourselves and support others.

In a culture of peace we need to better understand and respect the role of emotion. Painful experiences can pile up on each other over a lifetime. We may find the work of healing to be daunting in a distress-laden society, but the more each of us heals and clears the painful experiences in our past, the more distress-free our society becomes. In a culture of peace we notice when distressing emotions arise, ask for time to discharge them, then return to our work together with increased clarity.

Discharging and reprocessing memories from our youngest times or most significant incidents can resolve later memories, causing healing to cascade through our lives to the present. This stops them from intruding on us today. When did I *first* feel this way? When did I *most* feel this way?

I notice when I become distressed and ask questions. It often helps to start with less extreme memories to learn the techniques before applying them to more challenging incidents. But sometimes early or significant memories are so intrusive that one cannot think of anything else. Trust yourself to know what to work on.

To transform our lives and society, we need companions who know how to discharge emotion, clear our minds, search our consciences and exchange feedback. As long as you can stop and respond to feedback, you can stay resilient.

GROUP ACTIVITY: *Good Companions*
"Now we will practice Good Companions." Ask people to get into pairs and sit facing one another. Tell them that each person will get five minutes to practice being a good companion while the other discharges emotions, then they will switch. Read the Good Companions poster, then add, "A good companion stays in their core self in this time and place remembering the other's core self."

Good Companions

A good companion is a good listener who:

• Listens from the heart with relaxed, non-anxious attention.

• Pays attention to the other's goodness and capabilities.

• Notes distresses that arise to come back to later.

• Takes equal turns.

The other person will remember a difficult time. Do not remember the most emotional time, but something that still has some emotional traction. While you remember, do NOT speak but notice how the body can let go of the emotion and let it leave the body." The facilitator reads the Emotional Discharge poster. Note that human beings discharge emotion in the same ways everywhere, it is the healing, not the pain. Then add, "A good companion remembers their partner's core self and helps them return to the present time."

Emotional Discharge		
Emotion		*Ways the Body Discharges Emotion*
Grief	=>	Crying, sobbing, moaning, wailing
Fear	=>	Trembling, cold sweats, laughter
Anger	=>	Loud voice, sharp movement, hot sweat, laughter
Boredom	=>	Non-repetitive conversation, yawning, laughter
Pain	=>	Stretching, yawning, scratching

"If the person remembering stands, moves or goes to the restroom or outside, companions stand and walk with them. Wait outside the restroom. Please begin now. I will tell you when to switch roles." After two-and-a-half minutes, gently remind the group of their tasks.

- *"Let it go, don't hold on to it. Breathe. Make noises. Move. Do not hold it. Let it go. Feel the emotion leave the body. Let go of any tension. Soften anywhere that feels tight. Let it go."*

- *"Companions remember the goodness and capability of your friend. Stay relaxed, nonanxious in your core self. Remember the other's core self."*

After four minutes or more, tell the group we will finish soon. Then say, "When you're ready to finish, please stand up." Once everyone is standing, ask them to come back to the present time, to the here and now. Ask them to walk around the room, do a grounding, then to sit with their companion in different seats. Say, "Did you notice how walking and changing your orientation in the room helped you to come back to the present time? We practice coming back as well as letting go and being a good companion." Do a grounding technique. Ask everyone to check that their partner is back. Then, switch roles and repeat. Reflect in the large group. Ask what that was like? What did each role feel like? What did you learn? What will you do differently in your life?

Emotion is contagious and can overwhelm individuals and groups. Over time, we learn how to show but not dump emotional content in public. We tend our emotions in pairs or small companion groups that meet every one to six weeks to exchange attention, discharge emotion, clear our minds, listen to conscience and exchange feedback.

Physically expressing emotion in front of others challenges cultural inhibitions toward display of emotion. Around the world I hear, "Hush, hush, don't cry. It'll be okay." We need to learn to say, when appropriate, "Go ahead. I'm right here. It's fine to cry." As we become practiced, we learn to take a break, ground ourselves, remove ourselves from the situation or make a note of our reactive emotions to come back to later. Likewise, we may notice when others need to tend their emotions and ask the group to take a brief time in pairs or triads to discharge and ground. Our capacity to respond in the moment increases as we commit to regular companion sessions in pairs or small groups. We exchange attention in equal turns.

As we become more open about our experiences of violence, we change the power that it has over us. Violence garners power through surprise and secrecy. When we try to put violence out of our minds, deny, hide it or isolate ourselves, then distress amplifies. Resiliency requires that we practice facing and standing up to violence in our lives.

GROUP ACTIVITY: Stories of Violence

Say, "Now we will tell Stories of Violence." In the large group, brainstorm words associated with violence. Write them on a poster labeled Violence. Consider ways we have experienced, seen or noticed violence in our lives, directly, indirectly or through societal systems or social patterns. Then brainstorm words associated with nonviolence on a separate sheet labeled Nonviolence.

Ask each person to take a crayon and circle three words they experienced themselves on the Violence sheet. This illustrates how everyone experiences violence. Then go around the circle and invite each person to tell one story of one incident of violence they experienced themselves. Remind them to share only what they feel ready to share.

Storytelling Protocol

1. Where did it happen?

2. What happened?

3. How did it feel?

4. When was it over, at least that incident.

Say, "We will each practice using this storytelling protocol to tell a story of one event, not the background or consequences, just one incident. Where, what, how it felt and when it was over, at least at that time. If each person speaks for two minutes, it will take (calculate the time). As we listen, we should each practice being a good companion, staying relaxed and nonanxious in our core selves and remembering the goodness and capability in the core self of each speaker." Point to the Good Companions poster.

After every couple stories do a grounding. Stretch, look around, ask a random question or notice the space or an object, walk, move and check-in, then continue. After these stories, we often do not reflect in the large group. The group needs to move and play! We run and laugh, outdoors if possible. People discharge and ground themselves through play.

Some people say they have not experienced violence personally. But everyone knows pain, sadness and hurt. We can search our memories for the experiences that taught us those feelings. Civil societies are becoming more militarized, relying on and even glamorizing violence. In our workshops, parents, teachers, professionals and business owners tell horrendous stories of violence in homes, schools, workplaces and communities. Yet at the same time they compartmentalize, normalize and put violent incidents out of mind. Young children often face threatening behavior. Emotional outbursts, smashing things, hurtful words, piercing glances, ignoring or shunning and neglecting basic needs threaten young people's sense of safety and survival. Adults and older children often use threatening behaviors or outbursts as a quick way to get what we want from others.

The part of the brain that registers fear, the amygdala, reacts the same to threats of harm as it does to actual harm. This explains why threats work. Even a piercing glance if it produces fear of harm can be an act of violence. People use micro-aggressions, gestures or expressions designed to disrespect, control or threaten others to get what they want. They may or may not be conscious of this or of the costs to others. So they may have no insight or motivation to change.

Listening to others' stories of violence can make many shifts in individuals and groups. When we listen to these stories, we realize how violence permeates our families, schools and communities and causes lasting damage. We grow in compassion for ourselves and others.

First, we realize that violence is not just bad guys with guns. Violence can be in the way we talk to someone or look at them, even tiny gestures. We see the ways we use violence to get what we want. When we see violence in smaller, more pervasive forms, we can stop it from the start.

Second, we realize we are not alone, everyone carries pain, suffering, fear and sadness. We see how violence permeates our lives and society and erodes our culture. Then we can be more open. We can turn to one another in times of emotional hardship and become more resilient.

Third, we realize that staying silent and keeping secrets increases the power of violence. When we put up our guard, we become rigid. We lose touch with our core selves and our sense of compassion, flexibility and generosity. Sharing stories of violence helps us craft more realistic responses and ways to protect ourselves, without becoming rigid or callous. To pay realistic, honest attention to violence from our relaxed, nonanxious core selves robs it of much of its surprise, control and power. We do what we can to protect ourselves so we do not have to keep up our guard all the time. We can go about our daily business.

Finally, we realize that when we stop feeling alone and vulnerable, we can think and choose our own ways of responding. We do not have to respond to violence with fear and isolation or with rage and revenge. We can respond with many creative, compassionate, nonviolent means. Feeling more capable of protecting ourselves and more connected with others leads to personal stability, inner strength, genuine self-care, emotional regulation and effective self-management. We can live, free from addiction, self-harm or injury to or by others. Be careful, though. Do not to rely on telling stories of violence as a currency for bonding and intimacy. Exchange time with a good companion using the story protocol to not relive or reenact trauma. Let the emotion leave the body and heal. Sharing stories of violence to heal can create a tangible sense of equality, safety and trust, extend permission to raise a wider range of subjects and build resiliency.

Rely on Life's Transforming Power

People can find stories of nonviolence harder to identify than stories of violence. We take for granted the way we solve problems with nonviolence every day. We seldom notice when or how we do it. When we observe the dynamics of nonviolence in daily life, we gain a remarkable reservoir of resources and references. We feel more able to rely on nonviolent, peaceful solutions with confidence and enthusiasm.

GROUP ACTIVITY: *Stories of Nonviolence*
Say, "Now we will tell Stories of Nonviolence." Invite each person to take a crayon and circle three words they experienced themselves on the Nonviolence sheet. This illustrates how everyone uses nonviolence to solves problems. Then, in groups of four, invite each person to take three to five minutes to share a story of "a time I solved a problem nonviolently." As they complete their stories, give each group a poster paper with Turning Points written at the top. Ask each group to make a single list of what caused each of the four stories to turn towards nonviolence away from violence. Be specific. Name what was said or done. Do not retell the stories. Ask each group to read their list to the large group and post it on the wall. Reflect on this activity.

In moments of imminent violence, we may act quickly with surprise, humor or whatever stalls the violence and buys time to turn the situation. But this requires incredible skill and a hefty dose of good luck—and often fails. As the point of impact in violence approaches, the options for constructive, nonviolent responses decreases. The analysis of turning points shifts attention away from the point of violence or imminent threat to earlier openings for action, increasing the chances of peaceful conclusions. When a situation begins to feel tense or rigid, we can learn to point out, redirect, expose, object, resist or thwart a shift towards violence before it begins. We choose the type of power we draw on in any moment: creative or destructive. Violence may appear to have gains, but it only robs and leads to more violence and destruction. On the other hand, creativity can transform situations in powerful, regenerative ways with fruitful, lasting results.

GROUP ACTIVITY: Transforming Power

Say, "Now we will introduce Transforming Power." Point out the brainstorm sheets: Violence and Nonviolence. Ask the group to notice that Nonviolence means the absence of the things on the Violence brainstorm, "no violence." Nonviolence means not using violence yourself and standing up against its use in private or public life. Tape the word Nonviolence over the header Violence.

Guides to Transforming Power

- Seek to resolve conflicts by reaching for common ground.
- Reach for that something good in others.
- Listen before judging others.
- Base your position on truth.
- Be ready to revise your position if wrong.
- Expect to experience great inward power to act.
- Risk being creative rather than violent.
- Use surprise and humor.
- Learn to trust your inner sense of when to act.
- Be willing to suffer for what is true.
- Be patient and persistent.
- Build community based on honesty, respect and caring.

Alternatives to Violence Project (1975) AVPUSA.org • AVP.International

---

Note that the elements listed on the Nonviolence brainstorm need the absence of violence, but refer to the transforming power of life. Tape the word Transforming Power over the header Nonviolence. We call these transforming power, which refers to the power of love, truth, integrity, compassion, justice and so forth. Transforming power exists in everyone and every situation. We can open, rely on and follow its lead.

Note that everyone knows how transforming power operates. Point to the posted Turning Points. We live in peace most of the time in our daily lives. The Alternatives to Violence Project (AVP) has also studied stories of nonviolence and identified the following Guides to Transforming Power. Invite groups of three people to read these guides and bring questions or comments back to the large group for discussion. Inform the group that from now on our activities train us to rely on nonviolence and transforming power to create a culture of peace in our homes, communities and society. Reflect on this activity.

Once we see transforming power teeming through everything, no one can convince us it does not exist! Imagine I met you. Afterward someone tried to convince me you didn't exist. I'm convinced you exist because I've met you. Once I experience the transforming power of life, no one can convince me it does not exist. I'm no longer condemned to repeating old ways. I can arrange and rearrange things in ways that put me in touch with a sense of life's power. I rely on my inner sense of love and conscience to guide my decisions and actions. The Alternatives to Violence Project (AVP) developed a mandala that offers a starting point for practicing this in our daily lives.

GROUP ACTIVITY:
Mandala Interviews

Tell the group, "Now we'll look at the Mandala." Spread the six parts of the AVP Mandala out on the floor. State, "Experimenting with transforming power in our lives can feel like a lot. It's not clear where to begin. Here are a few, good places to begin." Invite everyone to stand by the mandala part they most need to practice now. Then invite people standing on each part to talk to one another about why they picked that part. Then ask those standing on Respect for Self and Caring for Others to push their pieces together and discuss the balance of the two. Then ask those standing on the other three parts to push their pieces together and discuss the balance of the three. Reflect on this activity.

⁓

We have one commitment:
to practice opening to and relying on life's transforming power to guide our private and public lives.

⁓

The ideas and practices from now on focus on one commitment: experiment with opening to and relying on life's transforming power to guide private and public life. As we gain more tools and skills, our ability to do this increases. Blaze Nowara filmed our work in Asia and produced the video *Silaturahmi: The Power of Visiting* (see FriendsPeaceTeams.org/AWP). He sought examples of people changed by this training and often heard, "Me! I changed. Completely!" An Islamic leader, Imam Saring, from the mountains of North Sumatra replied, "That's me! As a person considered an elder and called Imam, I used to be very violent. I refused to lose. But since I learned that living with violence is a waste, I have tried to become a better and better person, who is of benefit to everyone." He labored his whole life, lost everything in the war in Aceh and found himself unable to care for his children. Imam Saring had become a hard man. In a role play in his first workshop he played a pregnant teenager being beaten with a two-by-four, which he later confessed blew his mind. He now explains:

"If we want to live peacefully, we must begin with ourselves. We must learn to not fight over things that come up among us in our community, so stones don't clash with stones and shatter, only causing destruction. When we meet stones, we must look for water. If a stone falls into the water, it sinks down without a sound. This is the real nature of peace, which is good."

The film shows many people deeply changed by this work. Imam Saring's daughter, Ani, described the changes, "We were a hard people, very suspicious of anyone who came from the outside. We immediately beat them up. But now we speak to people, we don't just hit them first. We're more apt to ask, "Why are you here? What is it you want here?"

Many people who continue to perpetrate intergenerational cycles of violence do not think of themselves as violent. They say, "It's the people with guns who are violent. We're the victims." Or, "We're just defending ourselves." When they realize how they perpetrate violence, a conscious decision to use nonviolence can create enormous changes in their lives.

Through role plays we experiment with new ways of speaking, acting and responding to daily events. We do not dramatize a story or act out a predetermined outcome. Role plays allow us to experiment with transforming power under certain circumstances, explore creative ways of interacting verbally and nonverbally and develop new skills. It helps to disrupt the sense of being stuck in repetitive lives. We come to appreciate the wealth of decisions, responses and actions available to us.

GROUP ACTIVITY: *Role Plays*

"Now we will do Role Plays." In groups of five or six, select one true scenario you want to respond to better in daily life. Do not explain the history or plan a solution. Begin the role play at the turning point. Each person imagines they are in the real situation and emotional state and genuinely wants to rely on transforming power to find a good way forward. Remember transforming power may come through anyone: a child, bystander or authority. Do not use drugs, alcohol or weapons in the solution; they do not resolve violence in the long-run. Divide the roles among group members. Have each take a role opposite to their nature or experience. Ask them to select a name they have never used before. Make name tags with the role's name and position. Decide what each character is doing and feeling when the role play begins. Make a poster with a title, location and narrator (who reads the poster and plays a part). Make four columns: Name, Role, Doing/Feeling and Played By.

During the role play, once the situation escalates or de-escalates, the facilitator calls "freeze" to stop the action. Players stop like statues. Ask the audience what change they saw in body language, gesture, posture, words, action, movement or shift in atmosphere. Ask what caused the change. After two or three key insights, ask the players if they'd like to start again. If the facilitator sees no progress, ask the players to freeze. Remind the players that transforming power can come through anyone. Ask, "What are you feeling now? Do you have any ideas for how to open to transforming power in this situation or not?" If a player says yes, ask, "Would you like to try it?" If no, ask if anyone in the audience has an idea. Proceed once an insight is clear or someone has a plan. You may ask participants if they want to rewind and replay any part.

Once you've gotten a few lessons about transforming power in action, stop and ask the players if they are satisfied. If so, end the role play. If not, tell them, "The point was to learn how to rely on transforming power, not to finish the drama. We have learned a lot. Is it okay to stop now?" If not, ask what they need to be able to stop. When you bring people out of role, start with the most emotional person. Anyone who has fallen silent, become nonverbal or played a child should come out of role first. Ask players one by one: "Before coming out of role, do you want to say anything? (Listen to what they say.) Please stick your name tag to the wall (point to a location). Welcome back [participant's real name]. Is there anything you want to say as [participant's real name]?" If speaking to a role, speak to a player still in role or to the name taped to the wall. Do not address an audience member who already left their role as if they are still in that role! After they finish, say "Thank you, welcome back [participant's real name]. Please sit here (point to a location)." Reflect after each role play.

Anyone who has lived in a war zone or with domestic violence knows weeks can go by without incident. Then suddenly without sound or warning, the air thickens or your heart tenses in your chest. Within seconds screaming, shooting or smashing erupts. Just as one can feel the violence in the air before an incident occurs, so you can feel transforming power in the air as a sense of ease or delight. Transforming power is palpable. Practice noticing turning points and how to open to peaceful possibilities. As one young participant said, "They teach us how to be cool, but not be mean."

Commit to Practicing Peace

We developed principled friendships based on agreements, learned tools for telling stories of violence and nonviolence, and practiced noticing and experiencing transforming power. Based on this awareness, we each face the challenge of choosing peace and nonviolence, or not.

GROUP ACTIVITY: Write a Personal Commitment
Say to the group, "Now we will consider writing a personal commitment. Will you commit to relying on nonviolence and transforming power in your private and public life? If so, in your own words and language, drawing on your own history, conscience, ethics or faith, write your own commitment to yourself." Display examples:

- *I commit to experimenting with the transforming power of life— love, truth and integrity—in my private and public life for the well-being of the planet and its people.*

- *I commit to being my fullest, most authentic self and use my power in conscientious, purposeful ways to benefit all life and the Earth.*

"You may add to the statement one to three steps you plan to take. We never expect anyone to share your journal with others. Only if you want to, you may post your personal commitment on the wall." Reflect on what it felt like to write the commitment.

All the activities that follow are based on this personal commitment to experimenting with nonviolence and transforming power in daily life. An experiment requires a log or journal. Use the discipline of writing to test the insights you gain through solitude, silence, attention and experimentation. Also write about the feedback you receive from testing insights within companions and community groups. Test insights with people similar to and different from yourself. Record the implications of your insights along with the personal changes you make and their results.

PERSONAL PRACTICE: Keep a Log or Journal

Each person of love and conscience keeps a log or journal to record their experiment with transforming power in private and public life.

Journal Topics

- A personal commitment written in one's own words.
- Community expectations, agreements or road map for learning.
- Experiences of confidence and conviction in transforming power.
- Affirmations of your authentic core self.
- Notes of any distresses that need to be discharged or reprocessed.
- Implications for personal change and subsequent insights or practices.
- Open questions and feedback to explore.
- Questions and encouragements emerging from reflection.
- Sense of direction for right action and settlement of disputes.
- Any help needed, from whom, for whom and how to exchange help.
- Sufferings for conscience' sake and sharing of wealth.
- Letters of introduction for individuals, groups or communities.

This journal is not a diary or for therapeutic, artistic or professional development. Rather, keep notes to log or track your experiment. A journal is private. Write it for yourself and share only what and when you choose. Others should not ask you to share your journal.

We place our trust in the power of life, not based on blind faith or ideology, but based on experience, experimentation and feedback.

The results we reap as we live out our commitment reinforce our faith. We understand faith as a belief so strong it orders our actions. Be honest with yourself as you examine where you place your faith. What would happen if you put your faith in transforming power and invested in loving, just relationships and actions? Transforming power braids love and truth together. We listen to and follow love and conscience.

PERSONAL PRACTICE: Plan for Love

Plan how to love yourself, others and the natural world. Look for concrete changes needed to love more. Ask others what makes them feel loved. Plan to show love in the way they request, not only in the way you want to express it. Ask yourself what steps you can take to feel more loved. What can you do on your own or with others to love the natural world around you more? Write these concrete steps for loving yourself, others and the natural world, and describe the results.

PERSONAL PRACTICE: *Plan for Conscience*

Settle into silence and listen inwardly for what feels right or wrong and how to do the right thing. Be brave. Often you will not expect or even want what comes. You will have already yielded to easier truths. Prepare yourself to yield to whatever comes no matter what. Make a plan to apply the implications of these truths working within you. Write concrete steps. Notice which ones you resist, avoid or give up on. Notice the ones you take and how they change you.

As we reflect on our experiences, we make notes on our insights and the implications for our lives. We document practices and see how they change our lives. Love is not always as pleasant as we imagine. Love is often painful. Betrayal and heartache harden hearts from a young age. Negative messages heard as a child often stay with us and heighten insecurity, fear and avoidance. We often do not notice how much they undercut our lives, making us callous, hard, narrow, suspicious and self-sabotaging. At any age, negative messages about ourselves take a toll. Notice and discharge counterproductive messages to free yourself for love with courage.

GROUP ACTIVITY: *Whisper Circle*

Say, "Now we will do the Whisper Circle." Start by thinking of a negative message you heard as a child that stayed with you. Then think of the opposite, antidote or positive message you needed to hear instead. Write the positive sentence on a card without your name for others to read. Collect the cards and check that each statement is positive and legible. Ask half the group to sit in a silent circle. Give two cards to each remaining person, but not their own. Make sure they can read both cards. Ask them to hold one card in each hand. They each stand behind a seated person, bend forward and whisper the sentence in the left hand into the left ear of the seated person then stand. Watch one person to synchronize, bend forward and whisper the sentence in the right hand into the right ear of the seated person. Following the leader, move one person to the right. Repeat this around the circle. Then pause in silence. The people standing switch places with those sitting. Repeat for the second half of the people. Have tissues available, people often cry. Reflect on this activity.

Many people find it harder to hear positive messages than negative ones. "I love you." "You're beautiful." "You can do it! Go ahead, try." "I'm right here, don't worry." After people experience the Whisper Circle, they become more careful with what they say to one another, especially to children. Hearing words that affirm our goodness and our capabilities makes us feel loved. It softens our hearts, brings down our guard and helps us relax. We can open to vulnerability. The Empty Chair helps us notice how much we open up or close down to love.

GROUP ACTIVITY: *Empty Chair*

Say, "Now we'll do Empty Chair." Sit in a circle. "Think of someone who loves you and why. Each of us will stand behind our chair one at a time. Then speak as the person who loves us saying the person's name and relationship and why they love us. For example, I will go first." Stand behind your chair and say, "I am Fenna, Nadine's daughter, and I love Nadine because ..." Have tissues available. Reflect on this activity.

If you feel loved, you're lucky. Many people don't. Asking people to name a person who loves them may stir strong feelings. We may think of people who have died, who we wished loved us, who hurt us or we hurt them, or no one comes to mind. It may generate sadness over not having a lover or a partner. Emotion is contagious. Don't rush to rescue anyone. Expect the best and give them time to think. They do not have to choose a living person. Anyone may pass. This activity reminds us of how much we need to feel loved without demand or obligation.

Those who feel loved were graced with loving people in their lives or they worked hard for it, or both. Either way, they had to pay attention, invest, adjust, adapt, accept and forgive for love to last. They may have even needed an explicit plan to nurture their love. Still, if distress or violence intrude, even occasionally, they can lose that investment in a flash. Never underestimate the power of violence, even episodic violence, to destroy decades of loving investment. Love requires nonviolence. Nonviolence requires the absence of violence besides the positive attention and efforts. It's easy to take for granted the luck and grace of real love.

I remember the moment I realized the incredible implications of unconditional love for myself. I had two toddlers and a husband who spoke little English. We were both out of work. I was walking down a street in Tallahassee, Florida, and wondered if we might become homeless next month. I felt failure imploding. The shame was suffocating.

A few months before, I had run a large USAID educational development project in Indonesia. I asked the USAID Mission Director— in front of a dozen U.S. university consultants—what to do about the funds missing from my project.

The Mission Director asked, "Can they liquidate?" Meaning, can they submit receipts to account for the funds so they can draw more funds? In other words, can they cover it up?

"Sure," I said. "They're not stupid."

"Will a U.S. auditor catch it?"

"No," I said with certainty.

"Well then I don't give a damn. Your job is to move money. The more money you move, the more valuable you are to me," he said decisively.

Other consultants had encouraged me to be flexible, compromise and mind my own business. This shows they knew everything was not right. Yet still they considered the Indonesians the corrupt ones, not themselves.

The dynamics became crystal clear. Contrary to the project's stated educational development goals, the primary structural goal was to circulate money. Simply put, the U.S. becomes rich when more money comes in than goes out. But accumulating funds stagnates U.S. currency. Development projects pay funds back to U.S. universities, consultants, airlines, technologies and so forth. This circulates funds at a rate and volume necessary to keep currency stable. Development projects subsidize U.S. businesses and expand U.S. markets while stabilizing U.S. currency. Allowing theft of funds remaining in the country was irrelevant, but encouraged governmental officials to accept future projects.

The Mission Director's job was to keep the money moving and the opportunities to do so open. Suddenly, decisions on the project made sense. They were not sloppy, bureaucratic or complicated. They were consistent, precise and clear. Leaders approved recommendations that moved large sums of money fast and ignored or rejected recommendations that needed less money, moved slower or risked delays. So, I left the project. But then, to my surprise I discovered that many international consultants had married partners who controlled domestic school district contracts. I found myself blacklisted from most work in educational policy, in the U.S. and abroad. The level of professional collusion in corruption became conspicuous.

As I squinted through the Florida sun at the traffic light, I wondered if I would lose my self-respect if I became homeless next month? I had worked with and thought I respected homeless people. But how could I say I respected them if I did not respect myself if I became homeless? The question stunned me. To keep my respect for others under any circumstances, I had to keep my self-respect under any circumstances. This crushing realization emerged into a sense of immense calm.

I could literally feel myself choose unconditional love—for myself and for others. A huge wave of indescribable, unconditional love swept over me. In that moment I felt worthy no matter what. I could end up homeless, in prison, a success or a failure. But these outward signs did not define my worth or value as a human being. Everyone receives the same breath, heartbeat and life. This experience gave me a taste of what I came to know as the liberty of love and conscience. I no longer felt as if I would implode and die in shame. I felt free and calm.

This newfound depth of self-respect steadied my respect for life in unimaginable ways. Fear that failure would make me a social outcast fell away. I did not disappear. I remained a whole person. This allowed me to see others as whole people. Later, I heard Indonesians say when war or poverty forced them out of school and into labor they knew they would "never become a person." What a tragedy that people fear falling into a subhuman class when we cannot conform to or succeed. What a gift to be aware of being a whole, natural person on a whole, glorious Earth with enough for everyone!

I was still unaware, however, of the vigilance required to maintain this sense of value. Principled friendships based on agreements, as discussed earlier, may appear ordinary and simple, but they extend love in the world in astonishing, significant ways.

In a nutshell, to encourage love, practice stopping the body and mind and commit to personal and social transformation. Organize communities of practice and gather with others to learn, play and reflect. Greet people, make friends and affirm one another. Remind each other of basic agreements for peace and see mistakes as learning opportunities. Encourage good companionship, tend your core self, discharge distresses, share stories of violence and nonviolence and ask for permission to share other's stories. Each day ask what you need and how you may share the rest. Keep a log of experiments with transforming power in daily life. Make plans for furthering love and conscience and experience the power of these simple acts of goodness.

~

We have one commitment:
to practice opening to and relying on
life's transforming power
to guide our private and public lives.

~

Chapter 5

～

Visit with Oneself

Visit with, care for and get to know yourself. Put immediate, mundane matters in good order to make yourself available for more challenging or creative matters as they arise. With good attention from others, we can heal and change ourselves, strengthening our call for changes in others.

Care for and Get to Know Oneself

As we care for ourselves, confidence in our goodness and capabilities matures. When we feel valuable and self-confident we take better care of ourselves and make more loving, conscientious decisions. This upward spiral makes us resilient and able to take risks on behalf of ourselves and others. Jens Braun (2010) challenges the simplistic concept of safety first:

"As we engage in life, it is important to do so in a manner that cares for and nourishes our physical beings, but let this not be at the expense of our spirits and souls. Pain, even premature death, need not be invited, but seeking at all costs to avoid their entrance into our homes can well shut doors to the fundamentals of our humanity." He goes on to encourage, "Spirit first, family and community second, beauty and goodness third and safety fourth."

Living in war zones, we can find ourselves risking our lives for what is right, for family and friends and for the natural world. At the same time, lack of safe haven derails any other undertaking. Safe haven is a primary, basic human need for everyone. Basing decisions on love and conscience, not fear and avoidance, creates safe haven and a sense of security that liberates us to take risks on behalf of Spirit, family and community. We care for the beauty and goodness of ourselves, humanity and the natural world.

Physical care begins with regular sleep and hydration, the lack of which can cause extreme pain throughout the body. People often self-medicate distress with sleep deprivation because it numbs the body and reduces executive brain functioning similar to intoxication.

So first, we sleep enough and drink enough clean water. Then we make sure we eat nutritious food, bathe, clean, exercise, relax, interact, work, manage your household and have a goal or sense of purpose. We find meaningful occupation and seek counseling and medical care as needed.

The word "care" comes from the Germanic root meaning "grief, or to grieve and lament." Physical self-care also involves emotional self-care and self-regulation: grieving, letting go, discharging distress and recovering from addiction, domestic violence or any other form of abuse or neglect.

GROUP ACTIVITY: Stand on a Line

Tell the group, "Now we will Stand on a Line." First, brainstorm the ways to take care of ourselves to be well and to meet life's challenges. Brainstorm on a "Self-Care" poster. Sometimes we brainstorm on the "Zone of Adaptation" (below). Notice natural rhythms—awake-asleep, exercise-rest, talk-listen. In small and large ways we constantly self-regulate. Write items in the lower curve (rest) in green and in the upper curve (active) in red.

Then draw the lower dotted line and ask what this lower section called. In this section, write withdrawn/depressed and items for self-care in red. Then draw the upper dotted line and ask what this upper section is called. Write manic/hyperactive and items for self-care in green. Notice when you need to listen to and do what your body needs and when you need to do the opposite of what you feel like. When you are manic, you may need to calm down, breathe or meditate. When you are depressed,

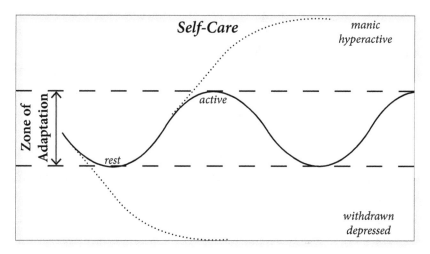

you may need to get busy, exercise or go out. Many people exacerbate our own extremes rather than self-regulate.

Ask the group to bring paper and pen or journals. Clear the center of the room. Post "100% enough" on one wall and "0% not enough" on the opposite wall. Say, "Stand from 100 to zero for how well you sleep. Without moving, put your eyes on the spot where you want to stand." Wait for everyone's eyes to be on a spot. "Okay, now move to the spot and look back and imagine one step you could take to make that change. Take notes." Repeat the sequence with sleeping, drinking water, exercise or take requests. Lastly ask: "How well do you take care of yourself in general?" After each one, invite them to take notes in their journals. Then reflect on the activity by asking in pairs what they learned and in the large group if anyone has any insights for us as a people or a culture.

We seek self-knowledge and self-care, not as ends in themselves but as essential ingredients for a peaceful life. David Johnson (2013, p. 28) notes how self-absorption "need(s) to be abandoned as quickly as possible with no regrets." This includes self-indulgence, self-congratulation, self-justification or self-pity based on an inflated sense of specialness. Beware of these pitfalls. Heal and cultivate your unique, genuine, true core self to the challenges of life.

Oddly, the more we heal the less special and more ordinary we become. Moshe Feldenkrais (2009) showed how letting go of distress and tension makes our gait so ordinary we become unidentifiable at a distance. Sometimes we fear that if we give up our pain we may forget the magnitude of past wrongs or lose our identity. People of love and conscience do not rely on pain to set us apart and make us special. We work to let go of distress and allow ourselves to heal and become ordinary. We turn our attention to understanding and expressing genuine, unique, creative perspectives and insights.

In addition, Feldenkrais encouraged "no extra effort." He showed how effort that does not turn into movement does damage. First, stop. This does not mean to go flaccid. Healthy body tone and mental alertness are autonomic and take no voluntary effort. Let go of extra, voluntary effort in your body, mind and heart, but stay alert and attuned. Second, exert only the voluntary effort necessary to carry out the desired movement. When we relax we can pay better attention to when, where and how to exert effort.

As we relax, we shift the work from the voluntary muscles made for movement to the bones and involuntary muscles made for posture. These muscles may be weak from disuse, so relaxing may feel tiring. Excess tension in the shoulders shifts the center-of-gravity forward. This requires muscles of the rib cage and abdomen to tense up and carry the weight of the head and upper body. Letting go of this tension moves the center-of-gravity back into the spine. The spine then bears that weight and effort, which is its natural function, improving spinal health. Our body stays healthy by moving then resting, not by over-exerting then collapsing.

Extra stress, tension and pain can become more familiar and stronger through habitual use than our natural, healthy selves. Wellbeing requires we rebuild our postural muscles and healthy self-image with confidence in our natural abilities. We practice letting go of extra physical and emotional effort—stress, worry, anxiety and fear. Then each part of the body can do its own natural function and each person can do their natural part. We learn to respect others to do their work. With relaxed minds and hearts, we offer attention with empathy and compassion, and notice if and when to offer feedback or help.

As our bodies, minds and hearts relax, so does our emotional intensity in social interactions. We become less susceptible to emotional outbursts, emotional contagion or taking others' distress personally. Our identity shifts from the drama of our wounds to our genuine, creative yet ordinary, core selves. We nurture and strengthen our core selves and let go of pain and suffering. We function as our perfect part of the perfect whole of life and work to create community and society that supports this. Contrary to common misconception, perfectibility does not mean doing everything on one's own without flaw. It means being one's perfect self, with genuine goodness, capabilities, weaknesses and flaws, as our perfect part of a living whole.

This ordinary, healthy life with no extra effort produces great beauty and peace, deep self-respect and connection with others and with nature. We wonder why we did not stop the extra effort a long time ago!

PERSONAL PRACTICE: Plan Self-Care Based in Self-Knowledge
Dedicate time to stop and listen inwardly to get to know yourself and attune to your inner knowledge tempered by love. Make a plan for self-care and self-knowledge. Focus on one to three actions at a time. Redraw your core self every three to four months. Note what helps you grow more relaxed, nonanxious, joyful, unselfconscious, uninhibited, loving, clear, honest, fearless, courageous, confident, connected, compassionate, valiant, adventuresome, intrepid and genuine.

Braid together an inner sense of love and conscience through silence, solitude, reflection, counseling, self-care, self-soothing, listening, learning and recreation. Both love and conscience grow within relationships. Sharing good attention contradicts old experiences of abandonment or isolation and supports us to bring our whole selves to meeting life's challenges.

Meet Regularly with Companions

Companion groups exchange attention among two to four people who meet on regular intervals every one to three weeks. Groups choose their own interval and duration. Some people prefer pairs allowing more time for each person. Others prefer small groups allowing less time for each person but hearing from more people.

GROUP ACTIVITY: *Companion Group Sessions*

"Now we will do Companion Group Sessions." Gather in pairs or small groups of three or four. In your group, ask whether light touch or hugs are comfortable or not. Allot time to settle into silence at the beginning and end of each session. Divide the remaining time equally among the members to take equal turns to receive attention.

When *offering attention*, *remember to:*

- *Be a good listener: stop, turn towards the other, follow their meaning and imagine what life is like if what they say is true for them.*
- *Listen from the heart with relaxed non-anxious attention.*
- *Pay attention to the other's goodness and capabilities.*
- *Note when your distresses distract you to come back to later.*
- *Stay grounded in present time and help your companion fully return.*
- *Test where messages come from, restate or offer feedback as requested.*
- *Take equal turns.*

Do not take on another person's story, interrupt, tell your own story, indulge in curiosity, try to figure it out or fix it, give advice or over-sympathize. Do not become stoic, either. Interact in gentle ways to balance your partner's attention between the painful memories and the wellbeing of the present. Do not try to amplify or stifle the other's release of emotion. Nod, make light sounds, touch (if agreed to) or ask brief questions to balance attention between the past and present. Do this to encourage emotional discharge and sustain attention on difficult memories. Restate or offer feedback if the person requests. **When receiving attention,** *remember to:*

- *Stop, settle into silence, let go and listen inwardly.*
- *Discharge and learn from emotional distress.*
- *Speak about experimenting with love and conscience in your life.*

Print or post the Companion Group Questions. During your time, speak to relevant questions or consider each to spark unanticipated insights. Seek insights and direction essential for yourself now, not general truths for others. Record and read insights or directions that ring true for you to the group. Ask them to restate the main idea in your own words.

Companion Group Questions

- How do I experience transforming power in good and hard times?
- What do I need to have or let go of to stay aware of transforming power in every moment?
- What distress do I need to notice, learn from and discharge?
- Who do I rely on and who relies on me? How do I ask for or offer help?
- What guidance do I receive when I listen within to love and conscience?
- What are the implications for my private and public life and our culture?
- How can I use what I need and share the rest?
- What disputes can I learn from and settle?
- What fruits has this experiment yielded in my private and public life?

If fresh insights arise when you hear your words restated, then stop to give them time to sink in and change you. Resist the urge to engage in group analysis, which often leads to avoidance, not deeper insight.

If restating confirms the insight, ask others for feedback. Others state the part or parts in which they feel the transforming power. Record this information in your journal to use in your search for guidance.

After (and only after) the group affirms a statement for an individual, consider whether it rings true as essential for others also. People who resonate with the statement often find it hard to wait and not blurt out, "Me, too!" If you resonate, relax, affirm the statement and record it for the author first. Then add your signature if it's true for you too. If it rings true for the whole companion group, ask other companion groups to test it. If it rings true for them, ask a community group to test it. If it rings true for the whole community, publish it for society guidance.

Companion group methods often feel awkward at first, but become natural with practice. Don't be surprised if people talk, joke and trivialize this practice. But this robs us of the opportunity to practice and does immense damage to the group. So commit to the discipline of following the instruction, take your turn seriously and remind others to:

1. *Sit in silence and listen to the inner nudges of love and conscience. Resist collapsing into a stupor and let go of internal chatter.*

2. *Release distress from your body to heal and increase resilience. Resist reenacting, reliving or perpetuating old hurts and pains.*

3. *Describe the inner landscapes and outer forms of the experiment. Resist egotism, self-righteousness or discouragement.*

4. *Reflect back and offer feedback when requested.*

   Resist interrupting, giving advice or taking over.

Come back to the large group to reflect on this activity.

Companion groups offer an appropriate, regular time and place to tend emotion. But if emotional care takes over your full time and attention, seek the care you need from a doctor, nutritionist, physical trainer, spiritual advisor, peer counselor, professional counselor or trauma specialist. We balance tending emotion with bringing our full, clear selves to experimenting with love and conscience in community and society.

As we relax and open, we may find ourselves flooded by toxins released from relaxing and letting go of tensions and potentially unresolved trauma. Today many people live demanding, traumatizing, toxic lives. In such lives, needs can overtake the resources. General cultural competence may not be enough to meet the magnitude of accumulated need, distress and toxicity. Loving, conscientious cultures invest in physical and emotional well-being, not just managing and tolerating distressing, traumatic, toxic lives.

The regularity of the companion group meetings matters more than the characteristics, interests, personalities or experience of the members. Love and conscience manifest quite differently in different people's lives. If members genuinely practice love and conscience each in their own way, the group tends to nurture its members and bear unique fruits in each member's life.

GROUP ACTIVITY: *Form Ongoing Companion Groups*
Tell the group, "Now we will Form Ongoing Companion Groups." Make a 2 x 4 grid with two chairs along one side and four along the other (or use tape or string). Label the grid as follows:

	Pairs	*Small Groups*
Weekly		
Every 2 Weeks		
Every 3 Weeks		
Monthly		

Ask everyone to stand where they choose and form companion pairs or groups with others who want the same size group and interval. Plan when and where to meet every one to four weeks for three to four months. If a session is inconvenient, meet even if you can only take five minutes per person, rather than cancel.

Then meet with the whole community every <u>three to four months</u> to discuss the experience of companion groups, study patterns similar across groups and rearrange new companion groups.

Reach out to family, friends, coworkers and community members. Not everyone in a family, workplace, school or community needs to dedicate themselves to this practice. Similar to any art or sport, a few become players, more become fans and many make up the audience. Peace requires a few to become dedicated, some to take action and the sympathies of many. Everyone can appreciate the art of peace in our own way. Just letting people know what you're doing and extending an invitation expands awareness.

No companion should have hierarchical power over another—a teacher over a student, a guard over an inmate, a boss over an employee, or a parent over a child. And do not start a romantic relationship with a companion. If one arises, resist and seek outside advice and counsel. Transference, meaning substituting intimacy with a companion in the place of a former unresolved relationship obscures our core selves and leads to distorted relationships. This work offers a sense of safety and intimacy. New feelings of letting go of control, receiving help, being cared for or getting a break from carrying responsibilities alone may create attraction. Or we may have new feelings of gaining control or of feeling capable, needed and responsible. When romantic attraction entwines with these new feelings, the relationship depends on a rigid repetition of these roles. It's hard for it to grow into a relationship of two whole, flexible, healthy, complex core selves. These relationships often end in mutual rigidity and resentment.

Experiment with different groupings. Make plans, but base decisions on reality. People's lives change. No companion group lasts forever. People shift focus, needs and availability. People move, face life challenges and die. Do not apply pressure or impose judgment on anyone who opts out. It must always be okay for a companion to ask to stop meeting without judgment or punishment. Certain combinations are brief, others have staying power.

When the same people meet over an extended period, both the companion group and their communities get stronger. The capacity for discernment takes time to cultivate, which much mobility disrupts. The quality of attention in stable communities creates cultures where we want to stay. So don't give up or change groups that are working!

Value the Exchange of Attention

Once when I moved, I gave up a regular meeting with a dedicated companion. I had no idea how much losing her attention could affect my life! My life became like a ship without a ballast. Withdrawing the influences of her attention changed my inward landscape. I no longer had access to inward territories we had traversed together with such ease. The full power of our companionship only became visible in its absence.

The second time this happened was when another dear companion passed away. This time I knew her passing would change me and it did. The transforming power that had flowed through us into our relationships, activities and concerns shifted course. The ways we called on each other, the questions we asked and the experiments we tried in our families, workshops, visits and feedback had often surprised us. After she died, I could not match the richness of these unanticipated directions and outcomes.

Just before she passed away, she attended a talk I gave. She remarked, "You told me you couldn't describe this experience of experimenting with being inwardly guided by transforming power, that I could only know it by doing it. And you were so right! I've been doing it for five years now and it has changed me so much! I can't imagine what life would be like after doing this for ten or fifteen years, let alone decades! This is marvelous!"

A few months after she passed away, I received a call from another friend. She said, "I'm not sure why, but I feel like I'm supposed to pay attention to you." I smiled. What a gift! I readily accepted her attention, aware of its preciousness!

Creating a culture of peace requires some of us allow this work to take over our lives, through every life transition and stage. Those of us who choose this path need companions. We offer this power of visiting and attention to peace workers and nonviolence movements around the world with the support of the Quaker volunteer network of Friends Peace Teams.

Kind attention from another person contradicts self-doubt and trauma. As we learn more about trauma, we realize that the traumatic response sets in when we freeze, often because of a lack of loving, caring attention. We have learned to ask for good attention when we feel overwhelmed. We try to soften our rigidities from prior experiences and become more creative and agile. We persist in looking for a way forward without getting stuck or freezing. We ask for and accept good attention regularly, not only in times of need. Then we let go of our pain, forgive ourselves and others and heal. We can then reconnect with others and the natural world, which rebuilds a sense of trust in life and the strength to stand up to injustice. We return to our natural, flexible, loving, inquisitive, conscientious, delighted and delightful core selves with gusto and enthusiasm for life and society.

~

The people of love and conscience

find our protection in preserving peace,

not in making war, with each other and the Earth.

~

Chapter 6

⁓

Practice Peace in Daily Life

We avert and reduce violence by focusing on the precursors to violence starting with the first set of skills on the Road Map: friendship, affirmation, communication and cooperation. We integrate, embody and refine these skills through application and practice. Activities below introduce the skills, but a culture of peace requires we apply them.

Affirm the Good in Oneself and Others

When we meet others, greet them and get acquainted. Know and use each other's names, share something about yourself, ask something about the other and visit with one another. Apply the agreements and the expectations discussed in Chapter 1 in increasing depth, beginning with the first agreement to affirm oneself and others.

We cannot be friends with everyone on the planet, but we can be friendly with everyone we meet. We can be a friendly people by getting to know and building friendships with our neighbors, locally and globally. Then, when problems arise, we have friends to inform us or to contact before a problem festers or explodes. We have friends to work with in sensitive and effective ways. We call this grassroots quiet diplomacy.

Quiet diplomacy refers to connections across structural or historic divisions without publicity or fanfare creating opportunities for love and conscience to work among us. Visiting builds friendships, which leads to intimate knowledge, open hearts, humility, empathy, compassion, expectations for the best, loyalty and maturity. When problems arise, we do not shut down because we are not alone or unknown. Peaceful societies interweave quiet diplomacy at every level of governmental, professional and civilian life, at the highest levels and at the grassroots, involving everyone in the politics of peace. Even a few relationships among people of diverse backgrounds goes a long way toward preserving peace. Do not underestimate the power of friendliness as a foundation for dignity and civility. This foundation colors every other activity and skill that follows. Peaceful, principled friendships thrive on sincerity, honesty, integrity, justice, compassion, discernment and keen judgment.

Remember, people who have suffered prolonged violence, war, poverty or humiliation lose up to ninety percent of their vocabulary with positive words disappearing first. Along with friendship, we begin the work of peace by expanding your use of affirming, positive words.

PERSONAL PRACTICE: Use Positive Words

Brainstorm specific, positive adjectives and feeling words. Post them where they are visible. Decorate them to hang on the wall. Carry a list with you. Think of three, use them and see if the situation changes. Practice using them with yourself and others. When tensions arise, see if using five positive words reduces the tensions.

We agreed to affirm ourselves and others with no put downs or put ups. Affirmation puts no one below or above others, but upholds and encourages the genuine goodness and capabilities of each person. For many people, both parenting and schooling focused on detailed negative, corrective, punitive communication, as if getting rid of failings and problems was enough. Much less often we were asked to exchange detailed positive communication on what worked well for everyone. Our inherent gifts blossom when noticed and called upon, they cannot impose on others.

Affirmations do not elevate people through praise, admiration or boasting An affirmation does not place the ego above relationships or particular people above others, so they do not induce arrogance. We formulate affirmations to get to know, draw attention to and strengthen the goodness and capabilities of each person's core self and our relationships. The strength of an affirmation depends on its accuracy.

PERSONAL PRACTICE: Formulate Affirmative Statements
Name specific behaviors, actions or words that made the day or event go well or result in good outcomes. Name how that behavior or statement made you feel and the positive, natural consequences that follow from it. Affirm yourself and others after an event or task.

Do not underestimate the effect of affirmative statements. While humiliation leads to illegal and lethal behavior, affirmation deters, challenges and resists violence while it encourages, supports and sustains peace.

Listen and Speak with Empathy

Communication works best with people we know, with whom we have kept agreements, built trust and can affirm. If communication fails, return to these earlier steps. Share something about yourself, ask something about the other, discuss agreements or affirm the other person. This foundation is necessary to listen plainly to where words come from and speak plainly from one's best sense of what is right and true. Personal and social transformation depend on good listening.

We agree to stop, listen and not interrupt. When we listen, we do not speak. We communicate nonverbally through our bodies and faces, not through words. Stop the body and mind. Stop speaking, fiddling, moving, jumping to conclusions, figuring it out and trying to fix it. If anxiety and distress intrude, make a note of what triggered you to discharge later with a companion. Make sure you come back to it later or this method will no longer work because you will stop believing yourself. Stop again, open, be curious and track what the other person is saying or from where it comes.

We often forget to listen well to family members, friends and coworkers. Applying good listening skills with curiosity in what the person is trying to convey can have surprising, positive effects.

PERSONAL PRACTICE: Listen Well to Everyone

Every day at home, school or work practice good listening:

1. *Stop in your body and your mind and be relaxed and nonanxious.*
2. *Turn your body and face the speaker with love.*
3. *Track what the person says with curiosity open to the unexpected.*
4. *Believe the person and imagine life if what they say is true for them.*

Study when the quality of your listening changes by the person, setting or situation and ask yourself why. Notice when bodies close, open, tense or relax, who stands next to whom and which direction people face.

Without speaking, try communicating with your eyes, body and face. Experiment with how your body and facial language affect relationships and events. Practice speaking with your face before using your words. Check with people by asking, "From the look on your face, I assume you are feeling ____. Is that true?" "How do you think I'm feeling right now?" Their answer is always correct because the question is what you are nonverbally communicating to them, regardless of your intention. Try changing your facial expression until you convey to others what you intend to communicate. A good listener conveys interest and respect.

When someone introduces new information, give everybody time to discuss it in pairs or triads. This engages everyone in clarifying their thinking and developing their voice before using the information in public.

PERSONAL PRACTICE: Form Questions

Keep a list of interesting questions, such as those below, for getting to know yourself and others. Ask people these questions and listen to their responses for two to three minutes. Then share your response for two to three minutes. Thank them and move on, do not dwell. If they are reluctant to answer, share your answer first then ask them.

Conversational Questions

- Who do you respect and why?
- What have you done that makes you proud?
- What helps you get to know yourself?
- When is your true self most apparent or least apparent?
- What can others do to help you be yourself?
- What do you do that helps others be themselves?
- Who has influenced your beliefs and how?
- How are your beliefs visible in the way you live?
- How do you experience life's transforming power in daily life?
- When did you do the right thing even though you felt afraid?
- What injustice do you remember as a child?
- What rigid decision did you make as a child and how did it affect you?
- How do you see oppression operating in places where you take part?
- How does society encourage you to use unnecessary or unfair power?
- What one thing can you do to reduce prejudice?
- What way have you spoken up for yourself or someone else in public?
- What would you like to change about yourself and how?
- What is a positive influence in your life right now?
- Who can you turn to for help and how can you ask for help?
- What plans do you have to better your neighborhood?
- What hope do you have for the future? What steps will you to get there?

To remember these questions, answer them in your journal. Notice how your questions and answers change. Share this list of questions with others and ask for feedback on the questions themselves. When you have ten minutes to spare, ask someone a question of significance, "I only have a few minutes, but I was wondering ___?"

A good question can prove more important than the answer. Questions direct our attention. The art of crafting questions takes experimentation.

GROUP ACTIVITY: Concentric Circles

Tell the group, "Now we will do Concentric Circles." Ask people to sit in two concentric circles, the outside facing in and the inside facing out in pairs. We will take turns listening without interrupting and speaking to a topic for three minutes. Then either circle moves one seat to the right forming new pairs. We speak on four or five topics, beginning with an affirming topic such as, "A person I respect and why." Then consider two or three challenging topics around a theme. We close with a positive question on ways to approach the theme or share our plans. NOTE: With a group of six, sit three people facing each other in pairs. Then ask one person to stay in their seat as the other five rotate in a circle. This forms five non-repeating pairs.

Plain Listening. Plain listening refers to listening for where words come from. Then we respond to that which we sense rings true and authentic and let go of the rest. Our core self listens for another's core self. We ignore words that wander, distract, denigrate or inflate. We stay relaxed and nonanxious and remember each person is good and capable.

PERSONAL PRACTICE: Plain Listening

Notice where other's words come from. If words connect with your sense of what rings true, then listen and respond. If not, let them go. Do not get distracted by distress. When we speak out of distress, we often get the opposite of what we want. Name your best sense of where the words come from in as few words as possible. Ask if the other person concurs.

When I commit to a personal practice, I push myself to do it for six weeks. Then I consider how it shifts my habits, relationships, experiences and insights. Once when I was running a meeting, a tall, white male professor spoke with tremendous confidence and certainty. As I tried to listen for where it came from, I could only sense confusion. My anxiety grew, "This is not the time to experiment on others. You'll sound crazy in front of all these people!" But I recalled Sandra Cronk's warning. If you follow inward guidance you must yield. To refuse guidance plants a disease within. So, when he finished speaking, without qualifying myself, I said, "Thank you, I hear your confusion." But to save myself I immediately said, "Now it's time for a break. Let's come back in fifteen minutes."

Whew! I hoped over the break everyone would forget this non sequitur. At the end of the break, however, he approached me and said, "How did you know? I didn't know I felt confused! I thought about it the whole break and you're right. May I talk to the group again?" I nodded, "Okay." He apologized for his long statement before the break and shared how confused he was on the matter. Wow! This got the whole group on a better track and I was hooked. To name our sense of where words come from risks mistakes, but to respond to disconnected words leads us astray. Sincerity mitigates the risk honesty. So check your perceptions with others and ask for feedback, do not get over-confident.

Plain Speaking. Plain speaking refers to speaking from one's core self on what rings true and feels authentic without fear or distress. It means speaking directly person-to-person from personal knowledge unencumbered by mediating roles, positions or speculation.

When I was a preteen, my family built the farm house. We used no electricity, heated and cooked with wood, grew our own food, raised our own meat and honey and worked towards self-sufficiency. My parents both taught at the university. They had grown up farming and had read the book Small is Beautiful. I knew "simple" did not mean easy or uncomplicated, so what did it mean? When the dictionary failed me, I made a list of things I considered "simple" and "not simple."

Simple—direct relationships with the source of life. For example, apple pie made from apples picked in the yard, cinnamon taken from the bark of an Asian tree, grain gathered from the field ground into flour, lard from the butchered pig, salt from the mines and spring water. Place them in a metal pan in a cast iron oven and cook with slow-burning hardwood logs cut with a chain saw and split with an ax. All of these I can know in person and how to make it and compost the waste.

Not simple—mediated relationships. For example, a commercial candy bar made from ingredients, taken from land, produced through procedures, handled by people, wrapped in plastic and producing waste, none of which I can know in person or how to make or dispose of the waste.

From these two lists, I realized that "simple" involved direct relationships with people and the natural world through healthy, regenerative processes that lead to healthy products. These simple, direct relationships offer endless opportunities to become discerning, loving and conscientious. Mediated relationships are what Søren Kierkegaard called *The Sickness Unto Death* (1849). When we relate to each other through images we have of roles and positions, we lose the direct relationships between core selves where life's transforming power resides and moves.

PERSONAL PRACTICE: Plain Speaking

Pay attention to where your own words come from and speak from your core self. Ignore superficial reactions, thoughts or prejudices. Notice the source and purpose of what you say. Does it come from your core self and speak to other's core selves? Does it ring true and contribute to life?

Plain means unadorned without pretense, denigration or inflation. We come to know our true selves, the true selves of others and the matter at hand free of intruding distresses and distorting illusions. Then we can express our sense of the inner nature and relationship of things.

People who base decisions on their best discernment of what is true value plain speaking and listening. We recognize we can only know through our perceptions. But through exchanging and comparing perceptions, we arrive at greater insight and broader understanding. We refine our discernment through honest, balanced exchanges of insight.

People speak more or less depending on personality, style, knowledge or need, but in healthy, safe, peaceful settings people balance speaking and listening. We take responsibility while we stay open, which distributes resources and power. For a culture of peace, develop structures that help balance speaking and listening, such as:

- Begin gatherings with each person saying their name and one thing about themselves or the topic at hand.

- Take turns offering each person equal time to speak on a topic. Go around the circle for people to speak or pass. Or invite people to speak only once until everyone has a chance. And leave silence between speakers to let what each speaker says sink in.

• Share in pairs, small groups and the whole community.

These activities give people structured time to practice speaking in private and public and builds everyone's experience and skills.

PERSONAL PRACTICE: *Balance Speaking and Listening*

• *Notice how much time you spend listening or speaking in various relationships or settings. Question whether imbalances serve a healthy purpose or reinforce patterns of prejudice, privilege and oppression.*

• *Experiment with balancing your speaking and listening time and notice what happens. Invite others to experiment with this, too.*

• *Notice what you listen to or speak about, such as logistics, courtesy, personal or work transactions or humor. Track the time spent in each category of interaction during a typical day and record time estimates of those interactions in your own categories.*

• *Consider what you would like to listen to or speak about. Select skills such as affirmation, curiosity, exploration, self-care, care for others, care for the natural world, truth-telling or feedback. Pick one and look for moments to speak or ask about it.*

When Blaze Nowara interviewed participants from this training, he asked what changes they experienced. Most participants replied, "I learned to speak" or "I found my voice." A powerful tool for finding our voice is the I-Message format. It helps one explore, get to know and organize our experience by connecting feelings with concrete actions, words, consequences and needs. When we are emotional, we lose access to the language and analysis centers in the brain. As a companion, using this format to guide our partner's attention to helps us clarify these specific, concrete actions, words, consequences and needs.

GROUP ACTIVITY: *I-Messages*

Say to the group, "Now we will do I-Messages. Think of a persistent unresolved emotion you want to understand better. With a companion, write about that feeling in this format. Companions help the person write about specific actions and words rather than making vague references."

I-Message

__[Name of the person you are addressing]__ ,

I feel   ___(specific emotion)_____

when   ___(concrete actions or words)_____

because ___(concrete real consequence)_____

I need   ___(concrete actions or words)_____

---

1. " _[Name]_ ,"*Write the name of the person you are addressing.*

2. *"I feel ___" Select a word for your emotion. Consider whether any of the big four emotions apply: sad (loss), afraid (danger), mad (injustice) or bored (disconnected). If several emotions come to mind, you may need to write several I-Messages, one for each emotion.*

3. *"when ___" Write specific, concrete actions or words that led to your reaction.*

4. *"because ___" Write what real, natural consequences have or may follow from such behavior or language.*

5. *"I need ___" Write what actions or words you needed at that time.*

A companion can help you find the specific feeling and the concrete, specific actions or words that prompted the feeling. Sometimes I feel I will not survive small hurtful actions or words. My logical brain laughs at how ludicrous that sounds, but facts and feelings are different. The feeling can sound extreme or trivial to the logical brain. Do not exaggerate facts to express feelings. Practice using more specific, descriptive feeling words.

Then look for the concrete, specific actions or words that prompted the feeling. "When you were angry, lazy or mean," are abstract characteristics, not specific actions or words. Ask, "What was the person doing or saying?" If the writer looks blank, to spark concrete memories ask, "Where were you? Were you sitting or standing? Were you inside or outside?"

When emotional, our brain loses access to language, logic, analysis and chronology, inhibiting our ability to connect actions with consequences. Gentle questioning from a companion stimulates access to more of our capacity for understanding and expression. Questions can prompt our analytical brain to look for the answers. So always ask a companion to check your I-Messages, not only when you first learn to develop them.

A companion may ask, "Really? Was that really it, or was there something else? Is there something behind that? What might happen if they continued to do or say that? Was it damaging, dangerous, unfair or isolating?" Remind them that fear of the consequences not the actions or words often causes the emotion. When we state the consequences we fear, we often can understand our emotions. When someone has trouble stating what they need, ask, "Do you need to feel loved or to love them? To protect yourself or them? Is the situation fair? Do you need something restored?"

Write as much as you can, then ask a companion to help you make each part specific and concrete. Let them help you get to the root of the emotion. Read your I-Message to your companion. Then ask them to say it back to you in your words. Sometimes that feels right. You say, "Yeah, that's it!" If you do not find the root of the feeling, ask your companion to point out what they sense might be behind it (for you, not for them). Listen. Test their feedback by imagining if it's true. Pursue whatever resonates.

You may write I-Messages to yourself or to others, on positive or negative feelings, to understand your emotions or to celebrate or mourn someone or something. You may write multiple I-Messages to untangle multiple emotions arising from one event arising of various sources or potential consequences. Plain, simple language sometimes comes from going deeper and other times comes from stating the obvious.

In third grade, my daughter Sarah described her day, "We do this. We do that. Then we have lunch. Then I stand in the corner. Next we line up to go back to class ...."

"Wait, a second. Go back to "then I stand in the corner." What do you mean? Did that happen today?"

"Yep. Every day. I eat lunch, stand in the corner and go back to class."

"Why do you stand in the corner?"

"I don't know, the teacher just tells me to stand in the corner."

I scheduled an appointment to see her teacher. I arrived to a room with seven teachers at a table in a small conference room. They repeated several times, "She knows what she did. She can tell you."

I said, "Well I don't know, so you have to tell me!"

A teacher explained. For the last three weeks Sarah sat at the end of a long cafeteria table. She bounced her foot on the table leg shaking the table clear across the cafeteria. I was stunned. They could have said, "Sarah, I *feel* frustrated *when* your foot kicks the table leg *because* it shakes the entire table making it hard for others to eat. I *need* you to stop kicking the table leg." She would have stopped immediately!

Writing I-Messages can lead to many results. When I cannot find a real or significant consequence, I laugh and say, "Ah, get over yourself!" And let it go. Other times I find small actions or words can have huge effects or threaten significant consequences. Or I discover I am upset with someone for not giving me what I need, but I cannot even name what I need myself!

Listening and speaking improve with empathy. I learned to empathize so young it felt innate, but empathy is learned. I once asked a man, "How do you think a woman would feel?!" He looked stunned. "How would I know? I'm not a woman. I can't know that!" In his whole life, no one had ever asked him to imagine another person's feelings. I suggested he try. Stunned again, he could do it! A whole new world opened for him. My mother regularly asked me to imagine how my actions or words would affect others. She considered how plans might affect members of the household or staff. Empathy is a habit of thought formed in the disciplined of repetition.

Sympathy is *feeling with* others or feeling what others are feeling. Empathy draws on the experiences of sympathy to develop a cognitive *awareness of* other's feelings and needs. Compassion draws on empathy that becomes so strong that it moves us to action. We practice empathy by imagining other's conditions from their point of view and checking that our perceptions align with theirs. Empathy helps us to overcome egotism and self-centeredness and to assess the ethical nature of things.

PERSONAL PRACTICE: Ask: How Does This Affect Me and Others?
Ask, "How will it affect me or others? What would that be like for _ [person]_?" Will anyone remember this in twenty years?" Practice empathy through imagining how your words and actions might affect you or others, both near and far, now and in the future. Empathy

takes time and attention, but it deepens our awareness of life's natural consequences and tempers actions in positive, regenerative ways. Something may appear significant, but upon consideration is inconsequential. Something else may appear trivial, but upon consideration is consequential. If I won't remember it in twenty years, then let it go. If I will remember it in twenty years, then stop and pay attention.

Once developed, it becomes difficult to imagine life without empathy and uncomfortable or irritating to work with people who cannot empathize. To practice empathy, we extend our practice of writing I-Messages.

GROUP ACTIVITY: *Empathy*

"Now we will do Empathy." Write an I-Message with the help of a companion. In groups of four, each person takes a turn to read an I-Message. A person from the other pair, not their companion, restates the feelings and needs. Keep to the original words as much as possible, "I hear you feel __ and need __." If they respond, "Ah yes! That's it!" Then you know the statement resonates and captures a moment of empathy— the feeling that another person is aware of your feelings and needs. If they do not feel this response, then you can ask probing questions or add your best sense of what might be behind their words. Check whether their perception resonates with yours. If not, let them try to express their sense of what might be behind their words. Try a couple times to get to an "Ah yes!" Then move to the next person and repeat, even if you don't get to the "Ah yes!" Reflect on this activity.

Check your sense with others to confirm or adjust your sense of things. Speculation disrupts plain, direct communication. The experience of checking and having our perceptions corrected humbles us. We realize that even though we have become empathetic, we need to temper insight with humility, knowing we will sometimes get it wrong.

GROUP ACTIVITY: *A Problem I Face Right Now Is*

"Now we will do A Problem I Face Right Now Is." In groups of four, give each person a quarter sheet of paper. Ask everyone to write these

words in the same orientation (portrait): "A problem I face right now is …" and then complete the sentence. Each person folds their paper in half, then in quarters in the same way so the folded papers look alike. Shuffle the papers and redistribute them until no one has their own. Now one person reads one aloud and imagines what their life would be like if this were true for them. Imagine for yourself only, not someone else. Describe what you imagine you would feel and need under those circumstances. If your mind goes to someone else, then stop, go slow and try to imagine your own feelings and needs. Talk about yourself only. Do not hide advice for others. Then hand the paper to your right. The next person says, "I have that same problem, too." They read the paper aloud, imagine their life under those circumstances and describe what they might feel and need. Continue until everyone has spoken to that scenario. Then repeat with the next paper until each person has spoken to each problem. Reflect on this activity. In the reflection, ask, "What is the difference between empathy and advice?"

A preteen boy doing this exercise once read a problem and told me, with a giddy nervous laugh, "I can't imagine this!" I looked at the paper. It read, "A problem I face right now is that I am so smart that everyone makes fun of me and doesn't want to be my friend." The boy reading the paper had significant developmental delays. I told him to stop, take a breath and imagine he was born really smart. He looked at me with furrowed brows. I looked back with a confident, reassuring smile. He turned to the group and described how it felt to be so smart no one saw you as a real person. He described how he had real feelings and needed friends and connections. The boy who had written the problem looked dumbfounded. He could never have described his own experience so well. The boy speaking had never imagined such a situation. They became inseparable friends. Empathy is an awareness of feelings and needs, not strategies or solutions. To our surprise, learning to name feelings and needs without jumping to solutions improves communication and connections.

If you have never lost your voice, you may find it hard to imagine how disempowering it feels to lose or how empowering it feels to regain. But violence robs us of our voice. People who have lost their voice find it life-altering to learn empathy, plain listening and plain speaking. One female participant spoke only six words on the last day of her first workshop. She later became an inspiring facilitator and public speaker. Protecting her right to pass allowed her to stay, even when she could not find the words. She blossomed in her own time.

Appreciate Cooperation and Noncooperation

Cooperation builds on a strong foundation of principled friendships, affirmation and communication. We remember the steps in the Road Map for a Culture of Peace and invest in each step, then focus on the dynamics of cooperation.

GROUP ACTIVITY: Broken Squares
"Now we will do Broken Squares." Ask groups of five (or four) to sit in a circle with space to work in front of each person. Extra participants may observe a group's dynamics and remind people of the rules. Post:

Broken Squares Rules

GOAL: Work together to make five squares the same size, one in front of each person. RULES:
- Do not speak or use sign language.
- Do not take or ask for pieces, only give.
- Do not wave pieces around or set them in the middle.
- Give one or all of your pieces into another person's hand.

Broken Squares Pattern

Cut out these shapes from approximately 6"x6" squares for groups of five.

Reorganize the shapes in the envelopes for groups of four.

Give each person an envelope of geometric shapes with segments of the broken squares with the same letter. Ask them to wait for the instructions before opening the envelopes. Post the goal and draw five equal-sized squares with other shapes Xed out below them. Ask if they understand the goal is five equal-sized squares. Then explain the rules.

Once the group dynamics becomes visible, ask everyone to stop, set down the pieces and face you. Wait until they do this. Then say, "Notice your tension, anxiety and old distress patterns. Let go. Relax." Do a grounding: breathe, walk, look around, notice colors, look at your core self drawing and come back to this present time and place.

"Now, go slow. Practice being a good companion. Stay relaxed and nonanxious and remember everyone is good and capable. Smile, laugh and clear your mind. Focus your eyes on the five people in your group and how to make five squares together. Try to work together not alone. The way you put together your square may make it impossible for others to make squares. Look at what your neighbors needs and give them what they need. Remember you may give one or all of your pieces. Focus on how to cooperate not compete with your group members. The goal is to work together to make five squares the same size, one for each person not a square for yourself alone." Ask the group that finishes first to be quiet. You may mix their pieces and invite them to do it again. When each group has finished, reflect on the activity.

There are many ways to make a square, but only one way to make five squares. This means people who make a square fast often wait, frustrated with others for being slow. They judge others as less capable when in fact the way they put their square together made it impossible for others. They forget the goal is five squares. Even when reminded, they often won't break up their square. The words just do not register. They fear others will not give them the pieces they need to make another one even though one square is irrelevant, only five squares "wins." They often say later it never occurred to them to give their pieces away even when we repeated the instruction.

Other people hoard or get rid of pieces. The harder they struggle, the more they narrow their focus and ignore others, isolating themselves. They will not pass pieces making it impossible for themselves and others.

Broken squares serves as a powerful metaphor for community. Often the way we arrange our lives makes it impossible for others. Still, we view others as the problem and do not realize how we become the obstacle to other's success. Fear of not getting what we need blocks us from giving. Remembering our past failures and abuses, we forget generosity. As our vision narrows, we isolate ourselves and block possibilities for ourselves and others. This makes others angry, which becomes a self-fulling prophecy for an anxiety-ridden person. Broken Squares helps us recognize how fixed we become on our own needs while ignoring, shutting out, judging or abdicating responsibility for others. It can also help us recognize how fast everyone can get what we need when we readily exchange pieces. After Broken Squares do a fun cooperative game such as Paper Tear.

GROUP ACTIVITY: *Paper Tear*
"Now we will do Paper Tear." In groups of three to five pass a large piece of newsprint around the group without speaking. Each person will make one tear and pass the paper to the next person to repeat until the group tears the likeness of an animal. Continue until the groups have finished. Post the results on the wall or in a window.

Cooperation improves with deliberate practice. It draws on skills of friendship, affirmation and communication. We explore how our own idiosyncratic tendencies and patterns interact with others' and see universal patterns among us.

~

Non-cooperation draws strength from moral authority, sincerity and the fairness of the objection raised. When I hear a company mistreats its labor, I cannot buy their products without imagining the pain and suffering they cause. When I hear of tap water catching on fire, I cannot support hydro-fracking without imagining the losses people suffer for other's gain. We make deliberate choices to withhold or withdraw our support or participation. We realize the power of inaction and resistance not just the power of action and support. To get it right requires empathy and clarity to grasp the real repercussions of our choices.

PERSONAL PRACTICE: Choose Who to Finance or Boycott
Research the products you use each day from extraction to processing, transportation and retail. Experiment with reducing consumption. Stop using products with single-use plastic or nonbiodegradable waste. Select products or stores based on proactive information. Be driven by curious, not by anxiety. Invest in what you want. Divest from what you do not want. Share your decisions and reasons in public.

We value our freedom to speak and act in accord with our inward sense of love and conscience. Citizens have the right to be free of authoritarian restrictions on our political or religious views and ways of life. Citizens have the obligation to stand up against abuses of authority or power. Sometimes speaking the truth threatens our freedom or survival, but also liberates and enlivens us. We experience a freedom and joy from acting in accord with love and conscience that lifts the burdens of guilt, shame and distress. The liberty of conscience that results from moral action enlists more people of diverse backgrounds to reevaluate their positions and offer their support. People's movements that cast light on repression or exploitation expose perpetrators and bolster convictions.

In New York State, a mother lamented that a teacher was mistreating her son and other students. She planned to plead with the teacher to treat her son better. In her voice I could hear the fatalism. She did not believe the teacher would listen. She felt helpless to protect her son. I pointed out she was taking the teacher's actions personally, while in reality they were a public concern. I suggested she invite others to join her in going to the school to demand a kinder, friendlier, more peaceful school culture that showed respect for children. Her tenor, expectations and actions changed when she saw the problem as a public one.

People of love and conscience are kind to children. No one may mistreat children. This sense of "we as a people" grows over time as we consider the implications of our actions on our culture, not just on ourselves. Do not leave the public voice to others. Cultivate your public voice, speaking for a people and a culture. Check your messages with others. Exchange feedback and refine your message. And when laws or public institutions fail, take direct action. Withhold your cooperation, break immoral laws and enter your objections in the public record of the media, courts or public speaking. Organize peaceful strikes, boycotts, sit-ins, demonstrations and blockades or engage in other public forms of direct action and civil disobedience.

~

Aware of life's regenerative resources
that exceed human need,
we face our human condition without freezing,
open to transforming power.

~

Chapter 7

~

Tend to Emotional Well-being

We agree to tend emotions and our emotional well-being because our emotional condition affects others' lives and public life not just our own life. A culture of peace seeks ways to stop perpetuating pain and suffering and to heal in public. Since most people have dealt with subtle or extreme forms of abuse and neglect since childhood, maintaining a love for oneself in a way that infuses love for others and the natural world requires vigilance.

Many households experience addiction and/or domestic violence. So even if you have not suffered these yourself, the odds are that others have and may need reminders to make healthy, safe choices. Stop and discuss signs of abuse or neglect in yourself or others. Do not wait. Reinforce self-care tools. But if someone cannot manage on their own, encourage them to reach out to a 12-step program, peer co-counseling, counselor, specialist, shelter or other support. Take care of your basic safety, sobriety and self-care before moving on to the work in this chapter. Do not pretend everything's okay when it's not.

In addition, remember the agreement to refrain from put downs or put ups. Self-righteousness, self-aggrandizement and inflation of the value of our work are as detrimental as self-harm and neglect. Stay humble, regardless of where the work takes you. Develop skills to recognize, respect and learn from your emotions. Sit in silence and discharge emotion to clear your mind so you can experiment with transforming power, love and conscience and accept feedback that test your insights.

Practice discharging emotion and coming back to the present time, with equal discipline. We often fear being emotional because we don't believe we will recover or come back from it. The better we get at coming back to the present time, the braver we get at discharging and reprocessing painful memories. This makes us resilient. So practice grounding techniques to return to present time as seriously as you practice emotional discharge. Then sit in silence to let go, open yourself and connect with the palpable, refreshing presence of the transforming power of life.

PERSONAL PRACTICE: Sit in Silence, Alone and With Others

Set aside time to sit in silence, alone or with others. Let go, open and listen. Beware of using silence to escape, isolate or rest just enough to maintain an unreasonable life. When you sit in silence, let go of tension and stress, open to the healing power of life and listen for guidance. Sometimes sitting in silence softens and opens us in profound ways.

These lyrics got stuck in my mind, "Lay down your strain and stress and let your ordered life confess the beauty of Thy peace." Really? Is it possible to lay down your strain and stress and walk away? So I dug a hole in the black soil along a wooded path in Wallingford, Pennsylvania. I dumped my strain and stress in, pushed the black dirt back, tamped it down and walked away. Three days later, my heart began to race. I wanted to go back and dig it up. That was ridiculous! Physical withdrawal from stress hormones and adrenaline left me feeling lost, disconnected and meaningless. If my entire sense of orientation, connection, value and meaning came from a chemical addiction to stress. I didn't want it!

I chose this awful, dark limbo over a sense of connection and meaning gained only through chemical illusion. Once I recovered from the withdrawal, I developed real connections and a deeper sense of meaning. Then I wished I had given up the stress a long time ago!

As my daughter Sarah once said, "You can't keep your pain and get better too." After a pause, she added, "And I just don't think I'm ready to give it up." But when we are ready, we can just let go.

Discharge Distress Physically

Discharging emotion works the same for people everywhere in the world (Harvey Jackins, 1962; Peter Levine, 1997). We explored these in the Good Companions activity (p. 91). Emotional pain and tension trapped in the body numbs and suppresses physical sensation. We avoid feeling by holding on to distress, but then it erupts or forces its own way out. When we open to let go of the distress, sensation floods back. We discharge emotions with a companion so we do not dump our emotions on families, friends, communities and coworkers. We feel the pain as it leaves the body. Thus we often prefer to ignore and hold onto pain rather than let it go.

Emotional release occurs through physical release in response to a benevolent contradiction to falsehoods, injustice or harm. For example, feeling safe with a companion while remembering a time we felt unsafe often allows the emotion to discharge from the body and heal.

A companion may use a light touch, voice or attention to help the other person balance their attention between the inside and the outside, between the past and present. The companion gently brings the person's attention back to the distressing material the brain wants to avoids, while holding a steady reminder of the goodwill and safety in the present.

Emotions follow a sequence. Notice the primacy of grief. Unresolved grief obstructs resolution of other emotions. Once we grieve, we can let go of fear. After we discharge fear, we can let go of anger. And after we discharge anger, we can release apathy. Emotions—grief, fear, anger, boredom—serve as warning flags, alerting us to stop and notice feelings of loss, danger, injustice or disconnection. This emotional alert system draws our attention to real concerns and threats. Loss leads to grief. Danger leads to fear. Repressed grief or fear often leads to secondary anger. Injustice or pain, however, lead to primary anger. Disconnection leads to boredom or apathy and injury to physical pain.

Anger has two forms: primary and secondary. As a secondary emotion, anger masks grief and fear. When someone expresses anger, I often say in a sympathetic tone, "Yeah, how sad." Or "Yeah, that's frightening." The person often thinks for a moment, looks surprised and sobs or shakes. They ask how I knew. Once one releases grief or fear, secondary anger begins to dissipates.

As a primary emotion, anger is a natural response to pain, injustice or unfair treatment. We discharge anger through stomping, pacing, making loud sounds or sharp movements, lifting heavy objects, walking, running, working or physical exertion. But primary anger also discharges through taking action, standing up to injustice and speaking up for what's right.

Lighter forms of fear, anger and apathy discharge through laughter, as does joy and a zest for life. I remember one day driving down the road in the front passenger seat. I twisted back to talk to the other passengers who were Acehnese, Javanese, Malay and Batak. They were laughing raucously. Through the back window I saw military trucks carrying armed personnel. They grew up in war, so this was normal for them. They had been shot at, tortured and seen loved ones killed. I pointed to the truck behind us and asked, "How can you laugh under these conditions?" They looked at the truck, then back at me with huge grins, "They can take a lot from us, but they can never take our laughter!" Their laughter discharged intricate nuances of emotion and kept them well in the face of extreme violence.

The first time I offered to share tools on trauma recovery and resiliency, a group of peace activists agreed to experiment on ourselves. We had worked together during the war in Aceh and felt safe with one another. Contrary to my lifelong dedication to regular sleep, the night before the workshop I stayed up all night laughing hysterically from supper until dawn. I had never laughed so hard or so long! Phrases from that evening put us into fits of hysterical laughter for years. I realized the power of laughter to discharge a whole range of emotions and draw us into a joy and zest for life. Young people who face daunting challenges discharge stress and strain daily through running, laughing and playing with their friends. Adults might find that playing helps us discharge emotions, too, soften rigid patterns and become more creative, flexible and open.

If we do not take action to gain insight and prevent the threat, then distress patterns repeat and eventually become rigid and habitual. Such patterns lead to self-doubt, confusion or self-disgust. If we indulge emotions without taking action to protect ourselves, we can relive and reenact the patterns, amplifying the painful emotions and behaviors. Reliving trauma without discharging it can lead to serious dissociative disorders.

To tend emotions, we let them go, discharge them and learn from them to heal. If we face them with good attention from someone who shows confidence in our goodness and capabilities, we can get curious, flexible and creative in seeking solutions and taking action.

PERSONAL PRACTICE: Express Emotion

To counteract cultural inhibitions, show emotion yourself, encourage others to show emotion and exchange good attention. When someone tears up, do not say, "Hush, hush, don't cry." Say, "It's okay. I'm right here. Go ahead and cry." Commit to companions. This is a commitment to heal, not a license to over-tax, disrupt, hold hostage or abuse others with excessive emotional outbursts. Resist emotional contagion, stay relaxed and nonanxious. Notice the goodness and capabilities of others. Balance attention to the past and present, inside and outside, tragedy and goodness, fact and feeling. Respect the other's ability to let go and discover their own way forward.

People of love and conscience practice with companions. We do not do this alone! But when we have no companion, we do the best we can.

PERSONAL PRACTICE: Take Time to Feel

Before I had companion groups, I set a timer for whatever time I had (10–20 minutes) and allowed myself to feel. I reminded myself to let feelings pass out of my body, not to hold on to or wallow in them. I gave myself time to cry, shake, scream or stomp, whatever I needed until I felt done or the timer rang, whichever came first. Then I got up, washed my face and went back to work.

Time set aside time to heal helped me recover from horrific events. Yet this individual approach has a fundamental flaw. Distress sets in when we do not receive good attention when we needed it the most, so feel overwhelmed. An attitude of I-can-do-it-myself reenacts, repeats and reinforces this distress pattern. Invite companions to give you good attention. Remember the first time you ever felt a particular emotion or a prominent memory and discharge it. This can take the salience out of the emotions and stop them from intruding. Reenacting or reliving loss and pain, however, can worsen the distress, so focus on feeling the distress physically leave the body. Let go and heal. If you do not improve or are in crisis, then seek skilled care.

Since emotion arises to protect us, when we notice, learn and respond with due care, the emotion recedes. Emotion may or may not respond to current events. Events may trigger the emotions of past threatening, unresolved experiences. So each person reacts differently to the same event.

PERSONAL PRACTICE: Seek the Source of Emotion
When emotion rises, stop and check for a clear, current loss, danger, injustice or disconnection and take action. If the emotion does not recede, ask yourself, "When was the first time or most significant time I felt this way?" Take that material to your companions to talk and discharge on those experiences. Let the emotions leave your body. Then bring a clear mind to current insights, implications and solutions.

After a person discharges, the companion helps the person return to the present time by reminding them to notice colors, textures, smells or arbitrary facts. These grounding techniques distract the mind from the past and back to the present. Do not stay inside in the memory, come outside in the present. For example, describe an object, notice where you are on the planet, look for colors, play, walk or run.

If we cannot find the source of the emotion, distressing thoughts, feelings and behaviors repeat forming distress patterns. We can only disrupt these patterns when we decide to do so, but we often cannot do it alone. Do not personalize these powerful patterns to yourself or others.

PERSONAL PRACTICE: Do Not Take Other's Emotions Personally
When emotions get directed towards you, remember not to personalize them. If you feel yourself taking it personally, remember their reaction

is often from their history and yours is often from your history. Pay attention to the feelings that their emotions bring up in you. Take your feelings to your companion to discharge them. Then speak directly to the person with a clear heart and mind. Recognize their emotion as their own, not yours. Resist emotional contagion.

Distress forms rigid patterns through repeated recounting or reenacting, often with only one answer or one way of seeing or doing something. An internal voice says, "I must do it. It must be me. It must be now. It must be this way." Since distress patterns are rigid, notice when you or others get rigid and stop, open and soften. Rigidity comes from real needs and hopes that did not get met when we got hurt in the past. We say, "Well, I guess to survive, I must …" My rigid childhood decision was, "If that's the way it is, then I guess I must do it on my own." As an adult, I still do many things on my own, but now I try to notice when it feels rigid and I soften, reach out to others and seek collaborators. If these needs and decisions are not discharged then the needs may become frozen and form into chronic, insatiable behaviors. Since our emotional brain has no sense of time or capacity for analysis, we cannot realize that these needs and hopes are in the past and can never be met in the present, no matter how much we try.

PERSONAL PRACTICE: *Notice and Soften Rigidity*
When you get rigid, stop for a moment and notice the feeling. Do not trust your certainty about who's to blame. Stop, breathe, soften, take time away, relax. Bring the event to your companion session. Remember your youngest or most pronounced memory. Discharge those emotions until your mind clears, softens and becomes flexible, then bring fresh attention to the matter at hand.

As we heal, human tragedy remains tragic but no longer carries the emotional charge or control over us. We do not forget what happened, we may remember more, but the memory feels like a "normal" memory, distant and flexible.

Human failings, faults, pains and sufferings create the cracks in our egos through which we can see life's transforming power. This experience instills conviction, which deepens our experience of life's resources and serves as an antidote to egotism and trauma. When we lean into life's abundance and generosity, we are no longer overwhelmed by our human failings and needs. We are humbled and grateful for the abundance and resilience of life. When you feel overwhelmed, look around, notice your surroundings and stay engaged. Lean into your confidence and conviction in the goodness, capabilities and resources of the transforming power within and beyond you.

Build Resilience to Emotional Trauma

Trauma disrupts good self care and hospitality. As we militarize society, communities become more violent and the media bombards us with stories of violence, increasing primary and secondary trauma. We begin to show symptoms of trauma and take them as signs of personal failing. Discouragement and self-denigration inhibit our self care. On top of painful news and events, we punish ourselves. We cannot remember, concentrate or make decisions. We lose touch with a sense of our integrated core selves. But when we read the symptoms of trauma written up on the wall, we see that everyone experiences these symptoms when overwhelmed.

GROUP ACTIVITY: Stress, Distress and Reactions
"Now we will brainstorm Stress, Distress and Reactions." Brainstorm examples of "Stress", ordinary, common strains in daily life such as being tired or late, traffic, illness, children or deadlines. Then brainstorm "Distress", extraordinary, uncommon pressures in life such as death, loss of a job, homelessness, major illness or accident. Brainstorm "Reactions to Distress", how we respond after distressing news or events such as feeling numb or confused, can't remember, can't talk, sleeping too much or too little, tired, isolated, crying, loss of confidence, irritable, angry, enraged, empty, distrustful, paranoid, nervous, anxious, repetitive talking or addiction. Sit back and look at the three lists. Then discuss what you notice. Ask, "What is your distress level right now on the SUD Scale?" Note that even low levels of stress starting at #4 disrupt functioning and learning. One need not lose control at #6 or higher to

notice the signs. Remind the group of our agreement to "tend emotion." Invite the group to do a grounding technique and ask when they are in their core selves. Ask the group to request a grounding when they notice themselves or someone else seems distressed or when the stress rises.

Subjective Units of Distress (SUD) Scale

0. Asleep–feel relaxed, no distress.

1. Dozing–very relaxed, day-dreaming or mind-wandering.

2. Relaxed–at home, on vacation, on a stroll or so forth.

3. Normal stress–pleasantly focused on a task or activity.

4. Mild distress–feel tension, worry, fear, apprehension, anxiety.

5. Mild to moderate distress–unpleasant feelings but in control.

6. Moderate distress–very unpleasant feelings, able to function but feel sick to one's stomach or achy.

7. Moderate to high distress–lose concentration, disrupted breathing and physical discomfort.

8. High distress–lose capacity to think, make decisions or problem solve.

9. High to extreme distress–thinking is substantially impaired.

10. Extreme distress–panicked, terror-stricken, non-coherent.

If distress in the group rises to a mild-to-moderate level (#4-5), stop a moment and play or do a grounding technique. If distress rises to the level of moderate-to-severe (#6-7), discharge emotions in pairs for three to five minutes for each person. Then do a grounding technique or play.

Definitions of Trauma

1. A perceived threat that overwhelms usual functioning or adaptability with a sense of terror or helplessness, constricting attention to self-preservation.

2. A mental state of collapse and disorganization that occurs when one cannot resist or flee a perceived threat instilling deep patterns of emotional distress.

In the large group, read the definitions of trauma. Point out everyone reacts this way when overwhelmed by circumstances. Reflect on this activity.

When we see these reactions as normal, we do not feel confused or ashamed. We become curious about what happened. We learn how to reprocess traumatic memories stored in the emotional brain to give the thinking brain access to them. The emotional brain does not have language or ability to sequence or analyze. When someone says, "Just talk about it," we may sit there dumbfounded, unable to talk or write anything concrete or coherent. Traumatic memories flood. It feels as if they just happened, continue to happen and will never stop happening. The brain wants to understand, but cannot make sense until more of the brain gains access.

GROUP ACTIVITY: Stories of Trauma

"Now we will do Stories of Trauma." Find a partner with whom you feel comfortable. Then think of one difficult emotional incident, distressing enough it has stayed with you, but not so distressing you cannot think or learn (#4–5 SUDS). You will share this event with your companion and a facilitator. If the event happened repeatedly, select one incidence. Each person will have five minutes to tell the story. Do not explain the history or consequences, describe just the incident using the Storytelling Protocol (see p. 93). Hold five blank sheets of regular white paper in landscape orientation. Write these five numbered sentences, one at the bottom of each page with enough room to complete the sentence.

Five Sentences

1. I was startled when …
2. I froze when …
3. I did what I was told or what I could, which was …
4. I knew it was over, at least for then, when …
5. To feel better, I …

Then notice at what point in the memory the body felt startled, frozen, obedient, out of danger or in self-repair. Step through the memory.

Remember one body sensation at a time. For each sensation, stop and look around the memory. What concrete, physical things do you see, hear or smell? What was being said or done? Write what was happening physically. Do not write vague, general or emotional statements.

This is difficult because the part of the brain that stores traumatic memory has no language or ability to sequence. So ask a companion for help. The companion asks what did you see or hear next to help put the story in order and checks that you completed each sentence with concrete things you can see, hear, smell, do or say. If the sentences are vague and emotional, ask, "Were you sitting, standing or lying down? Were you indoors or outdoors? What could you see, hear or smell? Who else was there? Where were they? Where were you? What were you or others doing or saying?" Direct them to write down the details. Ignore emotions. Focus on linking physical body "feelings" with physical events.

Check the sentences with a facilitator, then draw a picture for each, adding details. Once someone finishes, invite everyone to add speaking bubbles for any thoughts or statements and to put the core self drawing on top. Invite people to take a silent break. They may come back and add more details as they wish, but please do not distract people still working.

When everyone finishes, demonstrate the final step to the whole group.

Each pair finds an empty wall. One person sits in silence in a chair facing the wall and hands their stack of papers to their companion. Then sit in silence and watch, do not help. The companion tapes their partner's core self and five papers in two rows on the wall, then steps back in silence. The person in the chair looks at their papers. When they are ready, say, "Okay." The companion reads the words written on the page pointing with their index finger to the words. Start with the writer's affirmation name and words on the core self, then the sentence and word bubbles on each sheet. Do not add, elaborate, explain, converse or make jokes. When finished, step back and wait in silence. When they are ready, say, "Okay." The companion takes down the papers, removes the tape and returns the papers. The pair switches roles and repeats. Reflect on this activity and ask, does the memory feel different now than it did before?

We reprocess memory by putting the story "out there" on paper, then re-entering the memory into a different part of the brain visually by seeing the drawings and audibly by hearing the words. It literally draws iconic images from the emotional brain and re-enters them into the thinking brain, which can then help with language, sequencing and analysis. We do not forget what happened. In fact, we may remember more, but it becomes a "normal memory" rather than an emotionally charged one. We use words and place it in time to make sense of it. We are no longer speechless, condemned to the feeling in perpetuity or suffer a sense of shattered meaning. The memory joins other memories we can analyze and use. The emotional, iconic memory no longer floods, taking us unawares. We do not replay the entire thing every time and lose faith in everyone and everything. The whole, integrated mind regains control.

Rehearsing, reliving and reenacting distress patterns reinforces past hurts and pains. The body brilliantly uses avoidance and denial to partition hurtful memories, but in doing so erodes resilience. When we face, discharge and reprocess hurtful memories we can recover and heal.

When we reprocess primary trauma, we become more resilient to secondary trauma and to potential future traumas. We can break the cycle of piling new traumas onto old ones and learn not to freeze in the face of challenging events and to ask for good attention at the right times.

Eric Gentry, who coined the term secondary trauma, writes in *Compassion Fatigue: A Crucible of Transformation* (2002):

"... no one is immune to the effects of secondary traumatic stress— some cope better than others and some hide it better than others—no one remains unaffected. If we simply refuse to address the issues of self-care and tend to our own resiliency, we may be lucky and "catch on fire" quickly, have our crises and make these necessary adjustments in our life. For those who are less fortunate, they get the slow burn. They get to watch their relationships slowly disintegrate because they can no longer tolerate intimacy, or witness their effectiveness as a caregiver dwindle because they are unable to hear one more story of abuse, or experience somatic symptoms (including weight gain, alcohol/drug usage) so intense that they can no longer find comfort inside their own skin."

We experience secondary trauma from hearing traumatic stories, witnessing violence and interacting with or caring for traumatized people. Secondary trauma instills patterns indistinguishable from primary trauma. If we take in real news, become concerned citizens, care for others and face human tragedy, eventually we suffer secondary trauma. As media permeates our lives, everyone in society shows these signs. Without tools to prevent it, people withdraw or become apathetic. We no longer want to hear, see, think or face life.

I looked at the faces of several hundred people in a lecture hall in Miami. I recognized their facial expressions. I'd seen them before in war zones! I thought of the symptoms of trauma: frozen, short of breath, tired, confused, numb, obedient, sad, forgetful, frantic, fearful, insecure, isolated, impulsive, indecisive, erratic in sleeping and eating, lazy, crazy, repetitive, compulsive, needy, paranoid, suspicious, anxious, distrustful, enraged, vengeful, guilty, ashamed, self-critical, empty, inarticulate. When these symptoms intrude, we can think of nothing else. So I gave examples and asked the group, "Do you feel this way?" Everyone nodded.

We can recover from secondary trauma by discharging and reprocessing primary trauma, by staying relaxed, nonanxious and engaged, not freezing. In addition, Eric Gentry noted that taking a big breath and relaxing the floor of the abdomen on the exhale helps us to ground ourselves and prevent secondary trauma.

PERSONAL PRACTICE: *Relax the Floor of the Abdomen*
Find the point of your hip bones in the front and your sit bones in the back. Notice the trapezoidal space in between them. Take a deep breath and relax that space in the floor of your abdomen as you exhale.

If you are holding fear or anxiety, you may need to go to the toilet when you relax. We agreed to take care of ourselves, which includes letting go of distress. So get up, move around, wash your face, go to the restroom and take proper medications. Take good care of yourself.

We can prevent secondary trauma by staying in motion, observing, noticing, inquiring, problem-solving, taking action and speaking out. Restorative justice reminds us that injustice decreases everyone's safety not only the victim's. What victims need is for the public to declare an injustice happened, it was wrong and should not have happened, then prevent further injustice. Getting to know one another and speaking up in public against injustice can prevent trauma, both primary and secondary.

GROUP ACTIVITY: Speak Up

"Now we will Speak Up." Form groups of three. Give each person three to five minutes to tell a story of something they saw or heard that made them sad or mad. After hearing the stories, select one scenario and write a public statement as a group using the format below. Then arrange the room theater style. Each small group comes to the front together and reads their statement out loud in strong voices, then posts their statement on the wall. Reflect on this activity.

Speak Up

1. We are speaking to ____name of person or group____.
2. What happened was ____concrete actions or words____.
3. Why it was wrong was <u>concrete loss, threat, injustice or inhumanity</u>.
4. It made us [sad / mad] because ____concrete, real consequences____.
5. What has to change is ____concrete actions or words needed____.

We see and hear stories of injustices daily. It takes time to choose which ones to address together at this depth. The experience of doing this in a small group provides discipline and a format to support effective group processing. Consider meeting to develop the statements further to send to the newspapers, representatives or relevant groups.

A culture of peace requires we learn and practice resiliency tools and share them with others. So we practice good companionship, discharge emotion, ground back in the present time, reprocess memories, relax the floor of the abdomen and raise our voices.

Reintegrate the Parts of One's Life

Trauma wounds our sense of connection. To reconnect within ourselves and with others takes time. We need to build on small successes, and reconnect by mourning significant losses.

GROUP ACTIVITY: *Memorial Sculptures*
"Now we will do Memorial Sculptures." Post, read and discuss the definitions of loss, grief and mourning.

- **Loss:** *Something or something important to us no longer in our lives.*
- **Grief:** *Deep sadness or sorrow in response to a significant loss.*
- **Mourning:** *Time with family or community to honor and pay our respects to whom or what was lost.*

Ask participants to give examples of significant losses. Note how earlier we learned to grieve through crying, sobbing, wailing and moaning. Now give examples of mourning. We have many ways to mourn deaths, but how do you mourn divorce, loss of a job, moving, homelessness or exile? Brainstorm: wakes, funerals, feasts, making books, slide shows or videos, making an altar, planting a tree, commissioning artwork, hanging photos, hosting a party, taking a pilgrimage and so on.

Stand in a circle. Invite everyone to remember a significant loss and something they loved or valued in who or what they lost. Use people or props to create a sculpture that honors who or what they lost. Once someone makes a sculpture, ask the person to step back and look. Ask, "Does this represent what you loved or valued?" If not, ask them what they loved or valued. If it does, ask, "Do you want to say something?" Then, invite the group to walk around the sculpture slowly and silently viewing it from every side. Return to the circle. Give everyone a chance to make a sculpture. Reflect on the activity.

In war zones people lose the right to assemble with people unrelated to them. So we lose the opportunity to mourn our losses. This obstructs grieving and recovery from trauma. Oddly enough, in commercial societies people also lose the opportunity to mourn. Mourning becomes a lost social art as mobility disrupts family and community cultures and employers (or our own busy-ness) constrain time. But mourning helps us reconnect, reintegrate and heal. So consider planning time to honor your significant losses with others.

Another way to integrate within ourselves is to draw or note major life events along a timeline of past, present and future. To put emotional events outside oneself on paper along a timeline helps place them in sequence. It depicts how life goes on and brings our integrated, whole brains to understanding them.

GROUP ACTIVITY: *River of Life*

Tell the group, "Now we will do River of Life." Each person draws a river on a large sheet of paper. Use one-third of the river for each the past, present and future. Ask people to draw or write three to five formative life events in each section. Then add more later if time allows.

PRESENT

PAST   *drawing*   FUTURE

group members (audience)

River of Life

Name _____   Helper _____

Date _____   Recorder _____

Past Inner Resources:

Past Outer Strengths:

Present Inner Resources:

Present Outer Strengths:

Steps to Take:

Now gather in groups of four or five. Place three extra chairs facing each other with a sign on each: past, present, future. Select who will speak first. The speaker selects a helper to represent them and a recorder to write what they say on the form below. Ask the speaker to:

1. *Sit in the PAST chair. Describe three life events that made you who you were in the past.*

2. *Sit in the PRESENT chair (while your <u>Helper</u> sits in the Past chair to represent you in the Past). Describe three life events that make you who you are today.*

   - *Speaking to your Past self (to your Helper sitting in the Past), name the inner strengths and outer resources in the past that made the present possible. (The <u>Recorder</u> writes these words.)*

   - *Switch places with the <u>Helper</u> (so the Helper moves to the Present). The <u>Recorder</u> gives the paper to the <u>Helper</u> to read the inner strengths and outer resources that got you to the present in your own words.*

3. *Sit in the FUTURE chair (while your <u>Helper</u> stays in the Present to represent the Present-day you). Describe three life events that make you who you are in the future.*

   - *Speaking to your Present self (to your Helper sitting in the Present), name your inner strengths and outer resources in the present that made the future possible. (The <u>Recorder</u> writes these words.)*

   - *Then the facilitator adds, "BUT, you must remember to ...." And ask the speaker to name the steps they need to take to achieve this future. (The <u>Recorder</u> writes these words.)*

   - *Switch places with the <u>Helper</u> (so the Helper moves to the Future). The <u>Recorder</u> gives the paper to the <u>Helper</u> to read the inner strengths and outer resources that got you to the future and adds, "BUT, you must remember to ...." And name the steps you need to take.*

4. *Hand the drawing and the Recorder's notes to the Speaker and invite them to make a small sculpture to represent the future, if they wish.*

Each group member takes a turn as the Speaker. Reflect on the activity.

At the AVP-International Gathering in Guatemala, five of us spent five hours doing this activity on an extended lunch break. To limit the time, we ask people to draw three to five life events in each the past, present and future and note three inner strengths and outer resources. This integrates major life events and we give ourselves fabulous advice! We discover we know what we need to do, we just have to do it!

The ability to form self-reflective statements is crucial for our healing and well-being. If people have trouble forming self-reflective statements when naming their inner strengths, do not rush them. Use your best empathy. Follow their lead. Ask them to imagine if they had inner strengths what would they be?

Once a person colored CURIOUS large and bold at the top of the past section, but could not name a single inner strength. As she sat there blank, I tried to draw her attention to the paper. I pointed to the word as I asked her if she saw any inner strengths in her past. She persisted in saying no. After waiting, I added, "But you wrote curious. Yes?" She looked blank, "No." Luckily I did not push it. I gave her time to work on her own words. It turned out others called her curious, but she did not identify that way. Remember, we cannot presume to know another person. They find the answers inside themselves.

Even after we discharge emotion, reprocess traumatic memories, mourn losses and reintegrate memories, splinters of past traumatic experiences work their way out. When that happens, we may feel we are right back where we started: threatened, overwhelmed or frozen. When our core self feels unable to cope or out of control, a part of ourselves takes over for our protection. We classify these parts into three categories: managers, firefighters and child exiles.

When a part shows up, thank it for its protection! Ask what the core self needs to learn. A lifetime may not be long enough to repair and reintegrate severely wounded parts. Managing the internal parts is sometimes the best we can do. Yet if the core self acknowledges the real threat and suggests an effective strategy, the dissociated part often softens and reintegrates in relief. This may mature the core self, reintegrate split parts and heal wounds.

Dissociated Parts as Protectors

Managers: Fragmented competence, keep exiles from waking up and remembering pain and distress: perfectionist, pleaser, codependent, compulsive care taking, judge, organizer, ruler, servant, anticipating and meeting other's needs, passive, striving, disengaged.

Firefighters: Reactive activities, keep the exiles numb and distracted from their pain, to control them from flooding: drinking alcohol, taking drugs, eating, self-harm, risk taking, thrill seeking, spending, sexual acting out, anger, rage, day dreaming, suicide, sleep.

Child Exiles: Young wounds, deep frozen feelings, sensations, beliefs and experiences, pushed away young that flood if triggered: shame, loneliness, fear, hopelessness, isolation, terror, worthlessness, locked in the past, permanently damaged.

~ Lee Norton, Center for Trauma Therapy, Nashville, Tennessee

A culture of peace respects and learns from emotion, but plans and acts from our core selves. We aim to be well and live full, integrated, peaceful lives. A mature, integrated core self, confident in meeting daily demands without extra effort promotes health and wellness.

PERSONAL PRACTICE: Learn from and Reintegrate Parts

When you sense a dissociated inner part take over, try to stop speaking, making decisions or taking action and get quiet.

- *Name the young wound, fragmented competence or reactive activity from the list of Dissociated Parts as Protectors.*
- *Ask the part to tell its story. Why did it appear? What does the core self need to learn or do to unburden the part and keep you safe?*
- *Remind it you're older, more insightful and capable, than you were.*
- *Make notes in your journal on each part: name them, record their answers, draw them and learn from them.*
- *Ask a companion to sit with you to listen, ask questions, restate your words and offer reflection or feedback as requested.*

Seek professional help to better understand, but especially when needed.

Experiencing my own struggles with my parts has helped me notice them in others. It enables me to appreciate how much work it takes to learn from our distress, mature in our core selves and become relaxed and nonanxious. We do this as a personal activity with a companion, not as a group activity, and seek professional support when needed. It takes practice and skill to reintegrate dissociated parts into our core self.

To create cultures of peace we experiment with personal transformation by opening to life's transforming power. We listen to one another, discharge emotions, reprocess memory and reintegrate internal parts. We encourage clear thinking, exchange feedback and discern our paths forward together. In pairs and small groups we get to know and mature our authentic, unique core selves.

We can offer each other feedback and guidance because love and conscience are universal and recognizable, even in their varieties of unique expressions. Paying attention to and recognizing love and conscience in another person helps us recognize love and conscience in ourselves.

Tending to emotions enough to become discerning requires physical stamina as well as knowledge and skill. So sleep well and take good care of yourself. Avoid addictive or mood-altering substances and remove yourself from domestic violence. Reduce or eliminate nicotine, caffeine, refined sugars and carbohydrates to support emotional stability, regulation and well-being.

~

When adults playfully explore our worlds,

especially with young children,

we can heal and learn in ways

that create cultures of peace.

~

Chapter 8

~

Learn
Through Play

Peace needs the capabilities, flexibility and creativity that education develops. Likewise, education needs the safety and freedom peace offers. When the brain feels safe, it opens to learning through curiosity, exploration and discovery to create meaning and comprehension. This enriches our human capabilities of discernment and insight to meet life's challenges without violence.

Without good attention, our natural goodness and capabilities go undeveloped. We stay immature. We fail to meet the increasing demands of survival, stability and peaceful relationships. Failing in a peaceful society, we feel incompetent, insecure and fearful. We revert to the most expedient power, violence. Violence and stress further erode our capabilities. Then we rely on charm, deceit and image, which leads to more violence. War survivors found the empowerment and resiliency training transformative but inadequate to succeed in a peaceful society until they developed more versatile cognitive, social and physical skills.

We learn and develop our capacities when we feel safe enough to be curious, open and exploratory without retribution or abandonment. We can bring down our guard and throw ourselves into creativity with abandon. Through play we take risks, both children and adults. We explore the world, test knowledge and understanding, develop flexibility and adaptability and create connections and patterns of interactions. We test through controlled demolition—knock down, tear up or otherwise experience destroying things. We plan and negotiate approaches to protect ourselves and our possessions. Learning through play develops capabilities to engage in our social and natural surroundings.

We cannot engage in play and reap the benefits of its learning if we feel unsafe, rigid, distressed, closed or defensive. Insecurity and danger close the cerebral cortex. We memorize, mimic or imitate but cannot understand, comprehend or form meaning. Distress patterns set in and dissociated parts take over. Learning lacks a sense of playfulness when driven by distress, but exudes a sense of playfulness when driven by confidence.

The developmental, creative play that supports fundamental learning involves open exploration and experimentation without specified purpose beyond the enthusiasm, enjoyment and freedom of the play. This play draws on the skills described so far in this book and puts them into action:

- Stop inwardly to notice and pay attention.
- Listen, look, touch, smell and observe.
- Open inwardly to curiosity and delight.
- Discharge emotion through movement and laughter.
- Create story lines and narratives.
- Explore or experiment with others and with materials.
- Integrate the inner and outer parts of our lives.

On this foundation, play activities can develop our social, linguistic, physical and psycho-emotional capacities. Voluntary, engaging activities support practice and experimentation with materials without dread of their consequences.

Through play we generate new uses of resources, ideas, products and purposes and experience intelligence, imagination, growth, adaptation and maturity. Developmental play in this sense serves what Fromberg (1990, p. 223) calls the "ultimate integrator of human experience." The play activities rely on the work of educators such as Dewey, Parten, Piaget, Vygotsky, Montessori, Bruner and Ashton-Warner along with many others.

Loris Maliguzzi (1920-1994), who founded the Reggio Emilia approach with parents in Reggio Emilia, Italy, wrote the poem below to guide their activities.

Hundred Languages of Play

The school and the culture
separate the head from the body. ...
They tell the child:
to discover the world already there
and of the hundred
they steal ninety-nine.
They tell the child:
that work and play
reality and fantasy
science and imagination
sky and Earth
reason and dream
are things
that do not belong together.
And thus, they tell the child
that the hundred is not there.
The child says:
No way. The hundred is there.

~ Loris Maliguzzi, Reggio Emilia, Italy
translated by Lella Gandini

Play teaches us to trust ourselves, others and our place in the world. Jean Piaget (1972, p. 27) wrote the following about teachers:

"Children should be able to do their own experimenting and their own research. Teachers, of course, can guide them by providing appropriate materials, but the essential thing is that in order for a child to understand something, he must construct it himself, he must re-invent. Every time we teach a child something, we keep him from inventing it himself. On the other hand that which we allow him to discover by himself will remain with him visibly."

We find this true for any adults, including parents. Perhaps there is something to be said for taking the time to reinvent the wheel! Play allows for exploration, experimentation, invention and innovation.

Play to Recover from Violence

The Early Years Organization of Northern Ireland supported by the World Forum Foundation captured the interdependency of peace and education. Adults and children who playfully explore the world with an inward spark of wonder, awe and joy heal from violence and learn to live in peace (Connolly and Hayden, 2007).

I once watched a group of hundreds of Acehnese women act like two-year-olds. They were skilled. They managed families, processed salt fish and did other complex tasks. But the stress of thirty years of war and a massive tsunami eroded their basic cognitive capacities. They followed one- or two-step instructions, but not even three. When given five steps of instructions, they did the first one or two and the last one and dropped the rest. They performed these complex tasks using imitation, repetition and muscle memory. They did not generalize, innovate or generate new approaches or methods.

After the tsunami, a charitable organization with the best of intentions unloaded a few hundred single-burner kerosene stoves. Over 300 women were present. Every one of them needed a stove and the group had brought plenty. A man on a make-shift stage spoke to the women, "My name is … I'm from … We brought stoves." If they had handed out the stoves at that point, they could have distributed the stoves with ease. But he went on and on. The women's eyes glazed.

A woman noticed one blue stove in a sea of red stoves. She wanted it. So she put it under her scarf and looked around humming. Her eyes looked away with a nothing's-going-on-here expression.

A woman next to her craned her neck, "What do you have?"

"Oh, nothing," she replied, looking away at the treetops.

Other women tugged at her scarf.

The first woman pulled away. She ran down the path. The crowd sprang a leak as the women ran after her. The man on the stage glanced over, furrowed his brow and glared back at center of the crowd. He talked faster to hold the group's attention.

Word traveled through the crowd, "She got a blue one." Women looked around for another blue one. "I want a blue one!" Frantically looking but not finding any, the women huffed and folded their arms on their chests. "If I can't have a blue one, I don't want one!" they retorted.

As news traveled through the crowd, the women turned their backs. An entire crowd of hundreds of women walked away from the stoves. In disbelief, the humanitarian workers loaded the stoves back onto the truck. I heard them complaining, "How arrogant! They just walked away!"

As I watched this crowd, I recognized the single variable thought common among two-year-olds. They only hold one thing in their minds at a time. While they think of color, they could not think of shape or function, namely "stove." Later that evening, as these women sat on slabs of cement or cardboard left by the tsunami, I'm sure they mulled, "Hmm, those were stoves. Darn! I could use a stove right now." In that moment they would forget the color. I reeled at the magnitude of the work needed here—it might take 300 years to bring this community back from decades of war and deprivation. So we had better get started!

Everyone agreed that if the war came back it would start from this region. To preserve peace would require massive educational and social investment. They needed to start with the basics: clean drinking water, trust in life and each other, trauma resiliency and developmental education. And everyone was in need: teachers, parents, families, leaders, professionals, workers, fishermen and farmers. The entire adult community needed basic sensorimotor activities to develop hand-eye coordination, three-dimensional perception and object permanence such as empty-fill activities; paint, sand or water play; peek-a-boo or hide-and-seek. They needed to string beads by color and shape, sort, sequence, pattern and create representations until they could play with signs and symbols.

People who engage in developmental play for a single hour each week for six months advanced their thinking and skills so much it changed their lives and many others along the way. But sometimes their thinking and behavior became so strange and inexplicable to others, they became ostracized. We warn people to look for ways to include local leaders, extended family and community members as much as possible.

Even the technical staff of the Indonesian Directorate of Early Childhood Education reported that after six months they had trouble communicating with their colleagues and families. I asked, "Haven't you been sharing at the Monday morning staff meeting and with your families on the weekends?" We had planned that but did not monitor it. They confessed "more important things" took precedence. We encourage adults who engage in developmental play to share the ideas and activities with the other significant adults in their lives.

Empowerment and resiliency training were insufficient to advance a culture of peace in former war zones without including developmental play. The reverse was also true. Enthusiasm among the Acehnese after their empowerment and resiliency training led to setting up dozens of small, village play centers. They noticed that when empowerment and resiliency preceded developmental play, the parents and teachers maintained the learning activities and the community used protective, nonviolent actions with powerful results. But when we only did the developmental play training or offered empowerment and resiliency *after* the developmental play training, parents and teachers were unsuccessful. They rushed around setting out play materials for show when someone came to visit, but did not did not put in the time and effort necessary to make the changes or grasp the functions or benefits of the activities. Developmental play was insufficient without the empowerment and resiliency training first.

People who lived in violence learn to memorize, mimic and imitate. Teachers and parents who experienced threatening, punitive approaches to parenting and education have a hard time imagining learning activities other than drilling and recitation. Without doing empowerment and resiliency work themselves, they cannot relate to or meet the challenges of play. They demand drill-based instruction and view creative learning activities with suspicion for their children let alone for themselves!

Once we get someone to play for even ten minutes, they seldom want to stop. Play then stimulates learning, builds capacities and encourages peaceful relationships with both others and materials. With greater social skills, they can cultivate more peaceful, productive relationships. With greater physical skills, they can cultivate more peaceful, productive livelihoods. Still, people who have social skills and few other competencies resort to violence to cover up their frustration and sense of incompetence.

When engaged in developmental play, people connect with themselves, each other and the natural world and feel capable of providing for themselves and their loved ones. Skills lead to success without resorting to force, coercion, deceit or violence. As capabilities excel, people relax and open even more to learning. Communication, cooperation and production improve town meetings, business enterprises, dispute settlement, community welfare and productivity. A culture of peace flourishes.

Peaceful development requires adults dedicated to changing themselves for the benefit of the children and grandchildren across generations, yet they cannot do it alone. They need long-term, consistent, caring attention and support from people with developmental advantages.

Organize Play for Adults and Children

We begin by inviting teens and adults to play cooperative, social games. Participants let down their guard, accustom themselves to others and gain new experiences. Cooperative games involve interpersonal and group challenges. Some games may involve materials also, such as throwing balls or using construction materials. The games may be rudimentary or complex and may or may not involve touching. Each one creates lively, visceral experiences of self and community and builds trust along with a multiplicity of skills.

GROUP ACTIVITY: *Cooperative Games*
After an activity requiring thought, concentration or focused attention, take 5-15 minutes or longer to play. Notice what game is needed, short or long; sitting, standing or moving; or with or without touching. Before introducing touch, build trust and ask permission. Judge no one's preference. Adapt activities for those who are not comfortable standing, moving or touching. See examples of these games in Appendix IV.

We alternate social cooperative games in large groups with developmental play stations in pairs or small groups. The former practices social skills while the latter practices physical skills with materials and tools. Activities include coloring, painting, clay, art, water, sand, ballgames, puzzles and so forth. Organizing these activities requires materials and space that the social cooperative games do not. Although some materials get consumed, others last. Materials require storing, hauling, arranging and cleaning and so take regular time and effort.

People who enjoy and commit to this training, often end up using the materials to set up an ongoing play or cultural center. Some rent, buy or build dedicated space, while others collaborate with an established child care center or preschool. The successful ones receive tremendous support from their families because they see the benefit of these activities for their extended families and communities.

Whether in a home, school or community setting, we prepare three types of play: sensorimotor, dramatic and construction. Each kind of play has macro and micro forms, for example:

- **Sensorimotor:** Large newsprint on an easel or wall with paint and thick brushes, and drawing paper on a table with crayons and pencils.

- **Dramatic:** Clothes for various roles, and dolls with a doll house.

- **Construction:** Large blocks on the floor, and small blocks on a table.

Play activities include materials for each kind of macro and micro play, both outdoors and indoors, to develop gross and fine motor skills. People of any age go through the same developmental stages, beginning with open, fluid play and moving through structured social and materials play. Adults and children play through song, movement, stories and activities with people of a similar age and developmental stage and mixed ages and stages. Different play activities with people of different ages and backgrounds help participants develop and reconstitute capabilities, reevaluate rigid patterns and experiment with new patterns of interaction which creates culture.

GROUP ACTIVITY: Play Sessions
Say, "Now we will do a Play Sessions." Prepare materials and activities to support three types of play: sensorimotor, dramatic and construction,

both fluid and structured in macro and micro forms. Buy two to six of any equipment to support two to six people playing together in pairs, triads and small groups. Offer enough materials and equipment to support play places for three times the number of people playing. This allows choice and easy movement among activities. Offer enough time and space for the ideas to grow, extend, expand and deepen.

Play Stations
(number of play places)

1. Clay and tools (for 4-6 people)

2. Finger paint (2-4)

3. Oobleck (2-4)

4. Water with liquid soap and whisks (2)

5. Newspaper for crushing, ripping, making balls (4)

6. Drawing with pencils, crayons, pastels (4-6)

7. Painting with watercolor, ink and pencil (3-6)

8. 250 unit blocks (2)

9. Two sets of Tinkertoys or 1,000 LEGO ™ pieces (4)

10. One package of Set (4)

11. Two kick balls and three to six juggling balls (4-6)

12. Beads and strings (2-4)

13. A box of sidewalk chalk (4)

14. 6-12 story books and pillows (2-4)

15. Gardening area and tools (2-4)

16. Sewing area, cloth, supplies and patterns for simple products (2-4)

17. Repair center, supplies and items needing repair (2-4)

NOTE: *This example of 16 play stations offers 45-68 places to play. When divided by three, equals enough places for a group of 15-23 people to play. See Appendix III: Learning Activities for more activities and materials.*

Welcome people to the play space with genuine delight. Show them where to store bags or personal items away from the play materials and spaces. Point out the Agreements to Practice (Chapter 3) for new people and to remind everyone to practice them. Without these agreements, play can go awry. Tell a new group to remember they need three things to play: drinking water, movement and loving attention. Then introduce Agreements for Play and the materials. Be brief and clear. Go into detail later as issues arise during play time.

Drinking Water. Play requires perpetual decision-making. The decision-making part of the brain, the frontal lobe, generates energy from water. Drink water often. Also, wash your hands with soap and sweep and dust the play space often. One person drops over 600,000 dead skins cells per day that feed microbes. When inhaled they cause respiratory illness. Good health, especially drinking water, protects learning!

Movement. Gross motor neurons enter through the center of the brain and spread out throughout the entire thinking part of the brain, the cerebral cortex. Schools and universities maintain sports programs because gross motor activity improves our capacity to absorb new information and create new patterns of thought and learn. Movement protects learning!

Loving Attention. When we feel safe, our cerebral cortex opens and engages in thought, creativity and learning. When someone looks up from doing a good job and sees a smiling, encouraging face, they continue to make connections and expand their learning. Safe, loving, encouraging attention protects learning!

Agreements for Play

- Choose an activity and make your own decisions.
- Take care of and share the materials and the space.
- Focus from start to finish.
- Tell someone about it when you are finished.
- Use your words softly and listen to others.
- Clean up when finished.
- Enjoy playing.

Agreements for Play. Use these agreements in natural conversation so they become second nature. As a person finds a place to put their stuff, ask them, "What activity will you choose?" Once they choose an activity say, "Let me show you where these materials belong and how to care for them." Introduce materials, even simple paper and crayons. Ask, "Do you know what or how much you need?"

Notice when people follow the Agreements and thank them. Notice when they do not and remind them. Demonstrate what an agreement means. Say, "You don't need a handful of crayons. You can take one or two and return it to the center when you finish. Set things where everyone can reach, to support yourself and others." Use language from the original Agreements to Practice from Chapter 3 whenever natural. The Agreements for Play are concrete ways of acting and speaking. It takes six to eleven weeks for an entire group or a class to follow the Agreements for Play. Once the group follows the agreements with consistency, we may begin play sessions by introducing one important characteristic. Since characteristics are abstract concepts, help form understanding by identifying and sharing concrete examples of each characteristic, one at a time.

GROUP ACTIVITY: *Characteristics*

Say, "Now we will look at Characteristics." Post the Characteristics. Sit in a circle. Brainstorm examples of how we see one of these characteristic expressed in daily actions and words in private and in public.

Characteristics

- Loving and respectful
- Polite and friendly
- Disciplined and responsible
- Sincere and grateful
- Persistent and patient
- Humble and compassionate
- Listening and honest
- Enthusiastic and joyful

Taking turns, ask each person to describe when they saw that characteristic in themselves or in others. Keep this activity short. Thank the group. Suggest they look for this characteristic during the play session or use materials to represent the characteristic in a story, poem, drawing, painting, sculpture or song. Enjoy the play!

In Indonesia, when I ask a group of children the meaning of respect, they salute me. When I ask a group of adults, they look confused. When I tell them that their children would say it's like this, and I salute them, they laugh. Honestly, that is what they think of too, but they sense there should be something more. Then we brainstorm things we say and do to show respect. In Indonesia when you arrive or leave you go and greet the oldest person, you offer food to others if they pass you while you're eating and you offer tea to a visitor. There's no universal way to show respect, so be creative and make it up. This is culture, creatively meeting human needs that have no universal response. We may also talk about how acts of class division—who is served or not, who waits or not, and so forth—show disrespect and prejudice.

In the U.S. when I ask children what loving means, they often squirm and pretend to hug and kiss sexually as they have seen on television. When I ask adults, their responses vary widely from kindness, to confusion, to, "Well, we know what you mean, but lots of people will sexualize it, so maybe we should find another word for it." We brainstorm ways we show love to others to reclaim the concept, such as notice others' needs, share about our day, stop and offer attention when needed, and so forth.

Discuss what characteristics we want in our lives. Post them, think about them, talk to others about them and make them a part of our conscious daily lives and relationships. A culture of peace requires we use these words and translate them into private and public action.

Greeting. Greetings matter and set a tone of respect, safety and delight. Greetings are cultural, not universal, so we create our own ways to greet, notice how others respond and adjust. We want to communicate to each person that they are respected, safe and appreciated. Convey that with your facial and body language, say it and ask others if they feel respected, safe and appreciated. If not, ask them what would help them feel that way.

Notice if you and others feel love toward others and loved by others in the space, and make a plan for making the space a more loving place.

GROUP ACTIVITY: Greetings

Say, "Now we will practice Greeting." Ask, "Is it sometimes hard to meet new people?" Many people nod, "Yes." Ask, "Do you know why? Because greetings are not universal. You either follow, lead or make it up." Ask for a couple volunteers to show the group how they greet each other. Do children, adults or teens greet each other this way? No! Show us how others greet each other. Ask people in pairs to show each other how they prefer to be greeted. Discuss why and compare. Then have the pairs show other ways to greet and welcome others. Practice welcoming people to a play space. Show them where to put their things. Invite them to choose one thing to play. Show them how to take care of the materials. Ask them to tell someone about what they did or made when they finish before cleaning up. Then switch roles. Reflect on this activity.

Valuable practice occurs both in how we arrive and leave a play session. Consider cleaning up the materials and the space as a significant activity, not a nuisance, distraction or burden. It expresses love, care, respect and attention and builds important skills. Welcome and enjoy the time to clean.

GROUP ACTIVITY: Clean Up and Classify

"Now we will Clean Up." Give players a three-to-five-minute warning before cleaning to allow people to complete their ideas and creations. Tell them they have ten minutes to clean, so they do not have to rush. Select and play specific music when you clean to bring joy to this transition. Give them simple, natural, quality cleaning supplies. Point out how to classify or group various materials on a shelf or in a cupboard. What items are friends? What items do we use together? Can we store them together? Use your words, make it explicit but let them do it. Do not just do it yourself. Try different ways to organize. Notice ways to group unit blocks that look nice versus ways that display mathematical relationships. Notice ways to sort dress-up shoes to use one variable (color, function or size) or multiple variables (men's, women's or children's shoes by color and/or size). Discuss interesting aspects of organizing.

People often dislike cleaning. Sometimes they have no experience with it, so do not know how. Other times they have never been offered the time to build the skills and enjoy it. Cleaning requires more skills than we imagine. Often adults impose awful experiences of cleaning on young people. Transitions create confusion, anxiety and stress. Work and play get interrupted so we cannot complete our thought or idea. Disappointment or discouragement sour the moment. The time, space, supplies and attention may not support easy cleaning or develop the vast skills needed. When we clean, we sort, classify and create patterns. People with strong classification skills forget they learned them. They bring increased order into their environments. Without strong classification skills however, sanitation projects fail. People cannot sort plastics, metal, glass and paper from compost and garbage unless they can classify.

The women in the story of the kerosene stoves gravitated to playing with large wooden beads when they played. They did not string them. They filled bowls with them, carried them around, dumped them out, put them into things and lost them. These types of sensorimotor exploration comprises eighty percent of developmental play. We need extensive experience with materials and tools to understand and use them. Social and physical skills build on that foundation.

Eventually these women made necklaces of random beads or pulled a few beads on the end of the string making the sounds of a dog or a train. This early stage of dramatic play develops representational thought.

Later the women noticed color and strung one color. Shapes stand out when the beads are one color. So then they strung a single shape, such as spheres or cylinders. Then a few of them made patterns and presto, they had a two-variable thought: color and shape (red-sphere, yellow-cylinder). Young children go through these same stages of development!

Once we see a person, of any age, making a two-variable pattern, we know they can understand letters and learn to read. Without two-variable thought, they may imitate, but cannot comprehend meaning in the letters.

Multivariate thought strengthens classification. They no longer throw everything into a huge cardboard box or into the corner of the room. The prior disorder in their homes and play centers reflected the absence or weakness of multivariate thought, not laziness or disrespect.

Every six months, I would "clean" the play center with the teachers and parents. Every time the group's classification skills improved. Their skills became more sustained and then more detailed. Creating patterns with three variables—color, shape and size—builds capabilities beyond those of most people in the world.

We seek activities to build such basic functions and skills:

- Object permanence (peek-a-boo and hide-and-seek).

- Multi-step instruction (dress-up, storytelling, crafts).

- Multivariate thought (bead stringing and sorting objects).

- Classification (sorting and clean up).

- Patterning (puzzles, pattern blocks, and tangrams).

The Chinese tangram puzzle is a square cut into one rhomboid, one smaller square and five triangles. We can reassemble the pieces to form a vast number of different figures. Look for any traditional crafts, games or puzzles that enrich development.

The strongest indicator of the developmental levels of a child is the developmental level of their primary caregivers. Increasing the developmental levels of parents does more to support a child than any time we spend with the child. The greatest rewards come when we play together: children, parents, teachers, community leaders and neighbors—everyone!

The Early Years Organization of Northern Ireland supported by the World Forum Foundation contends that adults and children must playfully explore our worlds to heal from violence and war and learn to live in peace (Connolly and Hayden, 2007). Peace and education need each other, and both need a genuine, inward spark of wonder, awe and joy in life.

Everywhere we did the empowerment, resiliency and play training, children later excelled in school and won local and regional awards. They established closer relationships with adults, who became more confident, capable, peaceful and successful. Still, play centers were hard to sustain without persistent attention from outsiders. Local people could sustain activities when both male and female community leaders committed. This usually occurred when two generations wanted to pass on to their grandchildren the huge, constructive changes they experienced.

Connolly and Hayden's seminal publication, *From Conflict to Peacebuilding: The Power of Early Childhood Initiatives* (2007), presents case studies from eight countries. In each case, early childhood play made essential contributions to recovery from war and violence. Their experiences resonated with ours.

Involving men and village leaders was a key lesson at the Garden of Mothers and Children Centers for overcoming historic blood feuds in Albania. The case resonated with our experience: sustained progress requires the support of both women and men. Their Centers established Fathers' Boards to support training for men on children's rights and developmental needs. Ingrid Jones, the Garden's Director, described how they "placed a big emphasis on raising people's awareness that it is very important to have a positive, calm, and stimulating environment for children, and that the men do have a very crucial role in the early education of children, in their development, and in their care" (Connolly and Hayden, 2007, p. 28). Their manual for fathers, *Roli I Baballareve Ne Mirerritjen e Femijeve* (The Father's Role in Raising Children), is the first publication that runs out at a parent conferences. It covers basic tasks that men, or anyone in the family, can do to support pregnant and nursing mothers and young children.

Jones and her team realized that to create fundamental cultural change required working with local officials, village elders or leaders, both male and female. Doing the developmental work with themselves and other adults generated a respect for the dignity of everyone. They sought nonviolent approaches to protecting human rights for everyone to reestablished a secure peace. The community could not have achieved these changes through protesting or confrontation.

Organizing activities in flexible settings, including child-friendly spaces at therapeutic feeding centers in Chad, significantly contributed to recovering from civil war and internal displacement. This resonated with our experience in Aceh, North Sumatra and Central Java. "Child-friendly spaces are physical areas where children and their caregivers can feel safe and take part in structured and unstructured activities. The spaces are mainly aimed at children from ages 0-15 years, although adult programs are also available" (Connolly and Hayden, 2007, p. 45).

In poor, rural Indonesian villages, women who invested their time and energy in their own development often established play centers or preschools. They reached out through volunteer village health clinics for weighing, feeding and immunization of children. Once or twice a month women could exchange information and practice activities at these clinics.

The needs of children and families extend well beyond the end of a conflict. Peace gets declared in the instant of signing a cease-fire or an accord, but recovery takes a long time. Child-friendly spaces help communities heal and increase confidence as they help their children.

Peace or violence are passed down. As noted by the Early Years Organization of Northern Ireland, Sioban Fitzpatrick and Eleanor Mearns supported middle-class, private preschool providers investing in children's access to better education. When violence erupted in Northern Ireland, the organization became a community-based movement to unite parents of every backgrounds around the interests of their children, rather than around political divisions and privilege. As an unfunded women-run organization, they "flew under the radar." They protected safe, peaceful spaces for children and adults to gather, learn and explore social and physical worlds. They came to realize the power of having a membership from across the political divides. This unique opportunity to explore diverse attitudes and experiences allowed them to form social leadership with significant social impact. They contributed to the peace dialogues that followed the cease fire and could overcome long-standing prejudices and violence and stop passing them on to their children.

Play to Invest in Development and Justice

Communities prosper as we invest in empowerment, resiliency and developmental play. But as we prosper, we often lose touch with what got us here and our need for one another. If we lose touch with transforming power, play degenerates into control, entertainment, thrill-seeking or escape and education into an investment for personal gain. We buy play through sports, lessons, programs, entertainment or competition. We store children in play centers while adults are too busy and separate them from the larger social fabric. Children become entitled or a liability, increasing the stress and underlying violence of society.

Prosperity ends up eroding the developmental capacities that made us prosperous. Secondary trauma introduces a pervasive, low-grade dulling of senses and flattening of relationships. With so many demands, we cannot stop, relax, open up, let go or play with abandon and delight. Sequestering play into limited, often privatized or closed spaces, with only the youngest children and a minimal number of adults, robs us of its renewing invigoration. We crash, shut down, escape and seek thrills as we squeeze play into smaller and smaller times and places.

Even people with the capabilities to create cultures of peace often dislike others' who do not share their awareness or perspective. We forget where we came from and how we developed. Cycles of violence, oppression, exploitation and injustice create an "us and them" mentality, which we reinforce as we struggle not to become "one of them." Prosperity degenerates into exploitation and patterns of oppression passed down to our children, discouraging any hope for a better society.

Just as we realized the interdependence of peace and education, so must we realize the interdependence of social development and justice. Development alone does not ensure social responsibility, honor or fairness needed to resist oppression and injustice. Justice alone does not ensure human development, insight or capabilities needed to put opportunities to good use. Social justice happens in an instant through the way we think, act and treat one another and the Earth. Social development on the other hand takes time and practice through individuals and communities to society. Play not only supports development, it changes the way adults interact with children and can break patterns of violence and oppression.

Adults often think they know how to play so they can skip this part. Or play is a luxury they cannot afford or an uninteresting waste of time. But once I get the adults to play, I often ask, "What's the difference between seeing the play and playing yourself?" They reply, "Totally different! Totally, totally different!"

Focus first on exploratory play with a sense of adventure and surprise. Use tactile materials such as paint, sand, water and clay. Observe the world. Look for activities that bring the senses alive.

Many ordinary work activities—gardening, construction, repair, cleaning and so forth—offer ample opportunity for free play and exploration when we bring a playful, exploratory approach to the work. Setting up our homes, community centers, reading rooms, libraries, clinics or schools with times, spaces and materials to play helps make sure we continue to grow, adapt and mature. As we look for opportunities to include others, we become more secure, open and available to others.

Mike Fellows, a world-renowned mathematician and computer scientist, worked with children before their minds got rigid and forgot how to play. *Computer Science Unplugged!* (Bell, Witten and Fellows, 2015) presents how to play with even advanced knowledge. It shows that through play children can grasp concepts as complicated as intractability, sorting networks and cryptography. The book uses stories, "presenting math and computing topics through story-telling and drama can captivate children and adults alike, and provides a whole new level of engagement. Mike's activities are about thinking outside the box, whether sharing the unknowns of computer science and mathematics with elementary school children or running a mathematics event in a park" (Wikipedia, April 2017).

Creating and protecting opportunities for play takes social discipline and investment. In our experience, when adults arrange enough relevant materials—not too easy or too difficult—in a loving environment, then players experience great joy and delight.

Adults try not to decide for young people or do it for them. Older people may model ways to play and interact without telling younger people what to do. We offer attention and value a light touch with engaged, appreciative attention. Then the players take over and protect one another.

When we open new play centers, we stop children as they leave and ask them what is in their pockets. We remind them to leave the play materials or toys here. They often return items because we remind them without punishment. Instead, we explain that if we leave the items here we can play again tomorrow. Before long, they remind one another and protect the play space.

Feeling relaxed and nonanxious eliminates most discipline problems. The way we arrange an environment can eliminate many threats to people, materials and their products. Still, we have stressful and joyful times. When stress arises, often a glance is enough to calm someone or divert their attention. If not, a gentle reminder of the agreements and a request to change may help. When reminders do not work, redirect attention, invite people to take a break or do to something else. Still, the art of disciplining oneself or others takes great sensitivity and experience. We need to know when to disrupt a behavior and when to allow it time to adjust on its own. We will not always get it right.

If distress takes over, then stop, offer time for emotional discharge or go to a quiet place to rest or sleep. Many problems stem from exhaustion and over-stimulation. Arrange a space with pillows, picture books and soft, quiet toys where anyone may rest and relax. People of all ages appreciate a way to take a soothing time-out when they need it. Some adults close the door and take a ten-minute "power nap." They will play or work again when they are ready. Practicing loving, pragmatic, matter-of-fact approaches to the discipline of children or ourselves carries over into our adult relationships.

M. Dahlan, of East Aceh, declared without hesitation, "We will not make peace with each other, until we make peace with the Earth." As long as we feel disconnected from the Earth, we will continue to abuse it and each other. Play can serve as a powerful agent to reweave our social fabric with others and our ecological fabric with the natural world.

Achieving peace and nonviolence today requires we offer as much attention to the way we interact with the natural world as we do with other people. Reggio Emilia, Waldorf schools, Expeditionary Learning schools, Outward Bound and Free Community Schools lead this dedication to explore the natural world.

~

Everywhere, from Indonesia to the United States, violence erodes human capabilities. It leaves gaps in our abilities to think that impede our ability to generalize, innovate or trouble-shoot, even as we engage in higher-order functions. Violence closes the heart to compassion and justice and destroys relationships with other people and with the natural world. Empowerment and resiliency transform, but without developmental play, with a gentle yet effective approach to discipline, they will fail. We return to deception and violence. Play remains essential for recovery from violence, human development and preservation of peace. Communities that invest in both peace and education as well as both justice and development document our work in public record to create a vibrant, healthy, playful cultures of peace.

In cultures of peace, we approach our lives with an inward openness, tenderness and affection for the whole of life. We practice flexibility, humor and creativity as we connect and reconnect with each other and the natural world in ever-changing ways. We approach work playfully and lovingly free to take leave without ill judgment or retribution. We reach out, check in and stand up for one another. Life begets life, creating and connecting whole, true core selves with one another and with the transforming power of other life around us.

"Be Like a Bird"

My daughter, Sarah, taught me this traditional song, adapted from a Victor Hugo poem, passed down to us from Michael Cicone on the album *Only Human* (Kallet, Epstein and Cicone, 1993). It reminds me of the ups, downs and risks of life, as well as our ever-present power to live free and fly!

> *Be like a bird,*
> *who halting in her flight,*
> *on a limb too slight,*
> *feels it give way beneath her;*
> *yet sings, sings knowing she has wings;*
> *yet sings, sings knowing she has wings.*

Love life, in joy!

Part III

~

ACT ON CONSCIENCE:

Living Peaceful Public Lives

Loving people, who practice peace and nonviolence in daily life, engage with each other in conscientious, discerning communities.

~

With humility, shortcomings lead to

conviction and compassion.

Without humility, shortcomings lead to

humiliation and violence.

~

Chapter 9

~

Be Aware and
Available

Transformed by a living sense of power, resilience and playfulness, we discover we need to transform our public structures to function with others. Experiencing transforming power in every moment builds the confidence and conviction to allow love and truth to guide our decisions. We bring our whole, core selves to both our private and our public lives. This confidence and conviction prepare us to act on conscience, liberate ourselves from oppression and create discerning communities.

The confidence comes from experiencing life's generous, creative power in the glorious, mountaintop moments as well as the still, quiet, all-is-well moments. The conviction comes from experiencing this power in the times when we feel inadequate, exhausted or guilty.

Stay Aware
of the beauty, joy and love of life in every moment.

Order Daily Life
How do I experience transforming power in good times and hard times?
What do I need to have or let go of to stay aware of transforming power?
How can I put my life in order so I am available and prepared?

We can create cultures of peace when we approach daily life with the clarity of confidence and conviction, not obscured by guilt and shame. We direct our attention to life's beauty, joy and love and order our decisions and actions based on what rings true.

Cultivate an awareness of the beauty, joy and love of life's transforming power in every moment. Select what you must have or let go of to keep this awareness. Then allow this inward experience of life's transforming power to shape your outward life in a way that makes you available and prepared.

Become Confident

Awareness of life's transforming power in good times increases our confidence. I experienced this transforming power as a young child, running in the fields and creek beds, hiking in the mountains and listening to my parents reading or singing. We engaged in daily life—made curtains, cleaned house, washed dishes, explored nature, viewed a vista, farmed and taught. Whatever we did, we did in joy. We let the younger ones take part as much as they liked or let them explore on their own.

I felt the power, goodness and capabilities of life within and around me as a young person. Morning came with the sunrise. The door was always open. Everyone was a potential friend. Men registered as conscientious objectors to war from World War II to the wars in Korea and Vietnam. Educated women raised brave, bold children. We lived on our land. We studied in village schools and land-grant colleges, grew our own food from the soil and manure, built our homes from the trees and rocks and soaked wooden strips in the creek to bend for spinning wheels. We raised sheep, and carded, spun and wove their wool. I got over two hundred bee stings, and still loved the honey. I never wanted for clean water or fresh food. The night sky was so dark at times I felt part of the Milky Way and could see the Northern Lights. The ground water was so clean, endangered purple salamanders thrived. I lived in an aboriginal dream where life teemed with transforming power.

As a young adult I moved into a world that obscured the transforming power of life, love and conscience. I married into a family with multigenerational trauma and sought my way in a militarized, commercial society. To regain my awareness of it did not come easy.

PERSONAL PRACTICE: *Track Awareness*

Write in a journal the percentage of each day during which you can keep your awareness open to transforming power. Try to increase the percentage, then try to keep it stable. Let your awareness increase on its own, without extra effort, to become an habitual awareness. Notice and write what you feel when you live in and from your authentic, core, true self. Explore transforming power's various qualities: good, capable, authentic, compassionate, caring, calm, clear, courageous, curious, connected, creative, worthy, peaceful, present, relaxed, unrestrained, unselfconscious, uninhibited, non-anxious, loving, honest, bold, brave, fearless, confident, valiant, adventuresome and intrepid.

Let go of extra effort. Discharge grief, fear and pain. Be carried into the pure love that is so generous it gifts life to you incessantly. Notice your heartbeat and your breath, the unconditional gift of life in every moment. Spend time with others who share this awareness and life experiment. Several companion groups may gather to form a community. For all its challenges, a community supports keeping this awareness alive.

A *Gathering for Silence* reinforces our practice of rooting our lives in life's transforming power. We often open with 10 to 20 minutes of silence. Or gather for silence once a week. We may sit longer in times of challenge, change or need. It takes about 20 minutes to stop, let go and open inwardly. It often takes another 20 minutes or more to listen for and express guidance that arises. But we may meet longer if insights build among the people gathered. Regular practice of stopping in silence leads to greater insights as individuals and a community. Stop in your mind and body each day. Gather and stop in silence as a community once or twice a week.

GROUP ACTIVITY: *Gathering for Silence*

"Now we will do a Gathering for Silence." Pass out cards (below). Ask someone to read the card out loud. Ask for questions. "Okay, let's settle into silence. Please do each step to feel how each affects us as a group." This takes about 20 to 45 minutes. Reflect on this activity.

Gathering for Silence

- *Gather* in a circle and settle into silence.
- *Stop*, let go and be present.
- *Open* inwardly to life's transforming power.
- *Listen* inwardly and let insights work on you.
- *Write* personal insights, implications or distresses to consider later.
- *Speak* to any insights for the community or society.
- *Change* based on your own and other's insights.

If an insight applies to yourself, don't speak about it. Keep it inside and let it work on you to allow it to change you. Consider its implications regardless of how inconvenient, undesirable or intimidating they appear. Write it in your journal and experiment with it. Sometimes speaking about an insight replaces action. Test the insight by experimenting with it in your life, then share it with others.

If you sense an insight is for others or for us as a people, then stand and share it in the silence. When others speak, do not respond to their insights. Sit in silence, listen and let their insights work within you or let them go. Consider implications for yourself. Make a note of distress that arises and what triggers you, but only if you will attend to it later. If you do this, the distress will subside at the moment knowing you will attend to it later. If you do not, next time your distress will intensify.

Take time later to try to name the specific words or actions that triggered your distress. Complete an I-Message (Chapter 4) to seek the root of your response. Note concrete consequences and specific needs. Then discharge your distress with a companion. As insights and implications for us as a community or as a people come to you, share them with your companions. If the companions concurs, bring them to the community.

A Gathering for Sharing, aka Claremont Dialogue, often meets every month or quarter for up to 90 minutes. We come to know each other on matters of consequence. Sit, stop and open to transforming power. Listen inwardly to speak plainly from one's core self and listen plainly to where others' words come from. Leave silence between speakers. Note and tend distresses that arise. Seek your best sense of what is loving and true.

GROUP ACTIVITY: *Gathering for Sharing*

"Now we will do a Gathering for Sharing." Pass out cards (below). Ask someone to read the card out loud. Ask for questions. Tell the group to sit in silence and speak out of the silence until everyone has a chance to speak. Then say, "Okay, let's settle into silence. Please do each step to appreciate how each step affects the group." This takes 45 to 75 minutes. Reflect on this activity.

Gathering for Sharing

- *Gather* in a circle and settle into silence.
- *Read* a question, encouragement or statement.
- *Ask* "Is anything unclear?" Clarify as needed.
- *Speak* from your own experience and best sense of what is true.
- *Leave silence* between speakers.
- *Offer everyone a chance* to speak before speaking again.
- *Listen with empathy,* stay open to learning and changing.

Once insights or themes emerge (ideas repeat):

- *Everyone speak again* on what rings true for us as a people.
- *Record* collective insights or implications for later testing.

Schedule a regular monthly Gathering for Sharing on: *"How do I experience and keep my awareness of transforming power alert in every moment? How is transforming power shaping, guiding and changing my life?"* To get to know how each community member experiences transforming power, keeps their awareness alert and is guided by love and conscience helps us form a loving, conscientious community.

A community may host Gatherings for Sharing on a specific topic, insight, practice, advice, question, direction for the community or dispute among its members. Encourage every community member to attend these sessions. Important topics may require a few gatherings to hear everyone's comments and questions. When you think you have covered a topic, meet one last time. This final gathering will either settle into silence to appreciate and affirm the results or go to a whole new level of sharing. The latter has happened so often I come to expect and look forward to it.

Discover Conviction

If our awareness of transforming power occurs only during good times, then it becomes indistinguishable from ego and can even inflate egotism and self-righteousness.

Hard times offer a very different awareness of life's transforming power. Vulnerability strengthens us. We realize that transforming power reaches far beyond us. We can lean into and rely on it even when we fail, make mistakes, get lost or are inadequate.

GROUP ACTIVITY: Step into the Circle

"Now we will Step into the Circle." Begin by playing 5 to 6 rounds of Big Wind Blows using topics that help the group get to know one another. Then ask the center person to rejoin the circle and say, "Now we will change the rules. One person will step forward." The facilitator steps forward as an example. "That person says 'step into the circle if ....' and names an experience that shaped their life." The facilitator starts with an example, such as: "Step into the circle if you have ever been present when someone died." Or "Step into the circle if you have ever experienced violence in your own home." The facilitator continues, "Then anyone who has had this experience steps forward. We practice empathy by imagining how this experience effects someone's life." Stand still a moment. "And imagining what life is like if this experience had never happened to you." Stand still a moment. Then ask everyone to step back. Invite others to step forward. Do not rush. Give everyone time to think. People will step forward if they are ready. Consider and honor each person's example. Ask the group if anyone has another example before ending the activity. Keep going until no one responds to this prompt. Reflect on this activity.

Lives oriented to personal accomplishment lose this humbling awareness of everyone's limitations and frailties. When we fail or feel inadequate or guilty, human needs can outstrip resources. We can become overwhelmed and freeze, so our mental capacity collapses. Unmet needs from that time become frozen because that part of the brain cannot analyze or place them in time. The brain shuts out these negative memories. But the longer we live the more avoidance and denial lose their utility. Distress accumulates and intrudes on our thoughts. We continuously reenact the past to try to change the outcome and meet those frozen needs.

Ironically, when we make ourselves vulnerable by sharing losses and fears with companions, we see beyond ourselves to the omnipresence of the transforming power of life. Our needs no longer outstrip the resources, so we are less apt to become overwhelmed. We discover we can reintegrate memory into more parts of our brain and so can analyze and sequence them in time. We no longer have the urge to reenact or change the past. Memories stop intruding and begin to "feel normal." We become resilient.

GROUP ACTIVITY: *Transforming Power in Hard Times*

*"Now we will do Transforming Power in Hard Times." In groups of 2-4 do a Companion Group Session. Settle into silence at the beginning and end. Give equal time to each person. During your time be silent, speak, discharge and/or ask for restatement or feedback. This session focuses on the question: "**How do I experience transforming power when I fail, am inadequate or make mistakes?**" Remember to let the emotions leave the body. Do not hold on to them. Balance your attention to the past and present, the inward and outward, your failings and your goodness. Remember to return to the present time after each person shares. Reflect on this activity. Offer extra time for journal writing.*

Many people find sharing hard times with a relaxed, nonanxious companion both exhausting and elating. Our failings and shortcomings offer an exhilarating awareness of transforming power within and beyond us. We can see beyond our own egos. Our minds clear, our hearts melt, our bodies regain feeling and the joy of life floods back.

When hidden away and repressed, such experiences lead to humiliation that injures our sense of dignity and self-respect. Losing self-respect robs us of respect for life, which opens the way to violence. The path away from humiliation is humility. When we experience the value of life beyond our own egos, we experience human weakness and frailty as gifts not as failings. We come to love and respect our whole selves.

Convicted of limitations, failings and mistakes, we can open to a direct, personal experience of power beyond human ego, understanding or control. This deepens and strengthens our experience with and understanding of life's transforming power. We come to rely on it despite all opposition and against all odds. Our mistakes and weaknesses serve as "the cracks where God comes through." We find beauty in our imperfections, see the gifts of others and find we are complements to each other's gifts and needs. We no longer have to fear the whole truth. Integrity—in its varied forms of honesty, authenticity and consistency—reflects our perfect, genuine selves, and how we fit together into a perfect genuine whole.

We come to love and value life and realize we are lovable and loving. Then we can be honest with and trust ourselves and others over an image or desire. And we find the courage to overcome our fears and learn to rely on one another with true humility, appreciation and compassion.

~

With humility, shortcomings lead to conviction and compassion.
Without humility, shortcomings lead to humiliation and violence.

~

To allow life's transforming power to shape and guide my decisions, I practice staying aware of this power, even when I am weak or confused. This full experience of life's transforming power balances strength with kindness, integrity with love and justice with compassion.

Make notes in your journal or log on your experiences of both confidence and conviction in good and hard times. Let go of stress and fears. Reconciling with one's human limitations holds the key to experiencing life's full abundance and peace.

Transform Private and Public Life

Note in your journal or log what you need to have or to let go of to stay aware of life's abundance and power. Notice what helps or impedes your awareness. When you lose touch, bring your attention back. Word and action matter whether you are alone or with others.

PERSONAL PRACTICE: Ask What I Need to Have or to Let Go Of
List what you need to have or let go of to stay aware of transforming
power in every moment. For example, invest in particular relationships
and give up others, live within your means, settle debts promptly,
simplify your schedule, quit particular occupations or take up others.
Do not list everything, only the ones you need to stay aware of life's
transforming power or life hands you. Experiment. Share your list with
others and listen to them. Acknowledge and record when other's items
apply to you.

Tinker with the elements of your daily life until you maintain your awareness of life's transforming power in every moment. Tinkerers learn from experimenting with real-life application and adjusting. It takes a challenging level of honesty to accept and let go. When you find something works commit for three to six days, then extend your commitment to three to six weeks. Experiment with how it works in reality, not only the concept.

Items may apply to one person, to a few people or to everyone. Test what makes a difference for one person with others to reveal the items everyone finds necessary.

GROUP ACTIVITY: List Questions and Encouragements
"Now we will List Our Questions and Encouragements." List the
questions we ask ourselves that have helped discover and maintain this
awareness. List what everyone needs to have or let go of to stay aware of
life's transforming power in every moment.

This awareness makes ourselves available and prepared to experiment with love and conscience in our relationships, habits and consumption. Do not strive to do everything. Experiment with your day-to-day activities, the resources you use and your relationships.

PERSONAL PRACTICE: Be Available and Prepared
Post these questions to consider if you are available and prepared and
reflect on them during the day.

Available and Prepared

1. Am I taking care of myself: my health, sleep, water, food, activity, curiosity, tranquility and balance?

2. What distress is intruding that I can discharge and reevaluate?

3. Is my heart open? Do I discharge my grief, fear, anger and apathy?

4. Is my mind open? Do I articulate my confusion, understanding, insights and sense of integrity?

5. Is my conscience open? Do I listen inwardly, experiment & change?

6. Do I love life and act on conscience for the joy of it in every moment?

7. Do I listen for what rings true, test it with others and enter it into the public record via writing, art, music, curriculum, law, court or news?

Be Available. As we put our daily lives in order and let go. We do not get busy, we get available. This allows us to be present and appreciate the beauty, majesty and diversity of the natural world. We can meet a peaceful life with each sunrise, available to respond to what the day brings with love and honesty. This bears the fruits of joy, peace, strength, compassion, beauty, truth and equality. To live in accord with our conscience leads to an amazing sense of genuine liberty.

The discrepancy between what we imagine and reality produces stress. When they match, stress dissipates. When they diverge, stress rises. Strain and stress recede as we let go of images and desires and move deeper into an awareness and acceptance of the natural world itself. Then we can be present to relationships with gratitude. To know, befriend and live generous and fearless in harmony with life's web creates an irrevocable sense of confidence, conviction and liberty.

PERSONAL PRACTICE: Haudenosaunee Thanksgiving

The Haudenosaunee people of northeastern North America give thanks to the people, Mother Earth, the waters, fish, plants, food plants, medicine plants, animals, trees, birds, winds, thunders, sun, Grandmother Moon, stars, teachers and the creator. Living in gratitude, our minds become one. One good mind. The Haudenosaunee Law of Peace, which influenced the U.S. Constitution, recognizes reason, righteousness, justice and health as foundations of peace. Learn your own traditional ways or create a tradition of your own for showing gratitude. Share it with others at public events. Seek opportunities to acknowledge life cycles in public. Hold your community to living in balance and harmony with each other and the natural world. Bring your minds together as one to greet and give thanks to each other and the natural world.

"Two Row on the Grand" canoe paddle has been a symbolic renewal of the Two Row Wampum—the original peace-treaty between First Nation and settler communities. The Two Row Wampum represents a treaty between the Haudenosaunee and European settlers for peaceful coexistence and mutual care of the land. At the close of the 2016 Paddle on the Grand River, Pamela Haines commented, "We feel the power of this group of people—Native and allies, men and women, young and old, friends and strangers—all intent on keeping a good mind as we traveled together down the river." Our collective good mind makes us curious and available to act on conscience and respond with love.

Stop a moment and consider this. How do we put our homes in order, not for comfort, complacency or distraction, but to be more alive, curious and responsive to people and the planet? Someone once yelled at me in frustration, "But this shouldn't take over your whole life!" A palpable silence descended. We could hear each other breathing. I responded, "Huh. I thought that was the point." Her eyes lit with surprise and recognition. "Oh, I see," she said.

Be Prepared. As we become aware and available, we limit obligations and let go of harmful relationships no matter how much we wish they were otherwise. We ask for what we need, share our gifts, engage in right livelihood and settle debts. As we put our lives in order, the source of our insight and guidance matters. We seek guidance from our best inward sense of love and conscience, not from acting out of:

- *Desire or convenience.* We often dislike, disagree with or don't understand the insight or guidance that comes, but can sense the power and life in it. Pay attention to what rings true, not what you wish were true.

- *Gratification or praise.* Life is already valuable. We do not earn value by doing this work. Nothing you can say or do will make us any more valuable than you are right now.

- *Distraction or avoidance.* Unless in imminent danger, we cannot rescue others from their own lives. We can only offer good attention to aid someone in finding their own way forward. Do not rush to help others to avoid or appease your own guilt about your privileges or misdeeds. Give up unnecessary or unfair power, use what you need and share the rest, even if it frightens or inconveniences you.

As we experiment with listening to love and conscience, we live from our curious, creative, intrepid selves and develop a wide range of skills. We cannot judge a person by the challenges life deals, but by the dignity with which they meet them. Do not try to help. Listen and offer friendship. Do not try to fix people. Be present in body, mind and spirit with respect. Do not advise people. Invite mutual relationships based on trust and forgiveness.

Make your decisions responsive to reality not to your desire. Seek enlivening arrangements, not obligated ones. Meet each moment with a fresh sense of adventure. Open to the unanticipated. Stay available to love and truth as it arises, unafraid of what it brings, valiant and courageous, tender and calm.

～

Aware of life's regenerative resources that exceed human need,
we face our human condition without freezing,
open to transforming power.

～

To become available and prepared simplifies life. We seek to live from the fruits of our own labor, exerting no extra effort and exploiting no one. We attend to our direct relationships with others and the natural world. This hones our discernment and builds a sense of security. When we know life's abundance, we do not feel overwhelmed. When we are aware of the rich relationships in life, we do not feel alone. We become resilient!

To preserve peace, we cultivate fluidity among the tiers of our attention to home, neighbors, community, society, ancestors, children, grandchildren and great-grandchildren. We shift attention from this geographic location to the planetary solar system, from this moment to the eternal, from ego to empathy. The finite, temporal human scale blends with the infinite, eternal natural scale. We increase our fluidity in shifting our attention across these scales. Like learning to drive a motorcycle or car, we may get overwhelmed looking to the front, side mirrors, rearview mirror, gear shift and dashboard. But the more we repeat this rapid shifting of attention, the more it becomes effortless.

Through practice we cultivate an appetite for the immense living power in the still, small movements—the creeping glory of a sunrise, the gentle rustle of a breeze, the meandering pace of grazing deer or the serenity of washing dishes. Nothing we do or say will bring about peace. Peace is already present. We preserve and protect the gift of peace by meeting our needs without abusing, exploiting or destroying each other or the Earth. Human beings are ingenious enough to figure this out, but can we do it in time to save ourselves from extinction?

We are still susceptible to the perils and pitfalls of our human condition—egotism, loss of self-control, indulgence and mania. Staying clear and strong in our awareness of transforming power allows us to preserve and protect peace in our hearts, homes and communities and to call for peace in human society.

~

As long as we can stop and
stay open to external feedback,
we can trust our inner sense of right action.

~

Chapter 10

❧

Visit with Others

Visiting with others without an agenda beyond goodwill and hospitality makes us available to care for, get to know and respond to each other's needs as they arise. It provides the time needed for love and conscience to affect our relationships, strengthen our social skills and weave a friendly, kind, generous and enjoyable social fabric.

Patricia J. Williams referred to philosopher Emmanuel Levinas, who "wrote that it is the face-to-face encounter that inspires one to serve and to give to others, for it 'involves a calling into question of oneself,' a critical attitude which is itself produced in the face of the other ..." (*The Nation* April 2, 2015 p. 10). Life's transforming power resides in these relationships. We bring our full core selves open to others' core selves. We open to the air, water and natural world around us. With each interaction, we step into the stream of history in a unique moment. In this sense, our every interaction makes history. Relationships form and transform us. As Manfred Halpern (1924-2001) wrote:

"Transformation is a process of participating in creation so that we may give birth to something fundamentally new that is also fundamentally better. However committed we may be to preserving what we have inherited from the past, trying to solidify and preserve any particular human situation becomes always an ever more costly fantasy. We live in a cosmos of continuous creation. We can nourish any experience which is already fruitful, loving, and just by asking and learning what is needed for its persistent renewal."

Many traditions recognize visiting and hospitality as central to a good society. Christians encourage hospitality to enrich spiritual life and Muslims consider visiting an injunction, welcoming and offering tea to the stranger. It involves spending time together. We prefer personal locations such as homes or public settings where people need not spend money to join. When we visit in each other's homes, we can get to know one another through conversation, recreation and play. Groups may be larger or smaller, spontaneous or scheduled, but we need both programmed and unprogrammed time for this work. We need time to listen, learn and collaborate on thinking and decision-making just as we need to rest, rejuvenate and enjoy one another's company. When we do so, we bond, and are open to listen and be available to what arises. Through visiting, we learn to develop and express love. We offer and receive love and can experiment with what makes everyone feel loved.

The hairdresser in our hometown, Jeanne Hyland, hears stories. When she hears of concrete ways to help, she acts. She goes to someone's home to do their hair after they return from the hospital, or she cooks for a family in need. One day, someone came in who had just come back from working on the Twin Towers site after 9/11/2001 in New York City. He explained, "We can only wear a T-shirt or a pair of work gloves for one day and they're ruined …. The soles of our feet burn as we work …. It was so much better when we chewed gum." After he left, she made a list: T-shirt, work gloves, insoles, gum and so forth. She taped the list to the side of her mirror and everyone brought in shoe boxes filled with these items. Through visiting, paying attention, caring and acting when right, without planning or stress, she helped us send just what was needed when they needed it.

Love and conscience are not thoughts. Love and conscience are both the inward motivation and the nature of our interactions with others and the natural world. Our loving and conscientious interactions create the community that love and conscience need to thrive. This then matures our capacities for greater love and conscience in an upward, reinforcing cycle.

Manfred Halpern (1987) encouraged us to ask what our thoughts or actions served. Nanik, founder of the Joglo Preschool in Java, Indonesia, noted that the intentions of people visiting mattered as much or more than the visits. Visiting with a concern for cultivating peace reinforces our own and each other's transformation.

The intent and quality of our visits and hospitality define the nature of our culture. We seek social patterns and customs that encourage visiting. No single prescription works in every community. But we recognize visiting and spiritual hospitality as a public not just a private matter. Visiting weaves the fabric of loving and conscientious society wherever we spend time, in our homes, workplaces, schools, studios or playgrounds.

Live with Integrity in Community

Every facet of life is an opportunity to seek integrity. Insight flourishes when we question ourselves and each other with openness, love and compassion, without accusation or taking offense. Once, in an exit interview I asked the supervisor why raising questions of integrity met with so much resistance. She replied, "Well that's natural. It's offensive to question another's integrity."

Surprised, I responded, "No, it's trained. Quakers ask questions of integrity about everything. It's the way we interact with the world."

"No, it's offensive." She retorted. "I committed my life to service and social justice and gave up my chances for wealth through business. It's offensive to question my integrity!"

"No," I came back, "it's trained."

The exchange illuminated a fundamental discrepancy in approach. In the ensuing silence, she grasped the implications of this. She remarked, "Well, I hope someday this office is a place where people like you can work."

I almost offered to stay, but realized she would soon feel integrity was a luxury she could not risk. She had not renewed the contracts of several long-term peace workers, and from this exchange I understood why. They asked questions of integrity and acted on the implications. She had misread them as offensive and insubordinate. Even if she wanted to try to change, as the director she feared taking risks. In her perspective, the office had to fortify itself and secure its position, then use its position to work towards the right thing. To act on a sense of integrity as a fundamental approach required too much faith.

Confidence in integrity grows more than good intentions alone when we get to know and align our lives with what is real. Small successes in doing this in our private lives, tested with companions in a community, hone our discernment. This leads to more successes and builds confidence in basing public decisions on love and conscience. Hierarchical organizations run independent of individuals' personal integrity.

In a fishing village in Aceh after the 2004 tsunami, village elders asked us to buy an irrigation gate for a mountain village. I assumed the village head must have a relative or someone to please. I explained donors wanted to help tsunami survivors, "So how can we help you?" They requested an irrigation gate for the village up the mountain. When I asked them why, they explained that when storms hit the shoreline, the mountain people take them in and feed them. An irrigation gate for that mountain village would double rice production, increase food security for disaster times and increase their trade of fish for rice in good times. Everyone I checked with agreed. To buy an irrigation gate for that specific mountain village increased food security along the entire shoreline.

The insights of these people, based on their intimate knowledge of their relationships with others and the natural world conflicted with our procedures and contracts. The office did not allow us to spend funds outside the tsunami zone even if our best discernment led to that recommendation. Later in Nepal, Friends Peace Teams organized disaster relief based on local, advisory and international discernment teams. We ran effective, smooth, well-placed relief based on the best discernment of the people involved.

When I got back to the U.S., I wondered, "What were the sources of my survival and food security?" I took an inventory of my minimal needs and looked for local sources in my local social and natural ecologies.

Today I buy far fewer things and most of them I buy from local people. This enriched my daily life. I may spend more on one item but I spend much less overall. And besides the items purchased, I make friends and create gratitude and good will. We cooperate on local projects and governance and help one another in times of need with ease.

A community of love and conscience cares for the group and the land in the same way we care for individuals. Through experimenting with life in this way, I learned more about local farming and production, government waivers to sell raw milk to residents and energy options for my home. We exchange experiences with neighboring communities and learn from place-specific, case-specific stories. "Box store" employees will never come to my home when I'm in need, but many local producers do!

Stay Open to Change

By nature, life is in constant change. Oriented to life's transforming power we stay open to, expect and welcome change. We are not fearful of change or annoyed by it. We ask, what obstructs my trust in acting on my best discernment?

Sometimes, we take risks for the right thing despite the fear and uncertainty of the outcome. When obstacles come up, however, one may try writing an I-Message to oneself, share it with a companion and ask for restatement and feedback. Or try doing "A Problem I Face Right Now Is," and use this prompt: "A problem I face relying on life's transforming power in every moment is ..." Empathy from others can help us imagine a wider range of how we might face our situation.

Advice seldom helps. Asking for advice often masks a self-put-down, "I don't feel capable. Help me." The response we need is, "I'm here. I know you're capable, and you can find the right path for yourself. You may need to discharge emotion or hear your thoughts restated. You may even need feedback on what parts ring true or not. But you can do it!"

However sometimes we can give stunningly great advice to ourselves.

PERSONAL PRACTICE: *Advice to Self*

Sit in a chair facing another chair. Pretend you are yourself in 5, 10 or 20 years and have "arrived" at being the person you want to become. Pretend you, at your current age, are sitting in the seat in front of you. Describe the future you have accomplished and name your current inner strengths and outer supports that helped you get to this future. Then add, "BUT to make it you must do X, Y, and Z." Write your strengths, supports and steps to take. Then give them to yourself. Switch seats. Thank your future self for the discipline, patience and persistence to arrive at that future. And promise your future self to use your inner strengths and outer resources to do X, Y, and Z.

We engage in and enjoy experimenting with our lives as a lifelong adventure. It keeps life from becoming routine. We delight that each moment offers opportunities to experiment, which ripple out with endless, intertwined repercussions. We align life with our sense of what is true and do not worry about getting everything right or feeling guilty about what we cannot do.

The people who taught me this practice by example attended to their own personal choices and what their lives or society laid before them. They exchanged feedback regularly. When they got together as a group, they experienced the sense of "group," "community" and "society" as real entities and took responsibility for active roles in them. They did not ignore or walk away from society or take it for granted. They knew we create our own societies through the way we think, talk and act. This consistent recognition of and attention to "the collective body" plays a large role in shaping the nature of our community. Collective bodies flourish with consistent care, attention and nurture, the same as individuals.

Mutual support in testing personal discernment strengthens our ability to discern a consensus of conscience as a community. Paradoxically, strength and stability in the community supports our openness to change. Communities who assume conscientious, loving options exist, and commit to ongoing personal change toward that end, have a much better chance of discovering and cultivating those options. People have varied gifts and interests, but we can come together in a concern for the condition of our society and planet. In this way, we can function on shared information, knowledge, perspectives and understandings in an ever-changing world.

Respect the Ecology of Practices

Conscientious, loving communities create cultures of peace through a social ecology of practices. The ecology of the comprehensive, yet manageable, set of practices in this book work together. They draw on their own outputs as inputs, which makes them regenerative, so able to restore health, wellness and peace to large numbers of people. This ecology of practice has created and sustains cultures of peace in a widening variety of locations.

Individuals, communities and societies work in self-referential cycles. Individuals shape their communities, while communities shape their society, and societies guide and shape the individuals. Because ecological systems use their own outputs as inputs, they can regenerate and adapt on their own. The simplicity of these self-referential structures generates life's rich, beautiful complexity.

We often think of these practices as a menu from which to pick and choose what suit us. But these practices function as an operating whole. A social ecology requires every part to function. You will not experience transformation by doing only the ones you enjoy, agree with, understand or want to do. You will experience transformation when you engage in these interdependent practices, even when they are inconvenient or uncomfortable, and let go of other competing practices.

In cultures of peace, individuals grow thanks to the attention and feedback from others in companion groups. Companion groups grow thanks to the attention and feedback from other companion groups in communities. Communities grow thanks to the attention and feedback from other communities. Society grows thanks to public record of the beliefs and practices that emerge and serve as guides to shape the individuals.

This self-referential ecology of discernment fuels adaptive and regenerative cultures. Each one of these integral practices works together in similar yet different ways in each unique setting. We cannot know these practices by reading about them or by good intentions. We only know them by practicing them moment-to-moment in real contexts.

The most developed people often have the most trouble focusing on this simple yet complete ecology of practice. We fill our minds and lives with too much. We want conscientious, loving lives along with every other power and convenience. When practices do not work or become too demanding or uncomfortable, we revert to old patterns rather than press on with new practices. Beware of our own competencies!

~

We can create peaceful, healthy, sustainable societies

with the liberty to act in accord

with love and conscience and

the justice to hold one another to

standards of fairness.

~

Chapter 11

~

Act in Community

Conscience is the inner knowledge of right and wrong with an inward drive to do what is right. It shapes the behavior that forms relationships, moving us toward regenerative, not degenerative, interactions. We cannot only know what is humane and fair we must do it. As Fromm describes (1981), conscience is interactions "conducive to life."

Conscience does not spring forth fully formed; it grows as we pay attention to it. Confidence, conviction and the inner peace they offer temper and shape our conscience. But for conscience to take shape, we experiment with it in our behavior, test it with others and observe its fruits.

We do not act on blind faith; we experiment with conscience in daily life. We no longer live in the guilt of a fallen people in a fallen world. Our attention turns to the liberty and joy of living as a loving people in a creative world. We engage in loving, just, compassionate relationships in ways that illuminate the futility of violence, humiliation and coercion.

Discernment helps us listen to conscience. This human faculty allows us to grasp the inner nature and relationship of things, even when obscure, that leads to keen insight and judgment. Conscientious people say "yes" to what seems right, and "no" to what seems wrong, and act accordingly. Organizations often focus on creating social solutions or fighting social ills. Discernment of conscience offers a rare platform from which to notice both—when to affirm and when to resist—with equal fervor.

When we resist what is wrong in its smaller forms, we prevent its growth into larger forms. Acts of humiliation lead to acts of violence. We could stop much violence if we spoke out against incidents of humiliation and refused to allow or support them in public. When we stay silent in the face of humiliation, coercion or violence, we fuel it. We can protect and preserve peace by learning to stand up and speak out, not freeze and become bystanders. Standing up may not resolve the situation, but staying in motion inoculates us to trauma and complicity, and invests in the long, hard work of a creating a just and peaceful society.

We claim our right and responsibility to define public life. So we combine experimenting with love and conscience with standing up against violence and social injustice. But to act on conscience, we first get quiet, connect and listen to our inner sense of the true nature and relationship of things. Young children explore their selves, adolescents explore the world and adults explore aligning the two. We shape our outward forms and relationships to reflect our inward experiences and insights.

Conscientious relationships challenge us to exercise our sovereignty as a natural person in the natural world and to meet the civic and ecological responsibilities that entails. We work within standards developed over time, while we maintain our independence of thought, speech and action. We challenge old standards and shape new ones. Yet when one's conscience conflicts with social norms or patterns, one chooses either to persevere in taking a stand or to extricate oneself.

Some people find ourselves blessed with strong families and/or communities who encourage and support us through our struggles. We understand relationships take time and work and trust them to be there for us if we invest. But strong families and communities re-configure. They wax and wane. Elders pass away. People move or commit time and energy away from family or community. We act out, take for granted, abuse and violate each other. Even strong families and communities can turn on one another. Genocides often occur among people who grew up together, and domestic violence takes place among loved ones.

Eroded relationships regenerate slowly. Damaged relationships may never recover. We may or may not receive encouragement and support when we need it. If you have not experienced shunning, cruelty, torture or exile, it's hard to grasp. Even more confusing, such tragedies often occur at the hands of people close to you. At an unconscious level, it's easy to feel that the victims probably play a part in their own tragedy. We do not grasp that people often face extreme trials through no fault of their own.

In addition, people of conscience may get labeled offensive, judgmental, aggressive, disruptive, or pretentious. We hear, "Who do they think they are? To be an adult means learning to compromise! Grow up."

Conscientious people invest in relationships. Still, we struggle to know how much and how fast to expect others or our relationships to change. Even with honest, rigorous self-reflection, it may be difficult to assess the source of a problem. Am I being self-righteous, naïve, impatient or lacking humility? Are others resistant to change, protective of privilege or afraid of losing control? How do we mitigate the real dangers of paralyzing self-doubt and insecurity and disrupt resistant, oppressive social patterns?

In such pivotal moments, we return to the practices of principled friendships. We rediscover the nature of companion groups and community feedback. Since conscience exists in relationship, remember that asking for attention from others and taking their feedback can help.

If you discern that egotism, self-righteousness or lack of humility motivates you, then invest in healing and strengthening your conviction. If you sense an urgency to resist violence, deception and exploitation and create humane, practical lifestyles, then connect with people ready to make those changes with you now. If you discern a real danger that others will retaliate against you, then invest in a pragmatic risk assessment and solidarity.

A person of conscience can find oneself isolated when taking a stand that can be discouraging. But do not give in to isolation. Since conscience only exists in relationships, we cannot outrun others in this work! In experimenting with conscience, seek ways to speak and act on truth within relationships. This offers the antidote to the fears and dis-ease that acting on conscience can cause.

Today's society poses another challenge. Monetization and corporate structures weaken personal relationships and rob us of vast opportunities for love and conscience. After the tsunami of 2004, money flooded into Aceh. Local people called this massive influx of money the second tsunami.

The environment could not absorb the funds, so organizations paid people to clean their own yards and children to play. They called this "cash for work." It devastated a culture already fragile from decades of war and isolation. Children who used to flock to newcomers, curious, playful and enthusiastic about activities and opportunities, suddenly looked at us with contempt. They would say, "Are you going to pay me?" This made visible the painful tragedy of shifting social attention from the living wealth of interactions to the accumulated wealth of money.

Nature distributes resources. Human beings trade those resources for money, which serves as a proxy for these free gifts of nature. Whoever extracts and processes them stakes a claim to them even though nature gave them freely to everyone. How do we maintain awareness and knowledge of the living wealth of direct relationships as corporations leverage our monetary system and obscure our relationships?

Cultures of peace flourish with well-distributed and well-timed resources so as not to become parched or flooded. We try to discern the right resource, in the right amount, at the right time for the most benefit. We each need a threshold of money to survive in today's society. Still, we cannot buy the life blood of a culture of peace: visiting, attention, healing, exploration, experimentation, learning and play.

For a culture of peace, conscientious people make decisions for love and conscience' sake. We shift our sense of security from accumulated monetary wealth to distributed living wealth. We find our security in investing in time, talent, intelligence, health, love and conscience.

To act on conscience, we first connect and listen to our inner sense of the true nature and relationship of things. We guide decisions by what rings true, the way a C-Note or true north does not waver. Whether we prefer, agree with or understand it does not make it more or less true.

Granted, perception limits human knowledge, so we cannot claim to know an entire reality or truth. But besides hallucinations, reality bounds our perception to its nature. We can perceive the infinite and eternal nature of life with its contradictions and paradoxes. Working together on what rings true brings people of love and conscience closer to reality and to what is true. We strive to act in accord with our best perception of the true nature and relationship of things.

Experiment with Conscience

Social norms and habits vie for our loyalty. Prudence requires we respect the evolutionary strength of social norms, but even a prudent and conscientious person should not allow social conventions to eclipse conscience. As we act on conscience and experience its peace, joy, security and fruits, we come to trust in it and will take risks on its behalf.

Through experimenting with conscience, we learn that truth does not come packaged to our size. Many times truth comes small and feels inadequate. "If I were God, it would be different." Or truth comes too big and overwhelming. "I thought I was ready for anything, but not for this!"

When we seek truths that fit, suit or look good on us, we miss the point of the experiment. Herein lies one of the greatest obstacles to the growth of conscientious persons and communities. We need to get quiet in ourselves, notice truths laid before us by the elements of daily life and then face them with honesty, not seek truths we prefer.

Sometimes we psych ourselves up before embarking on an experiment with conscience in our lives. We prepare ourselves to face uphill odds for conscience' sake, even to suffer. This may prove disappointing when the guidance directs us to put our mundane affairs in order. What? No courts, no prison, no glory? Buy less and settle debts. Turn off electronics and regulate sleep. Eat better food and drink cleaner water. Write, plan, talk, cook and clean. Care for the young and old. For many, life persists as usual. We make ourselves available and prepared to respond well, because we cannot act on conscience when we are too busy or distracted.

On the other hand, guidance may overwhelm us. We may feel ill-equipped. Often the first guidance comes on a truth we have avoided. We may need to let go of a relationship or take risks to change our occupation. We may need to stop paying taxes for war, eating industrial factory-farmed food or purchasing from exploitative corporate providers. The guidance may include an inconvenient cause or task not of interest or disruptive to our lives. We fear our world will implode if we acknowledge a particular truth. But we won't know what our conscience tells us until we listen, and we won't know how capable we are until we try.

Conscience leads us to act in accord with our best sense of what is loving and true. We act regardless of whether guidance leads to the ordinary or extraordinary, mundane or exotic, petty or overwhelming, consequential or trivial. We must be as honest with ourselves as we can. Quaker author Sandra Cronk described in a personal interview (1998) how once we make the choice to follow our Inward Guide, we must yield to its direction. To reject guidance for any reason—too much, too little, inconvenient or unattractive—plants a "dis-ease." The faint of heart should not embark on this journey.

When we live in accord with our conscience, we learn to trust it. Practice brings an effortless sense of peace. Even extraordinary circumstances can feel ordinary, yet stir up inconvenient complications. Hence the need for good self-care, emotional tending and feedback from others who are experimenting with love and conscience in their lives.

Sometimes we may suffer for what is true before it bears fruit. We maintain a healthy sense of personhood, value and strength rooted in the infinite and eternal transforming power of life. Imprisonment or pain suffered in the service of doing the right thing are bearable and worth suffering. We prefer it to a life driven by ego or privilege harmful to others or to the Earth. Life is valuable, no matter if it leads to poverty, wealth, leadership or prison. When we act in accord with conscience, we experience the adage "the truth will set you free."

Allow Conscience
to guide and shape my life.

Act on Conscience
What does my conscience reveal?
What are the implications for my private and public life?
What guidance does an insight offer us as a people?
What disputes do I need to learn from and settle?

Once grounded in our experiences of the transforming power and the liberty of living in accord with conscience, we choose to allow conscience to guide and shape our daily lives. Experiment with transforming power in daily life for the pure joy of it!

The danger of making decisions based on an inward guide lies in mistaking distress for inspiration. The distinction is inspiration can always stop and accept external feedback, distress cannot. To act from the distress caused by rigid or frozen shame or guilt leads to depression, anxiety, obsession, compulsion and hypochondria. To act inspired by love or conscience leads to mindfulness, curiosity and flexible interaction. Hence the directive to stop, listen and consider the feedback of others.

Nothing you can say or do will make you any more valuable than you are right now. Live for the joy of it. Allow love and life to wash in with every breath, every heartbeat and every ray of light. Become like a child marveling at the freshness of the morning air. Life gives us infinite ways to express insights in tangible, outward forms. Doing so becomes a central aspiration of and entertainment for a people of love and conscience. We begin by organizing our homes and workplaces to increase love and conscience. Then we experiment with reflecting love and conscience through our material possessions, activities and relationships. We follow love and conscience as it unfolds and opens before us. Respond to the questions to "Act on Conscience" (above) in your journal and with companions and community groups. Make notes on what rings true to you, to your companions and to the community.

What does my conscience reveal? Prepare and sharpen your mind, heart, ear, physique, compassion and logic. Then let them recede as a backdrop in the theater and let insight play out on the stage created by the openness and listening. Insight occurs in the living, creative moment of relationship. An insight often surprises us, not something we came up with, figured out or preferred. Life deals us insights. Do not seek to capture truth, seek to join in the constant movement of life's regenerative nature. Seek a convergence of the universal and the particular in your unique life in this unique moment. Although resonant with the stories of others, we each must find our own path.

PERSONAL PRACTICE: Write Insights and Ask for Feedback
Once a month, think back over the month and document your insights and learnings. Take out your calendar to see what you've done and learned. Then share your insights and learnings with a companion. Ask the companion to restate what they hear. If it still feels strong, ask for feedback on this question only: Do you sense transforming power present in this insight?

The more we act in accord with our conscience, the more insights follow. Over time we open further to inward guidance tempered by feedback. When we track, recall and consider experiences, we reinforce their lessons.

What are the implications for my private and public life? Draw conclusions from your insights on how to change your behavior. Consider the implications of insights for your home, work place and neighborhood. Honesty in addressing the implications in our lives can lead to unanticipated consequences, both delightful and daunting.

Apply these implications to your own life first. Experiment. Try out various ways to establish integrity between your new insights and the way you live. Test your intentions and imagination through real-life applications. If you need to slow down, cancel activities for six weeks. If you know you need to sleep more, set regular times to go to bed and get up, and do nothing during those times except lay there and sleep or relax. If you know you need to stop paying war taxes, then research and take the steps to resist (NWTRCC.org). Whatever your conscience reveals, do not belabor it, just do it and learn from the experience of doing it.

Document the changes and results to adjust, adapt and tinker. As changes in your life impinge on social patterns, explain your experiment with love and conscience to others. Ask them for feedback on a particular insight. Ask them how they respond to it and invite them to experiment with you. Reflect on the consequences, both expected and unexpected.

Persist in acting on your insights. Consider their implications and change based on feedback from within and from others. Let life's demands challenge and humble you. Do not try to do everything. One simple change affects many others. Take one step at a time. Accept and take the simple steps that life lays before you. Keep joy and delight close at hand.

Do not try to "earn your value." You are already valuable! Take up what comes, then rest. It's okay to stop sometimes. When we violate our conscience, we look for the roots of our actions in past pains, hurts and disappointments. Explore, discharge and reprocess this distress. Integrate the internal parts that have surfaced to protect you, maturing your core self bolstered by the transforming power of life. Then bring your full attention, intelligence and curiosity back to what love and conscience promise to teach you each day.

Conscientious changes in ourselves prepare us to notice implications for conscientious changes in social patterns. Just asking what implications a particular insight has for one's public life directs the mind to these possibilities. Sometimes I need to change the way I behave or speak; other times implications for my life may be much more pervasive.

What guidance does an insight offer us as a people? We seldom hear this question today. Asking this question changes a group. "Us as a people" shapes our worldview. What? We are "a people"? The modern, consumer society trains us to think and act as individuals, not as "a people." Who are "we" as "a people"? What makes us "a people"? We each have various group identities based on ethnicity, race, gender, location, orientation, religion or class. But the question remains, "What makes us a people?" To identify as a people changes our identity. We are the people dedicated to love and conscience in private and public life. We are the people who believe healthy, peaceful families, neighborhoods and societies are possible everywhere.

As we recognize, test and change our own behavior, we influence the behavior of others, changing social patterns. Yet peaceful ways to meet needs and desires often require more deliberate, collaborative thinking and decision-making. When an individual's choices resonate with others, it forms a whole greater than ourselves. These experiences change what we perceive as feasible or effective. We bring our playful, delighted, curious core selves to the work. Through relationships, we allocate, reallocate and adjust resources with speed and ease based on direct experience with real needs and good timing. Effortless acts can lead to extensive social change. When we make humane, healthy, sustainable decisions as a group, we experience a sense of joy, security, pride and relief. Tension drains out of our bodies. We feel more human and humane.

I saw this shift in a refugee community in North Sumatra. The leadership sent a few strong, armed men to meetings to discuss relocation of the refugees. After this training, they asked, "What power of nonviolence can we use?" To the next meeting, they brought thousands of unarmed men, women, children, reporters with cameras and former enemies to stand at their side. They agreed on a message, "No one should be made a refugee twice in one lifetime." This collective shift from violent to peaceful approaches changed the narrative and their community's historic trajectory.

PERSONAL PRACTICE: *Notice the Group as a Real, Living Entity*
Notice the palpable presence of a group, just as real as any individual. Trust builds when we notice, tend and protect the group as a body. Speak to specific actions, words or mannerisms that help or harm the group. Call or visit people who miss a meeting. Ask others their experiences of what strengthens or weakens the group. This discussion alone will further define and strengthen a sense of the group.

We only see a group when we are present. Others get to know us by comparing their sense of the group when we are present and absent. We only gain this larger knowledge of ourselves if someone shares their experience with us. Tell others how their statements or actions affect the group, not just how they affect individuals. Take actions that make the group safe and strong.

PERSONAL PRACTICE: *Write a Personal Commitment to Community*
Write a commitment to community in your own language: religious, spiritual or ethical. In your own words, express how dependent we are on our community, with others and with the land. We are as responsible for our social and ecological communities as we are for ourselves, our homes and our families. Consider what concrete steps you can take to create a loving, conscientious community and environment. Meet with a companion to exchange feedback. Always have at least one experiment underway with integrity in the community and the environment. Talk of conscience with people you interact with daily.

What disputes do I need to learn from and settle? We agreed to tend to our emotions and speak directly to another if a dispute persists. Take responsibility for unmasking, tending, discharging and reprocessing emotional distress that often masquerade as disputes. Once you discharge emotion your mind clears, which may end the dispute. Be prompt in settling remaining disputes since lingering disputes can do irreparable damage. As with mistakes, approach disputes as opportunities for learning.

First seek a truce to prevent future harm. A truce is better than ongoing harm. Then let go and open to creative solutions. Approach the person with the expressed hope of settling the dispute and reconciling the relationship. Ask for openness and honesty to allow the relationship to mend. Ask about differences of assumption, experience, feelings, consequences or needs. Empathize with the other person's feelings and needs and ask the person to empathize with yours. Affirm each other and affirm good intentions. Then open to transforming power. Do not press what you would prefer, agree with or even understand, but seek your mutual best sense of actions that could restore friendly, harmonious relations.

If people in dispute meet and still cannot settle their dispute, then bring one or two others to listen. This may be an informal group of friends or formal mediation or arbitration. Welcome feedback from others and take their feedback seriously. Ask yourself, "What if what they are saying were true?" Imagine this. Open to possibilities. If they refuse to meet, the relationship may be over no matter what you wanted.

We welcome change and embody the revelations and guidance received. Becoming loving, conscientious people can take generations. So we do not seek to settle into our life as we know it today or view change as a burden, annoyance or judgment of our past. Strive for nothing less than perpetual change. Expect to find new ways to survive, engage in and enjoy life beyond what we have hitherto imagined.

We learn that we can delight in—not fear—acting on love and conscience in our private and public lives. The more we listen to and follow our conscience, the more we find the words to speak up and the ways to change our behavior. Fear gives way to relief, and then to joy. We act with patience, tenderness and calmness, not rancor, irritation and rage. This sense of integrity makes us capable of calling others to love and conscience.

Experience the Liberty of Conscience

Take a big breath; let it out!
Look around.
Notice the light, the colors, the air, the surrounding life.
Stop reading. Notice this moment, here and now.

Shake off the ways you practice guilt or shame and let this sink in:
Imagine a lifestyle aligned with the natural, creative, generative flows of life. We will gain a tremendous sense of freedom and joy when the way we live allows the natural world and humanity to thrive!
Smile.

~

We can create peaceful, healthy, sustainable societies with the liberty to act in accord with love and conscience and the justice to hold one another to standards of fairness.

~

For many people, an attention to conscience dredges up a whole variety of distresses that lead us to avoidance, exhaustion or distraction. This intrusion of distress poses a great obstacle to a contemporary movement of conscience. We need to recognize, name and ask others and ourselves to discharge distress to clear the way for this work.

The entire issue of the *New Internationalist* (Issue 406, 2007), *Guilt Complex*, Adam Ma'anit describes how our society inculcates and capitalizes on guilt. From marketing to religion to governance to activism, this guilt arises from what Erich Fromm (1947) called the authoritarian conscience, "a fear for the authority rather than a representation of the individual's real conscience, the source of natural value judgments." Authoritarian conscience judges and punishes.

For many norms or creeds, Fromm notes, "Obedience is the supreme virtue, disobedience the supreme sin. When most people feel 'guilty,' they are actually feeling afraid because they have been disobedient. They are not really troubled by a moral issue, as they think they are, but by the fact of having disobeyed a command." Fromm (1981) compares this to humanist conscience, which he defines as "an intuitive knowledge of what is human and inhuman, what is conducive to life and what is destructive of life." We concur with Fromm's meaning, and understand conscience as an inner knowledge of right and wrong with an inward drive to do what is right, humane and conducive to life.

Ma'anit quotes British psychologist Penelope Leach (2013, p. 12): "Guilt is the most destructive of all emotions. It mourns what has been while playing no part in what may be, now or in the future."

Guilt and shame are not emotional or physical feelings, or even mental feelings, like intuition or a premonition. They are feelings of belief. Guilt is the belief that I did the wrong thing, while shame is the belief that I am a bad person. They prevent forgiveness because they are personal, not relational. Edwards (1995) described forgiveness as "giving up all hope for a better past." Forgiveness occurs when we reprocess a memory to place it in time, discharge the emotion and realize relationships constantly change.

A culture of peace shifts the authoritarian misappropriation of conscience to a sense of authentic conscience. The latter aligns our interpersonal creative capacity with the natural flow of life through relationships. This gives us a living sense of meaning, value and connection, a sense of love. Adam Ma'anit notes that motivation driven by duty or guilt at not meeting social standards oppresses everyone. Shifting motivation to inspiration and life-affirming actions makes everyone happier, healthier and more enthusiastic. People start "radiating a kind of positivity that is downright infectious."

No matter how wonderful this sounds, distress still intrudes. When you want to fall asleep, cry, shake, scream, run or self-medicate, then go ahead, but remember to reach out and ask for good attention. Discharge the grief, fear, rage and disconnection in the company of someone who focuses on your true goodness and capabilities. This will illuminate contradictions with your self-depreciating and distressed parts. A good companion stays relaxed and non-anxious and resists your emotional contagion. Impose good daily self-care. Go to bed. Wake up, make the bed and open the curtains. Drink water, eat vegetables and do the work before you. Do not let distress derail you.

Feelings of guilt or shame warn us when something is wrong or amiss. Do not suppress these feelings. Discover what is wrong and change it. If you cannot, remember the first time you had this feeling. After discharging emotions from that earlier time, check whether you have taken on:

- The fundamental lie that you are unworthy.

- The contagion of other people's distress.

- The self-righteous projection of your distress on others.

Resist persistent feelings of guilt or shame by reinforcing your awareness of life's worthiness, including your own value. Invest in a loving, compassionate, curious response or let go. Do not crumble. Reach out and exchange attention and feedback. Look for the source of what creates a sense of guilt, shame or anxiety and change it. Persist.

Experimenting with conscience in a community does not demand blind faith to a static "Truth" or judgment. To experiment with love and conscience nudges us to align ourselves to a true course with others committed to the same. We both find and lose ourselves in the love, compassion and joy of such communities.

GROUP ACTIVITY: Breakthrough

Say, "Now we will do Breakthrough." Ask everyone to stand on one side of the room. The opposite side of the room represents "living in accord with love and conscience in every moment." Randomly place one chair for each participant in the middle facing the group. Ask, "One by one step forward. Sit in a chair and say out loud, 'What blocks me from doing what I know is right is __[name your block] __.'" Record each block on a poster sheet. When everyone is seated, remind everyone we each have the inner strength to overcome our blocks. Invite people to stand up, one by one, face their chair and say, "But I have the inner strength of __[name your strength]__ to overcome this block to live in accord with love and conscience in every moment." Ask them to lift their chair and move it to the far wall. Record each strength on a poster sheet.

Invite everyone to make notes in their journals on their blocks and strengths. Ask them to add what they need to have or let go of in their lives to always keep their awareness of transforming power alert. Do not list everything, note only what is essential for you right now. When everyone finishes, ask them to gather in groups of three or four. Give each group a poster sheet. Ask them to combine everyone's items into one list. Report back to the full group. Reflect on this activity.

To act in accord with conscience requires listening for insight and noticing what obstructs us from our own natural drive to do what is right. As a people, we need to dedicate extensive, routine attention to this question. "What do I need to have or let go of to stay aware of transforming power and act in accord with love and conscience in every moment?" Use many standard methods, such as web brainstorming, fish bowl or discussion group formats to articulate and document your answers.

Exercise Sovereignty as a Natural Person

Although we begin with listening inwardly, conscience takes form through interactions with others and the natural world. We attend to changes in our own lives first, then to our relationships in community and the local ecology, and then to our care for society and the planet.

Peaceful society rests on shifting power away from institutional and corporate structures. These structures have no inherent faith, conviction, love or conscience. Citizens must take responsibility for the nature of the power exercised on our behalf in the public sphere. Citizens bring human love and conscience to bear on public life. That is to say, institutions and systems do not create peaceful societies, people do.

To practice conscientious living with others reinforces experiences of humanity. We gain a growing sense of our inherent, inalienable value, worth and dignity as natural persons on the Earth. *The Preamble of the Universal Declaration of Human Rights* (1948, U.N. General Assembly Resolution 217A) opens with this statement, "Whereas recognition of the inherent dignity and of the equal and inalienable rights of all members of the human family is the foundation of freedom, justice and peace in the world …." Extensive research, law, investigation and defense focuses on protecting our inalienable human rights. But a dearth of attention has gone to protecting our inherent human dignity and freedom of conscience. People experience dignity in several ways: being healthy and thriving, sensing the interconnected value among every life form and exercising the sovereignty the natural person. We encourage each of us to reach deep into our various traditions to explore our sense of human dignity, love and conscience.

Sovereignty of the natural person was the great experiment of the U.S. government and remains a critical foundation of international law. The supreme power or authority to govern resides in the people, ourselves. Juilliard v. Greenman, 110 U.S. 421 (1884) ruled:

"There is no such thing as a power of inherent Sovereignty in the government. In this country [U.S.A.], sovereignty resides in the People, and Congress can exercise no power which they [the people] have not, by their Constitution entrusted to it."

People often identify as members of a tribe or subjects of a crown. Yet the power of a tribe, monarchy, or state rests and lasts on the power entrusted to it by the sovereign people. But the people cannot act with impunity as natural persons. Our sovereignty resides in the law of natural consequences, which constrain our inalienable rights and responsibilities.

At the same time the U.S. considered Africans and women property and Australians classified native peoples as "flora and fauna." Sovereignty in this historical time remained oppressive. The people need a new constitution whereby we recognize the sovereignty of every human being and consider what powers to entrust to whom based on our 21st century experience and insight.

As peaceful people, we abide by the laws of the State, unless the State subverts, misapplies, oversteps or abuses its powers. Then we assume the obligation to speak out against or break false or unjust laws to enter our conscientious objection into public record. We take our responsibility to hold the State to the natural laws of love and conscience, knowing the State has neither. Only people can hold a system accountable to ethical or moral principles and standards.

Gregory Schaaf (2004) wrote *The U.S. Constitution and the Great Law of Peace: A Comparison of Two Founding Documents.* Mohawk Chief Jake Swamp, Cofounder of the Tree of Peace Society, wrote the foreword. After reading their book, U.S. Senators voted 100-0 to recognize the great influence of the Haudenosaunee Nation on the framers of the U.S. Constitution. While the parallels are undeniable, the contrasts are disturbing. For example, the first requirement of a Haudenosaunee chief is to be honest, but no such a requirement appears in the U.S. Constitution.

Many Europeans and Haudenosaunee strove to set up covenants to preserve the promise of peace. These covenants continued in people's movements for peace and justice. People around the globe looked to North America for moral authority in law, for good reason. But not only has our experiment in conscience fallen far short, its promise of peace remains elusive. As we moved into the "great age of prosperity," we abdicated civic responsibility for the corporation's promise of reliability, convenience and luxury. Many people have lost hope in the moral authority of the great people's movements for love and conscience, also for good reason.

To regain our confidence and conviction, we take active responsibility for our own sovereignty. We extend our sense of responsibility from ourselves and our children to humanity and the Earth. A movement of love and conscience may be the only way to restore real peace and hope.

~

Cultures of peace require the hard work of
vigilant, public resistance to the
dynamics of oppression.

~

Chapter 12

~

Liberate from
Oppression

A culture of peace becomes superficial and impractical without an awareness and understanding of the dynamics of oppression. Oppression passes from generation to generation. It affects everyone. Such cruel and unjust treatment disempowers everyone in systemic and persistent ways.

Oppression. Inhumane and unjust treatment, control, exploitation or invalidation of others that forms distress patterns in individuals and groups either to: 1) give in and be defeated, as if accepting or agreeing to it; 2) become the perpetrator, turning on others, especially younger, weaker people, to escape the role of victim; or 3) become a martyr or rescuer confining others to the roles of victim and perpetrator, maintaining access to privilege by ignoring it.

Oppression persists in schools, universities, companies, workplaces, communities, even families tell us which people to dismiss and exploit, and which to idolize and glorify. Practical application of our first common agreement, no put downs or put ups, becomes harder than first imagined. We need to change both our own prejudicial attitudes and habits and those of others.

~

Cultures of peace require the hard work of vigilant, public resistance to the dynamics of oppression.

~

Privileged people deny their role in the cycles of oppression with ease. They feel strong, capable, responsible and blessed, and assume they have worked for and deserve what they have. Others would have it too if they worked for it. They praise, commend, respect and admire people such as themselves, and do not see how oppression affects their lives. They are unaware of or unconcerned with the high costs of the privileges they reap.

People invested in privilege are often uncomfortable with the word. They complain that oppression is a strong word that does not apply to them or to a peaceful society. They ignore its operating dynamics and dismiss the word outright as excessive and inflammatory. They seek one job or skill to secure their place for making money. So they believe it is not their place to know or understand the larger system, or they think the system is too complex and beyond their capacity to understand.

Oppressors know nothing of the people they oppress. They do not realize how their restricted view blinds them to the realities of social dynamics. They view themselves as better than others, and so think it's only natural for them to decide for others. This justifies their right to more resources than others thus forming the fabric of modern oppressive society. They cannot see or do not want to admit that most contemporary institutions, on which they depend, presume inequality as normal and necessary. In these ways, privilege blinds. It makes them unable to generate consequential social action or solutions.

In contrast, oppressed people know everything about their oppressors. They know their language, mannerisms, customs and habits. An oppressed person's life often depends on their ability to read their oppressors and the larger operating dynamics with accuracy. Oppressed people often internalize, take part in and enforce their own oppression. They assume people such as themselves must be stupid, lazy, ugly, unlucky or untrustworthy. Otherwise why would people keep treating them this way? They may put down, humiliate, degrade or distance themselves from, even abuse, people like themselves. In this way, oppressed people often perpetuate their own oppression.

To overcome oppression, we must overcome both prejudice AND privilege. We must stand up against denigration of oneself AND others. To do this, we stand up against any claim for unnecessary or unfair power over others. This includes giving up our aspirations for privilege and our perceptions of privilege as respectable or successful.

This chapter invites us to overcome prejudice and recognize everyone as equals. Then it illuminates how everyone participates in the dynamics of oppression. It closes with the need to invest in the simplicity of direct relationships to overcome privilege and to meet our civic obligations through public witness.

Overcome Prejudice with Equality

To put people above or below others violates our first common agreement, "no put downs or put ups." We recognize the equal value and dignity of the unconditional life granted to every person and so call for the fair, just and equal treatment of everyone. The term equity draws important attention to fairness in the face of the damages of inequality. The term equality draws attention to the absolute value of each human being, which defies comparison. No one person can be more equal or more valuable than any other. We stand on the equality of every life and invest in the equity of fairness in righting the imbalances of former injustices.

We approach people under any conditions with affection and interest. This forms within us the resilience for the heavy political work of peace, the politics of no enemies and no sides. A culture of peace requires everyone, not just a chosen few. To extend this equal respect, value and attention to every person takes practice noticing the intrinsic value of life and calling on our own and others' core selves.

GROUP ACTIVITY: *Call Out Our Core Selves*

Say, "Now let us Call Out Our Core Selves." Invite everyone to take out their core self drawing, crayons, journal and pen to add to the drawing and write on the back on the following topics:

- *My core self is most obvious when___ and least obvious when ___.*
- *What others do that helps bring out my core self is ___.*
- *What I do that brings out the core self of others is ___.*
- *What I hope to remember is ___.*

In companion groups, give the group thirty minutes for each person to share how they felt or what they learned in this activity, and then compare what they say they need with what others say they need or with what they offer in order to learn from the variations. Reflect on this activity.

Societal patterns of prejudice, such as racism, sexism, ageism, ableism and classism, draw on patterns and habits established with those we love: siblings, friends and colleagues. Often these habits of interaction dismiss or devalue those around us. Even so-called loved ones may treat one another this way, although these habits do not show or engender love.

Prejudice. *A negative, hostile or unfair opinion of another person that causes injury or damage. Prejudice instills social distress patterns that reinforce prejudice, such as bias, bigotry, partiality, intolerance, discrimination, inequality and inequity based on race, sex, age, ability, class or caste.*

Once again, we revisit the first agreement to affirm myself and others, no put downs or put ups. When we dismiss and devalue certain people, we elevate and obsess on others. We need to notice when, how and to whom we over-extend or withhold our attention or goodwill. Prejudice established among those near us get amplified into patterns of prejudice in social groups. Changes in our private habits strengthen our experience of and confidence in the transforming power in everyone. We can amplify these patterns of respect for every person in our private life into public life.

GROUP ACTIVITY: Labels

Say, "Now let us do Labels." Divide into groups of four. Tape one of the following five instructions on each person's forehead without reading one's own: "Ignore me." "Tell me I'm right." "Tell me I'm wrong." "Encourage but doubt me." Ask each group to discuss where and what to eat for a dinner party. Don't try to finish. Experience this briefly, do not practice it. Invite people to come back to the large group. Ask everyone to sit with others with the same instruction on their foreheads. Ask each group how they felt, noting two or three of their main insights. Go from the most to least isolated: ignore me, tell me I'm wrong, encourage but doubt me and tell me I'm right. Ask, "How do these behaviors affect the group?" Do a hurricane to mix seats, then turn to a partner to discuss briefly who you treat or who treats you in any of these ways. Turn back to the large group and ask what instructions would we like to follow? Put new labels on foreheads: "Listen well and share honestly." Now return to the original groups of four to discuss the original topic of what to eat for a dinner party. Report back and reflect on the activity.

The people who had "ignore me" on their foreheads often say they felt confused, lost or still waiting for their turn. Upon reflection, people note how shunning or ignoring someone reinforces internalized oppression. They see how the sheer prejudice of ignoring others causes confusion and makes them appear less smart, fast or "with it."

Internalized Oppression. *To believe false denigrating, derogatory messages of oneself. Without an alternate explanation for one's subservient condition, one may subjugate, denigrate or sabotage oneself, people close or similar to oneself or members of one's own group.*

The people with "encourage but doubt me" may not realize what's going on. They try to follow, but often lose track or interest and want to leave the decision to others. Children and older women are often treated this way. Once they realize what's going on, it's very hard to counteract so they withdraw. The people who had "tell me I'm wrong" are often angry, envious of the "tell me I'm right" group and bitter. They may become confrontational or just want out. The people with "tell me I'm right" are either quite happy or extremely uncomfortable. Eventually they realize the trap. They can never participate in a conversation, because once they speak the conversation is over, people do not tell them the truth and their own behavior cannot change this dynamic.

The tragic patterns of oppression and internalized oppression amplify patterns from our everyday minor abuses of power. Parents, teachers and other caregivers of young children abuse their power to manage their own sanity and stamina. Interactions between adults and children define the type of power we get used to turning to and relying on to shape our interactions in times of stress or distress. We ignore young people, yell at them, tell them they are wrong and do not believe them. All the while we encourage and praise them, dote on them and idolize them. But often we do this without even paying attention, listening or noticing their core selves.

People of love and conscience pay attention to the ways we interact with children. We greet children as we meet and say goodbye when we leave. Listen with respect when children speak and get their full attention before speaking to them. Speak with respect and expect children to do the same in return. Sit in silence with children and practice stopping, so when we ask them to stop and sit still it means something real to them. We pace ourselves and our day to meet everyone's needs before the needs get out of hand. We offer ourselves and others a time out when needed.

As discussed earlier, we have to give up the cheap methods of ignoring, condemning, placating and elevating others to get what we want. We have to open to the transforming power flowing among our authentic, core selves. This applies to people of every age who we live with, pass on the street or meet in public places.

Gratitude for and attention to others similar to and different from ourselves contradicts prejudicial patterns. Notice how resentments and irritations towards others similar to us mask the frayed edges of our own sense of self-worth. Loving others similar to us pushes us to work through distress and allows us to love ourselves more deeply. We can then apply these patterns of respectful interaction to others different from ourselves. What if we paid attention to and appreciated everyone: store clerks, people on the street, children, employers, leaders and elders? To open our hearts and minds to the flow of transforming power in the direct relationship with each person in each moment does not drain but reinvigorates energy.

People often give attention to adults not children, the rich not the poor or the boss not everyone as a matter of habit. People who are used to receiving more attention than others often feel disrespected or insulted when given equal attention. Yet balanced attention enlarges and enlivens our lives. It disrupts oppression, even when that oppression masks itself as respect for one's parent, elder or boss. Everyone expands their understanding when we open to direct relationships, listen to and believe others similar and different from ourselves, and share our sense of what is true.

Illuminate the Dynamics of Oppression

My older brother was always smarter, faster and stronger than I was. I remember thinking, "Well, if that's the way it is, then I'll just do it by myself." To this day, I do many things myself and I leave or withdraw when stresses rises. Noticing this pattern allows me to take a breath and recognize I am not that small, weak child. I thank the distress for coming to protect me, but reassure it I have matured. I remember that I am good, capable and now able to take care of myself. This means I can stay here, with other people, without having to control everything or to leave. I stop, slow down, open to transforming power, smile and look for the best in the situation.

We store traumatic memories in a part of the brain that has no language, time or capacity to sequence or analyze. This part does not have access to the entire integrated brain forming our core selves. If these incidents are infrequent and counterbalanced with regular good attention, we may not suffer symptoms of trauma. But everyone has the seeds of trauma stored from childhood. This helps us understand and have compassion for others' tragedies and failings. The frequency and severity of overwhelming experiences predispose us to more extreme reactions later in life.

Inward Dynamics of Oppression

- We each begin young, small and weak. As young people, we experience unnecessary and unfair power or control exerted by adults. Unprepared and unable to stand up for ourselves, we may even experience physical or emotional harm. Adults may have been inattentive or unresponsive at moments when we needed love, attention and connection.

- Without good attention, young people may become overwhelmed in a moment of hurt, injustice, fear or loss. We may then make a rigid decision, "Well, I guess to survive, I must ...." We may strive to meet those needs frozen in our past, never able to fulfill them.

- Later in life, dismissive, harsh or unfair treatment may remind us of being hurt or ignored as a child. Old patterns of helplessness, powerlessness or disconnection may return, and we may act out of rigid decisions or frozen past needs, losing touch with our current maturity, strengths, goodness and capabilities.

- Distress patterns set in when circumstances overwhelm our ability to adapt. This occurs when faced with unanticipated or insurrmountable hurt, injustice, fear or loss, especially when caught alone without good attention from another person.

- When old distress patterns get re-stimulated, we may reenact past rigid patterns or decisions in several ways. We may become a martyr, rescuer or perpetrator. We may:

  - Internalize an injustice by self-denigrating, or even self-sabotaging in order to control when an attack occurs, effectively oppressing ourselves.

  - Shift the victim role to someone else, even in our own identity group of family or friends, constantly working to rescue others.

  - Exert power over others, escaping the victim role by becoming the perpetrator.

- Note how these actions can have momentary survival value, but serve no good function when imbedded in habit. When repeated often enough, they may even become embedded in our personalities and cultures. In an effort to avoid fear, failure and victimization, we may reenact injustice and pain in large groups over generations, despite our intentions. We may get stuck in old rigid patterns and decisions, and thus perpetuate oppression on ourselves, our loved ones and others.

- Modern society encourages us to aspire to and vie for unnecessary and unfair power over others and trains us to laud this as an accomplishment. Society assigns roles of power to some adults over others. In this manner, society trains us to aspire to become oppressors, ostensibly for everyone's welfare. But this spares no one from being hurt by or hurting others in powerful cycles of oppression.

- To counteract imbedded distress patterns, we ask for good attention when we need it, support discharge of emotions, and reprocess narratives of our youngest, pivotal and current painful experiences.

- This work strengthens us to stand up to, speak out about, and take action to resist injustice and oppression with clear thinking and discernment from our integrated, core selves, and to do so together.

GROUP ACTIVITY: Liberation from Oppression

Say, "Now we will do Liberation from Oppression." In a large group, read the text above "Inward Dynamics of Oppression." Ask people to take turns reading one idea at a time and ask if the idea is clear. Invite questions of clarification, not discussion or stories. Before or after reading the text above, depending on the group, conduct Concentric Circles speaking to the questions below.

Afterreading and clarifying the text, invite everyone to get into groups of two to four and divide a specified length of time equally for each to speak to the companion group questions below. Reflect on this activity. Offer extra time to write or draw in journals. In the large group, share final insights or implications for us as a people.

234 ACT ON CONSCIENCE: Living Peaceful Public Lives

GROUP ACTIVITY: Concentric Circles on Privilege

In concentric circles, share on the following topics:

1. *A rigid decision I made as a child and how it affects me today is ___.*
2. *How unnecessary or unfair power operates in settings that I'm part of is ___.*
3. *Ways in which I'm encouraged to use unnecessary or unfair power over others are ___.*
4. *A time I stood up against injustice or spoke up for myself or someone else in public was ___.*

GROUP ACTIVITY: Companion Groups on Prejudice and Privilege

In a companion group, discharge or speak on these topics.

1. *Rigid decisions made as a young person when I felt hurt or mistreated.*
2. *Ways I do not stand up for myself, but repeat old, rigid patterns.*
3. *Ways I internalize or believe prejudices against me or others like me.*
4. *Ways I aspire to or use unnecessary or unfair power over others.*
5. *Ways I resist or can resist the use of unnecessary or unfair power.*
Remember to do groundings and close with affirmations.

Allow as much time as needed. Do not rush. Invite everyone to write a personal commitment on liberation from oppression.

PERSONAL PRACTICE: Write a Personal Commitment to Liberation

Write a personal commitment to liberation from oppression in your own words. For example: "I will work to overcome oppression. I will discharge past hurts and injustices, speak up for myself and others, ask for regular good attention and draw on my intelligence, goodness and capabilities to resist prejudice and privilege." Or, "I commit to experimenting with love and conscience in my private and public life and to disrupt the dynamics of oppression." Invite people to post written personal commitments on the wall if they wish to do so.

We do not want to relive experiences of pain and suffering of personal or societal distress patterns. We want to become aware, discharge the emotions, reprocess the memories and bring our full, integrated core selves to healing and creating cultures of peace. People can then work together as whole, healthy communities. One's emotional condition is not only personal, it determines the nature of what is possible in a community. So look at everyone's core self drawings and practice working from there.

Apply tests of love and conscience as a measure of the legitimacy of humane decisions in stark contrast to the interpersonal dynamics of oppression. Liberty and justice take on substantial roles in our liberation.

Liberation. *Freedom from restrictions to thought or behavior such as war, slavery, incarceration, oppression, exploitation, occupation, domination or rigid social convention by another.*

Commitment to liberation from the brutality of any form of prejudice or oppression moves us to do everything in our power to oppose war, slavery, incarceration or exploitation. Humanity has taken steps to end public-sanctioned slavery and dismantle public-sanctioned prejudice. But we cannot break the cycles of oppression until we oppose both ends of the cycle, privilege and prejudice.

Privilege. *Use of unfair and unnecessary power over others without liability or obligation to others, often afforded legal impunity.*

When we quit aspiring to unfair and unnecessary power over others and expecting impunity, then alternatives to war, incarceration and exploitation become obvious. Ruth Morris (1998) offers a convincing description of the feasibility of ending incarceration and Paul K. Chappell (2012) does so for ending war. When will we take steps to end any public-sanctioned violence?

Overcome Privilege with Simplicity

Common usage of the word privilege refers to a rare opportunity or special pleasure, a good thing. But the root meaning of privilege derives from "private law," rights or advantages restricted to a particular person or group of people to speak or act with impunity.

Privilege exempts oppressors from liability for their actions or from obligations towards others. We should not consider the exercise of unnecessary and unfair power over others with impunity a legitimate source of opportunity or pleasure.

An opportunity, honor, blessing or gift has no need for protection as a privilege. We may be fortunate or advantaged, but we should not think of those gifts as privileges, free of obligation or responsibility toward others. Society needs to redistribute resources for social justice and development, without privilege. For our own and others' well-being and security we give up unnecessary and unfair power over others, both in aspiration and as our sense of success.

Development takes time and social investment, which gives certain people advantages over others. Oppression distorts and subverts the original purpose of any profession. Instead of discerning the real nature and relationships of things, professions devolve into securing privilege to prevent falling victim within an oppressive society. We need to devise ways to allocate resources to people engaged in developmental progress without ossifying their advantages beyond the substance or robbing social investment for personal gain.

We must advance legal integrity as we illuminate the damage caused by aspiring to privilege and the legal falsehoods created to protect it. People do not cure depression until they give up the euphoria of mania. So too, people will not end prejudice until we give up the thrill of privilege.

We can use the advantages created by the substance of development fairly for the benefit of all. Privilege is not the advantages, it is the unfair and unnecessary use of advantages without liability or obligation. Life's transforming power creates developmental opportunities. Privilege limits those opportunities to the few and offers legal impunity for abuses. Privilege does not create wealth any more than war does, both rob.

We can overcome privilege once we acknowledge the social and ecological obligations of developmental advantages and prohibit unfair and unnecessary use of their power. The implications of this run deep into the social fabric of our personal and public lives, from parenting to governance. We can devise ways to account for social and ecological resources and how to draw on them to achieve development without domination. We can design proper social obligations and constraints once we respect the power of discernment, creativity and ingenuity. Investment in these creates unlimited developmental opportunities, which result in advantages and real prosperity.

Development derives from the simplicity of direct relationships. Simplicity does not refer to easy or simpleminded, but to being grounded in real, direct, living relationships. Grasping the power of the simplicity of these direct relationships holds the key to overcoming privilege.

Simplicity. *Organization of life based on unencumbered, unmediated, direct relationships among people and with the natural world.*

Simplicity exposes the elegance and intricacy of living beauty. A simple life is rich with the wealth of relationships, love, knowledge, possibilities and creativity. We understand and incorporate simplicity as a measure of real human development. We recognize that richness lies in our knowledge of one another and the Earth, our inward drive for fairness and justice and our capacity for creativity, understanding, compassion and discernment. Our respect for the accomplishments of privilege shift to respect for the accomplishments of love and conscience.

In every way, we redefine success not as accumulation of material wealth and privilege, but as the abundance and generosity of the relationships in our lives. Our capacity to interact with each other and the Earth affords the great joy and liberty of living in accord with the transforming power of love and conscience.

Simplicity means we can see and relate to people as they are, not react to their position or role. We interact with natural not pre-processed materials in direct not mediated ways. This means plain listening and speaking, growing food in a kitchen garden, cooking organic food, building from local materials and making things to meet our daily needs.

The transforming power of life resides in these direct relationships as do the solutions for ecological and social sustainability. The farther we get from these relationships, the more we abuse and declare war on our own habitat. We then become poorer and lose touch with the power and fabric of our own lives.

Simplicity grows from conviction. We experience transforming power in the real, messy, tragic social and natural worlds. Simplicity does not make our lives easier. It makes life messier and less convenient. But it does makes life more elegant, fresh, alive and richer in knowledge, understanding, capabilities, relationships and compassion.

When I went to Aceh after the massive tsunami of 2004, I took a letter signed by my local Quaker meeting. The letter introduced me and commended me to their care. When I entered a village, I asked to meet the village head, a common courtesy in Indonesia. I delivered the letter and they read it with interest. "She brings with her our faith in the Living Spirit to bring life, joy, peace and prosperity through love, integrity and compassionate justice among those who live in simplicity, equality and nonviolence." Other foreigners built houses, bathrooms and boats, but local people pointed, "This! This! Can you do this?!"

For thirty years soldiers had burnt their homes to the ground many times. They wanted peace and recognized every word in this letter, except the word simplicity. "Simplicity? Why would you want simplicity? We don't want simplicity, we want to join the rest of the world, have power and be wealthy." Across the globe, people equate human progress with the ability to exploit and oppress others. Overcoming privilege becomes as strong a goal in the world as overcoming prejudice, slavery or war.

People's movements offer lots of guidance for facing human tragedy and struggle, but little or none for facing human prosperity. Hence, our commitment to the agreement, "use what I need and share the rest." Simplicity keeps development grounded in this transforming power of life. A simple life invests in learning, exploration and creativity, not in exploiting, accumulating and claiming supremacy.

In Aceh and the refugee communities across the border, we came together during times of war and struggle. Our pact was tangible. But prosperity made everyone too busy. Peace turned the focus to how much money they could each secure for themselves and their families. Exploitation, theft, secrets and lies emerged. They lost the camaraderie of direct, open relations. Evelin Lindner (2012) notes that people who excel in wartime often fail in peacetime; the transition is not as natural as one might imagine.

In a culture of peace, attention to love and conscience in direct relationships, although complex and challenging, bears the elegance and beauty of peace. In private and public life, we persist in asking, "What can we cut? What is outdated? What can we stop doing? How can we stop exerting any extra effort? How can we simplify?" The more we align with love and conscience the less distress, the fewer crises and the more we live into joy, liberty and justice.

Bear Witness Publicly

Today, we need to learn to understand and speak openly about oppression. Oppressors often think they have earned what they have and oppression has nothing to do with them or their surroundings. Privilege shields them from seeing the consequences of their behavior. They do not think of prejudice or oppression. Offended when accused, they wonder why others are not giving them the benefit of the doubt. They expect others to presume they are innocent unless proven guilty. Their privilege shields them from seeing their oppressive behavior while presuming the oppressed are guilty unless proven innocent, seldom receiving the benefit of the doubt. They keep their guard up so they never get caught by surprise or overwhelmed. Privileged people often find the word oppression excessive, inflammatory and uncomfortable. They suggest it only exists if we talk of it. But oppression is not extraordinary, extreme or inflammatory; it is ordinary, frequent and commonplace. We pass it on through the generations, sparing no one. As we learn more about oppression, we come to realize how it permeates society and thus everyone's life. We take steps to correct it and discharge the distress that drives its operating dynamics. We reject its privileges because we see the deceptiveness of the supposed benefits, the damage it inflicts on others and the heavy toll it takes on the Earth.

People experience oppression for many characteristics, such as race, ethnicity, gender, language, ability, class or education. Different combinations of prejudices work differently, so we cannot know another's experience. Prejudice may be blatant or subtle. To succeed in an oppressive society requires that we ignore, deny or repress memories of mistreatment. So identify how you have experienced oppression through prejudice or privilege around a specific characteristic, even if you have learned to ignore it.

To stop prejudice, privilege and oppression we listen to and learn from the experiences of those who are oppressed. With deep humility, we state in public that we want to end oppression, so we ask others to commit to exchanging feedback and discussing when prejudice and privilege arise. When someone raises a question or issue, we say thank you, stop and discuss it. Or we make a note and schedule a time to discuss it.

We treat prejudice as a warning sign. We stop and look for the source in ourselves and in others. First, we make sure there's not an impending threat for anyone. Then, return to the road map. Greet and get to know each other. Discuss agreements of behavior. Affirm one another and get curious. Ask for changes to overcome prejudice, privilege and oppression.

To notice and overcome prejudice, privilege and oppression taxes emotions and energy. We need to heal to do this work. Ask for the good attention of companions. Modulate emotions by telling stories in short segments. Discharge emotion, then discuss these matters with a clear mind. Intersperse groundings, play and rest along with the work. Reprocess memories through art, narrative and retelling. Tempered with these precautionary measures, storytelling and discussion can reduce rigidity and distress patterns and so reduce reenactment of oppressive behaviors.

GROUP ACTIVITY: Speak Out

Say, "Now we will Speak Out." In the large group, turn to a neighbor. Discuss times someone judged or mistreated you or judged or mistreated others yourself, and how that felt. Report to the large group on, "How can you identify and respond when something unfair occurs?" Invite people to think of one of their own characteristics that others often react to in hurtful or unfair ways. [In advanced variation, ask them to choose a couple characteristics and address the effects of their intersection.] Remember, we agreed to speak for ourselves only, not others. Invite them to take turns sitting on a chair or stool at the front and ask:

- What characteristic did you choose?

- *What do you like and dislike about being ___?*
- *What do you like and dislike about others who are ___?*
- *What do you never want to hear said or see done to people who are _?*
- *How can we support you as someone who faces prejudice for being _?*

Reflect on this activity. Reflect on the role of empathy and dialogue in testing our perceptions, and on how we can overcome prejudice when we look for and find transforming power in everyone.

Still, telling stories of violence and trauma has many pitfalls. Dialog can normalize injustice, reinforcing patterns of oppression without challenging and disrupting them. When people repeat themselves, go on and on, get lost or spread emotional contagion, we can reenact or relive events doing great damage to our minds, bodies and spirits. Stay grounded. When necessary, take a break, move, walk, run or do a physical activity.

As we commit to the challenge of correcting myths of oppression, we take good care of ourselves and each other. We speak up and take action against both prejudice and privilege and hold ourselves and others to standards of equality and simplicity.

~

*To reclaim discernment as a
foundation for social organization
offers one of the greatest challenges
and promises of our time.*

~

Chapter 13

⌒

Practice Discernment

Discernment is the human ability to comprehend the inner nature and relationships of things, even when obscure, that leads to keen insight and judgment. The ability to stop and respond to external feedback distinguishes discernment from personal distress or distortion. This exchange of feedback creates an influential social context which improves personal discernment, reveals collective patterns of insight and hones the nature of personal and collective judgment. Communities that rely on mutual discernment seek similar communities to exchange feedback on our collective insights and judgments. Discernment that guides our personal lives and relationships can extend into larger communities, organizations and society.

Discernment can organize collective thinking, decision-making and action. In the past, social movements, religious groups and professionals used discernment to seek solutions to real-life challenges. Yet they often took discernment for granted. It was the way they thought. When asked, they consider it idiosyncratic, not reliable or systematic. But that is not the case. Discernment improves with discipline and systematic attention. The results have a living structure—truth does not conform to social pressure.

A significant rise in population, technology and social complexity requires us to describe this formerly implicit approach. Begin by bringing people together to listen to one another and to stay open to learning from one another. This creates the conditions for arriving at a consensus.

Most people assume consensus means a convergence of opinion. Yet the *Merriam-Webster Dictionary* (2017) noted, "The phrase consensus of opinion, which is not actually redundant ... has been so often claimed to be a redundancy that many writers avoid it. You are safe in using consensus alone when it is clear you mean consensus of opinion, and most writers in fact do so." We may converge on a consensus of things other than opinion, such as a consensus of faith or of love and conscience.

Peace requires everyone, who have various opinions. So, pursuing a consensus of opinion does not a create culture of peace. It creates like-minded, special interest groups or cantankerous, frustrated groups. People of love and conscience do not seek what we prefer, agree with or understand, we seek what rings true. We focus on discerning a consensus of love and conscience, not a consensus of opinion.

After we stop and open, we listen to and learn from one another. At the point of decision-making, we shift our focus away from floating individual contributions to stating our best sense of what rings true. We recognize that only together can we find the universality of a choice or path. We discover the universal by seeing where and how our insights align with one another. When we open to what rings true, we can live into the fruitful, regenerative power of life, individually and collectively.

I often do not agree with the truth. If I were God, it would be different! But we can sense the love and truth of what is real. When we yield into our best sense of what rings true, we often find ourselves at a unanimity or convergence of insight. We do not arrive at this unified common ground by a convergence of opinion or interest or by coincidence. We arrive when we believe a reality exists that unites us and we strive to realize it.

A consensus of conscience leads to a sense of accord, unity and solidarity in sentiment, belief, feeling and action. We use a set of skills and community structures to discern a consensus of conscience. Listen and learn to trust and follow an inner sense of love and conscience. Yield to conscience in personal decision-making and actions. Test insights with others who are engaged in experimenting with love and conscience in daily life. This changes and prepares us for public discernment. Communities test insights to form a societal voice that offers direction to individuals.

This creates a self-referential cycle of discernment. Each part leads to the next: guidance for individuals leads to guidance among companions, among local communities and for society, which then offers guidance back to individuals. Many communities and organizations want to follow their best discernment but fail to engage in the scrutiny and discipline of personal transformation that prepares us for collective transformation. Only when we transform our private lives are we prepared to transform as a people or a society.

To discern a consensus of conscience, we rely on confidence and conviction in transforming power. The moment one recognizes transforming power, one can no longer put particular people above others or particular life form above others. Life is precious and interdependent. The moment we live in accord with transforming power, we no longer crave or aspire to unnecessary or unfair power over others. Life provides for our needs and we work together to meet the needs of everyone.

We each take care of ourselves, pay attention to love and conscience, act in joy and document what we believe and how that changes our lives. Our personal habits and activities affect the entire community. So we support and encourage each other through mutual companion groups.

Many leaders, whether professional, academic or spiritual, have relied on discernment to guide their work. They invest in getting to know the inner qualities of and relationships among people and things to develop keen insight and judgment. They gather and listen to everyone's insights of what is true, consider their sense of what is right and do it. Quakers call it a meeting for business. Indonesians call it *musyawarah*, intellectuals call it a smart advisory group, and tribes call it a council of elders.

Today we live under extensive regulations, often at the expense of getting to know real people or things. The law even requires corporations make decisions that are the most lucrative in the short run, not the wisest in the long run. When we buy from such sources we stifle love, conscience and intelligence. We are reclaiming the practice of discerning a consensus of conscience as a practical approach to organizing.

∿

To reclaim discernment as a foundation for social organization
offers one of the greatest challenges and promises of our time.

∿

In our work, words matter. We face massive work to disentangle violence or oppression from our language and perceptions. For instance, using discernment for organizing differs from managing or administering. Human beings have dominated first through fortresses and armies and later through management and administration. "Manage" comes from putting a horse through the paces of the *manège*, and "administer" comes from being a servant as in "minor" or lesser. "Organize" comes from the root word organ, instrument or tool, a more useful conception for this work.

Form Collective Stories

Group discernment begins by sharing and listening to each other's experiences and perspectives with empathy and discovering a story that encompasses everyone. Most of us have more extensive training and experience in developing our individual opinions than we have in developing collective stories. So it takes time to become good at it.

Picture Sharing (below) allows us time to create collective stories and make choices based on our collective stories. We see how our own story differs from the group's story on the same topic. To discern what rings true for a group does not mean imposing my perspective on the group or agreeing to someone else's. Personal and group choices do not negate each other. Our individual choices and perspectives remain, independent of the group's choice. They may be similar or they may be different, yet resonant. In a consensus of love and conscience, we seek "accord" not unanimity.

When our stories do not resonate, we seek a deeper truth. We engage in this practice because we trust that when we go deeper we will find resonance and strength. For us to make a collective choice, we practice getting to know who the "we" is as the basis from which "we" choose.

GROUP ACTIVITY: *Picture Sharing*

Spread out photographs provided by the facilitator. Invite everyone to choose a picture that represents transforming power to them. Ask them to share their picture and understanding with a partner. When finished, stand, stretch and breathe. Next, read and discuss "Discernment: Things to Notice."

Discernment: Things to Notice

- Create a story for your pair or group.
- A pair or group's choice does not change a person's or a pair's choice.
- Use silence and inquiry when useful.
- Notice differences between:
  … the picture or the story of how it represents transforming power.
  … selecting a picture or forming an identity as a pair or group.
  … giving credit or forming one voice.
  … listening to make one's own point or understanding each other.
- Notice:
  … emotions that arise.
  … when and how you speak or listen.
  … the experience of creating a story together.
  … similarities in personal stories, resonances in collective stories.

Ask each pair to pick a picture that represents transforming power for them as a pair and why. Remember to use silence, inquiry or discharge as you find out "who you are as a pair." The pair will share their picture and story with another pair. Take a stretch break afterward.

If time allows, ask each group of four to practice discerning which picture represents transforming power for them as a group and why. They should form one story, then share their group's picture and story with another group. After a stretch break, reflect on this activity.

The picture I choose for myself remains secondary to my understanding. In a group, the picture we choose remains secondary to our mutual understanding. Meaning, the time we spend shaping each other's perspectives and seeking a collective identity becomes more important than the specific decisions we make. To make choices, we first discover our collective story and understanding of what is true through listening to and learning from each other. Our choices represent our understandings, but our understandings drive our choices, actions and relationships.

In one long-term community, a member often left in the middle of a group discussion. Another member mentioned how much this detracted from and disrupted the sense of group and impaired creating a group understanding on which to base our decisions.

Since we had agreed to speak directly to someone when in dispute, the next time this person left the discussion I followed him. I told him his departure confused us and impaired the group's ability to function. He looked shocked. "But we weren't doing anything," he exclaimed. "We weren't making any decisions, so I thought I wasn't needed. I thought I'd do yard work instead."

It was my turn to look shocked. I explained how decisions became clear once we got to know each person on a matter. Only then could we see how we fit together and the decision would become clear. We could not do

---

Guides to Discernment

Commit to relying on discernment in a community to guide individual and group decisions.

- *Practice with other practitioners.* Test personal discernment with companions engaged in this practice for mutual support.

- *Help each other heal.* Ask for and offer good attention. Listen. Be present, relaxed and nonanxious. Discharge emotion. Focus on letting go of, not reliving, hurts. Notice how the clear thinking emerges.

- *Settle into silence.* Stop regularly. Let go. Sit in silence alone and with others. Sense the transforming power moving throughout life.

- *Seek and integrate feedback.* Ask for and listen to feedback. Take it in and allow it to work on and change you. Let go of what does not apply.

- *Test community discernment after personal discernment.* Cultivate and test personal discernment first. Then experience how collective discernment becomes easier, lighter and clearer.

that without everyone present to share, listen, learn from and change one another and form a "sense of the group." He had never thought of that. He returned with a fresh new presence and became engaged.

People of love and conscience extend this personal experiment into organizing public life based on discernment in voluntary organizations, businesses, schools and institutions. One such community created the Guides to Discernment.

My companion Vicki Cooley said (February 2006), "You told me this practice was something I could only know by doing it over time. That doing it would change me. You were so right! This experience changed me so much in just five years I cannot imagine what it would be like to practice this for ten or fifteen years, let alone decades!"

Colleagues who wrote this practice off as only applicable to religious or volunteer groups, now wish to study how it could apply in their organization. Individuals and small business find the practices demanding, but effective. We would love to hear what your community, organization or business learns from experimenting with discernment for governance!

Tests of Discernment

We trust an insight or practice when it:

- Reflects the flow of life's transforming power, not rigid or static.
- Persists in the silence, stillness and solitude.
- Emerges from and leads to simplicity.
- Appears trivial or impossible, not one's own will or desire.
- Has integrity: honest, authentic and consistent.
- Withstands the discipline of writing.
- Strengthens when companions restate or affirm it.
- Affirmed by community, regional and global gatherings.
- Appears in the texts of other's writings of love and conscience.
- Inspires writing, art, song, news, curriculum, law and court testimony.
- Bears the fruits of love, joy, peace, strength, compassion, beauty, truth, equality and liberty.

Test Discernment

Many traditions use tests of discernment. Among them, feedback and documenting have gotten the least attention. Although offering and receiving feedback requires great empathy and humility and risks misperception, it reaps tremendous results.

PERSONAL PRACTICE: Test Discernment
Post these tests of discernment where you will see them often or put them on a card to remind yourself. Reflect on them with companions and document your experiments with them in your journal.

Reflects the flow of life's transforming power, not rigid or static. Life's transforming power moves and generates life in every moment. The primary test of discernment comes from sensing how transforming power moves within something. The other tests of discernment are variations of this one. Love and conscience are not rigid or static. We do not say "debt is wrong." We say "settle debts promptly." A culture of generosity may lend and borrow to meet changing needs or circumstances, but long-term debt restricts our ability to respond to the realities of life as they change. As with any art, cultivating one's ability to sense how life's transforming power moves at any moment takes practice. The practice comes by continuing to ask, What is my sense of the transforming power in this? And compare our sense with others.

Persists in the silence, stillness and solitude. Sit in silence and open to the infinite and eternal. Stay in that place within yourself, try to extend the edges of that sensation to sense the infinite and eternal that infuses life in every form. Distress often gets narrow, edgy, urgent and agitated, then revolts when we try to stop. It does not tolerate silence. Silence eventually confounds distress. It loses its foothold and control and gives way to inspiration. If you cannot stop and be still, then invest in self-care, release distresses with a companion and get to know yourself. To test discernment, stop and see if an insight or direction persists. Focus on an insight in silence twenty minutes or more per day to see if it dissipates. Even when I am confident, by the fourth or fifth day I may find myself saying, "Wait. It was great! What was it?" No matter how convincing an insight was at the start, turn your attention to the ones that persist in the silence.

Emerges from and leads to simplicity. Simplicity stands apart from the other principles. In workshops, people ask, "Simplicity? I don't want simplicity, I want more, for myself and my children. Why would I want simplicity, let alone strive for it?" Peace requires a reorientation to simplicity, both as an idea and as a criterion for judgment.

～

Simplicity does not abdicate power through austerity or denial,
but derives power through direct relationships
with people and the natural world.

～

For simplicity's sake one may cook one's own food—not to be easier, but to brings us into direct relationship with others and the natural world. When we relate to the source of the ingredients, we develop skills and talents with the natural world. Since discernment relies on our capacity to grasp the inner nature and relationships of things, the more direct experiences we have with others and with nature the more acute our discernment becomes.

Appears trivial or impossible, not one's own will or desire. Insights and direction seldom come packaged to our size. As discussed above in Experiment with Conscience, insights and guidance may sound trifling when wanting more or overwhelming when unprepared. Trivial or impractical insights, if true, bear fruit when we act on them.

We often cannot trust rigid, willful or desirous thoughts. When we become rigid, impatient or willful, we need to tend to emotion to clear interior space that makes us more available in life. Since discernment relies on each other's capacity for valid, sound feedback, we have a deep concern for each person's emotional health, well-being and development. When we open to the movements of life, new insights often come. This increases our confidence in small and large insights or directions when they seem right.

Wealth comes in many tangible forms: time, health, talent, relationships, knowledge, capabilities and natural materials. It comes in many intangible forms as well: joy, peace, beauty, honesty, maturity, integrity, sincerity, love and much more. Direct relationships take on lives of their own beyond our control and tend not to conform to my will or desire. They expand our living wealth and we learn to trust them over our own willfulness or desires.

Has integrity: honest, authentic and consistent. In *The Testimony of Integrity*, Wilmer Cooper (1991) described three facets of integrity.

1. *Honesty* or accuracy, without exaggeration or flights of fancy, undergirds the healthy, prosperous functioning of civil society. The head of security for a clean drinking water project in Jakarta, Indonesia once said, "You know what stands between Jakarta and clean drinking water? Not the technology, the technology's available. Not the money, we have plenty of money. 1,800 honest people … If I could find 1,800 honest people, then twelve million people in Jakarta would have clean drinking water straight from the tap." It hit me. Prosperity in the United States resulted from the extensive honesty of ordinary people. Sure, opportunism, greed and exploitation permeate U.S. history, but people of conscience permeated the history too. It was their conviction that led to U.S. prosperity. In Indonesia, centuries of European colonial occupation disrupted the integrity of traditional systems and left the public treasury bankrupt. This created conditions ripe for corruption. Corruption wreaks havoc on education and public work because they defy direct supervision. When education and public works fail so does integrity in a downward spiral. Civil society prospers from honesty and integrity.

I asked Indonesians why they would work so hard to live in the U.S. when they could go back to Indonesia and have servants wait on them. They reply that "the schools and neighborhoods are so nice and reliable here." In Indonesia, one has to see the stamp affixed to its envelope, otherwise the postal attendant will throw the envelope away and pocket the money. When public systems work well, we take them for granted. We need to recognize, honor and celebrate honesty as the foundation of community wealth. Without honesty, business and society fail from the inside out.

2. *Authenticity*, genuineness and getting to know one's self, others and the natural world informs our ability to act. To become acquainted with our core selves provides a foundation for getting to know others. When we conform to social norms and images to belong, we lose touch with our core selves, others and our ecological home. Authenticity requires great courage. The more rooted in authenticity we become, the more valid and reliable, and the more fruitful our discernment becomes.

3. *Consistency* among belief, word, action and reality draws on honesty and authenticity to assess and align our beliefs, thoughts, words and actions with accuracy. This ability to align the parts of ourselves with the reality of others and the natural world creates the foundation for both learning and integrity. We learn when we can align representations with that which they represent. Through learning we increase our exposure to and interaction with reality. This exposure leads to more learning and deepens our capacity for integrity.

Withstands the discipline of writing. When one commits to experimenting with love and conscience in daily life, one needs a log to keep track of the experiment. A good experiment requires a good log. Mental clarity sometimes evades the test of writing. To get it down on paper, outside oneself, helps integrate and bring the entire mind to bear on the topic. If you dislike keeping a journal, think of it as notes or a log for an experiment. Write the simplest words, phases or sentences to track your experiment. The discipline of writing serves as an important test of articulating what you think you know. Overtime, writing exposes patterns, insights and results. When we write, we bring inward material into an outward form that illuminates, heals and motivates. It allows us to explore our choice of words and expressions, and to compare ours to the historical writings of others. It makes the results of our experiment accessible to others for feedback and accountability and for creating cultures of peace.

Strengthens when companions restate or affirm it. Feedback occurs as we cultivate discernment through conversation and sharing with others. Formal practices can then build on and leverage these informal interactions. People of love and conscience agree to offer and receive feedback. We test our discernment with others in small groups, moving on to larger groups if affirmed. Conscience forms in relation to others and testing conscience with others creates the community it requires.

Test insights or directions yourself before expressing them to others. Listen to your statements restated to you in another person's voice. Ask companions not to elaborate, interpret or improve on your insight when they restate it. Listen with curiosity to where others sense the transforming power is present or absent in your statements. You may experience great shifts at any of these steps. Forget everything you think you know or fear about doing this, just do it.

To know does not create a peaceful culture, we must embody that knowledge and seek the direction that comes with applied insight. Stop once you receive enough new information to continue application.

GROUP ACTIVITY: *Fishbowl Feedback*

Tell the group, "Now we will do Fishbowl Feedback." Ask people to bring statements of insight or direction that have become clear to them. Invite a volunteer willing to share their statement to sit in the center of the circle and invite two to four companions to join them.

1. *The speaker reads their statement and asks the companions to repeat it back in the speaker's words. To hear one's words in another's voice either makes us realize it's not quite right or it produces a sense of, "Yeah, that's it!" If the former, the speaker might restate their meaning to the companions. Clarify, but do not wrestle with it. The companions then restate the clarified statement without interpretation or improvement. If the latter, continue.*

2. *The speaker reads their statement and asks the companions for feedback. The companions say whether they sense transforming power in the entire or a part of the speaker's statement, not what they prefer, agree with or understand. Companions cannot say if it's true, only whether they sense transforming power in it.*

3. *Document the statement or the parts of the statement that the companions affirm. We document not to judge but as information on what others sense for the person's consideration. Include the speaker's name and the companions' names and date.*

4. *After completing this step, ask the group if the statement rings true for anyone else and if so add their names. Record this in your journals. If the statement rings true for the entire group, record it in the group's journal to bring to the whole community for feedback.*

Reflect on this activity.

Do not complicate this activity. Go slow and open to the unanticipated. People often remark that doing this activity feels totally different from thinking about doing it! Companions speak for themselves, not for the speaker. They offer information on their perspectives not judgment. Today, few of us have enough experience of offering good feedback, so resist taking mistakes or awkwardness personally. Another's perspective does not displace yours. So do not take offense, be curious. Everyone does not sense the same thing. Resist trying to be profound or right; this work defies ego. State your sense of the life and power in it and leave it at that, no more no less. Once the group has done two or three examples in the fishbowl, then have each person bring a statement forward to their companion group. Ask the groups to practice exchanging feedback.

GROUP ACTIVITY: Companion Group Feedback

Tell the group, "Now we will do Companion Group Feedback." Take written statements of insight and direction to a companion group to read, hear it stated back and receive feedback. The group focuses on whether they sense the transforming power of life in it. Record the parts the group affirms with the person's name. Then ask if it rings true for anyone else and if so add their names. Ask them to record that in their journals. If the statement rings true for the whole companion group, record it in the companion group's book.

Once I wrote a brief statement to a small group to ask for feedback. We gathered. I read the statement. People asked questions and I responded. One person said she felt baffled. She had come to the group convinced I was wrong, but she admitted that although she did not agree with or understand my statement she could palpably sense the life and power in it. It felt right. She surprised herself when she affirmed that I should go ahead. This was only possible because she committed to practicing discernment herself. If she had relied on her opinion, her assumptions of what was right or her predetermined position, she would not have been open to discernment. Discernment is a living reality, not a notion, idea or preconception.

Affirmed by community, regional and global gatherings. Take statements affirmed by a companion group to the community, and then on to regional and global gatherings if affirmed by the former groups. Publish what each affirms as guidance for individuals. Through these cycles of feedback societal direction emerges organically. In a culture of peace, insights do not belong to us alone. To test, offer feedback and record insights in companion, community, regional and global groups make our insights available to everyone, just as a tree makes its fruit available to everyone.

Appears in the texts of other's writings of love and conscience. Many communities have committed to organizing based on discernment. Our own direct experience becomes the key to grasping other's experiences. Life reproduces, but never replicates. Challenges and solutions display recognizable patterns within the specifics. We should see elements and movements of our stories in the stories of others who have worked to live loving, conscientious lives. We can test our insights and experiences against their historical record and gain new insights and direction. And we should document our historical record, both for the discipline to test our own discernment and to offer material for others to test theirs.

Inspires writing, art, song, news, curriculum, law and court testimony. Articulating one's insights deepens learning, heals wounds, and develops discipline. It also provides enough information for others to offer effective feedback. When we rely on and invest in discernment, not fame or fortune, misjudging comes at a high price. The validity of our discernment matters. Public expression provides a context and opportunities for broader feedback to refine the validity of one's discernment. The public record allows us to spread our learning to other parts of the world and other generations.

Bears the fruits of love, joy, peace, strength, compassion, beauty, truth, equality and liberty. When results of other tests are unclear, the final test is its fruits. Love and conscience prosper. Deceit and violence rob.

The joy and liberty of living in accord with love and conscience exceed imagination. If you are unsure, try it. Experiment with trusting and relying on doing the right thing in your life and enjoy its fruits.

Record Community Discernment

Communities use the same steps and tests of discernment as individuals in companion groups, but have a responsibility to preserve that discernment in public record. Although these practices are adaptable, at the beginning resist impulses to elaborate or adorn them, or strive for something more complex or difficult. Sometimes we find the simplest practices the most difficult.

Communities of love and conscience form from members who experiment with living in accord with love and conscience and test their experiment with companions. They schedule regular gatherings for silence, sharing and discernment as a community.

Gathering for Silence begin when a group gathers and settles into silence. (Review instructions on p. 188.) We stop and let go in mind and body, then stay a short while longer. As thoughts or anxieties intrude, let them go. It takes up to twenty minutes for the body and mind to settle.

Then, open to sense the transforming power of life. Sense it flow within and through you, your heartbeat and breath. Sense their source. Sense everyone's heartbeat and breath, and the transforming power of life within each person. The source that gives forth life teeming through the wind currents, water currents, carbon flows over the planet, drawing in the sunlight, creating the food we eat. Open to whatever name you use for it and that exists beyond name.

In this relaxed, openness listen for insights, directions or ways to settle disputes. If a message emerges, first ask, "Is it for me or for others?" If it's for yourself, open to the implications for your life and the steps to apply it. Make notes in your journal on the insights and directions that come to you. Test it in your own life before talking to others. If it's for others, then stand up and speak out of the silence to share it. Do not explain, elaborate or persuade. Speak in a clear voice, then stop and sit. Take the insights into your everyday actions, interactions or discussions and let them change you. A Gathering for Silence often takes 40 to 60 minutes once or twice a week. Routine works best, but beware of complacency.

Gathering for Sharing may follow a Gathering for Silence or begin with 10 to 20 minutes of silence. If the latter, remind people to stop, let go, open and listen inwardly. (Review instructions on p. 189.) Then read a question or statement, and answer questions of clarification. Settle into silence and reflect on your best sense of what rings true. Speak for yourself not in response to or for others. Leave silence between speakers. Give everyone a chance to speak before speaking again.

An inexperienced group may respond around the circle and pass if they choose. Then at the end return and give anyone who passed a chance to add something if they wish. An experienced group may speak as they are ready, giving everyone a chance to speak before speaking again.

Remind the group to practice good listening and companionship. Stop the mind and body, turn towards the speaker, imagine if what they say were true and open to being changed by it. Stay relaxed and nonanxious in your core, genuine self and listen for what resonates. Pay attention to what rings true. Ignore idiosyncratic distresses, opinions and distractions. Listen for new insights through rounds of sharing to explore what the entire group offers on a topic. When no new comments arise, ask everyone to speak a last time to what they sense rings true for us as a group, a culture or a people.

Open yourself to being changed by what others share. Once insights repeat without new ideas, allow ten minutes to settle into silence to close. A Gathering for Sharing often takes 45 to 75 minutes, but could take a few hours. Long-term communities may schedule them once every two to three months on an important community topic to seek the way forward together. We often gather once a month on the topic: "How is love and conscience prospering our private and public lives?"

As always, take the insights into your everyday actions, interactions or discussions and let them change you. Test insights by writing them in your journal or requesting feedback from your companions. Bring insights affirmed by companions to a Gathering for Discernment.

Gathering for Discernment build on the practices of Gatherings for Silence and Sharing. Open with silence, then test items in this order:

1. Individual's statements affirmed by a companion group.

2. Statements affirmed by an entire companion group.

3. Statements of disputes or direction within the community.

Use the feedback approach the same as companion groups. Listen, restate and record what the group senses is alive with transforming power. Consider if the statement applies to the individual, small group or the whole community. Only after that, seek a consensus of conscience on settlements of disputes within the community or on directions for the community.

GROUP ACTIVITY: *Gathering for Discernment*

"Now we will do a Gathering for Discernment." Read this card, clarify questions and follow the instructions. Reflect on this activity.

Gathering for Discernment

- *Gather* in a circle and settle into silence.

- *Read and speak* to statements one by one:
  1. Personal statements of insight or practice.
  2. Community statements of direction or dispute settlement.
  3. Concerns for sufferings, needs or prosperity.

- *Listen* to where the words come from and restate what you hear.

- *Offer feedback:* "Do I sense transforming power? Does it ring true?"
  If not, let the person reconsider or respond. If so:

- *Record* what they affirm with name(s) in a community book.

- *Ask,* "Is it true for others?" If so, record their names.
  If true for everyone, record it as a community statement.

- *Record* group statements, decisions and resource allocations.

- *Leave silence* after each item and at the end of the gathering.

Apply personal tests of discernment, including testing with companions, before requesting a community's discernment. If the question, encouragement, insight or practice persists and companions affirm it, then write it down to send in advance to the community group.

An individual or companion group brings a statement to the community to ask for feedback on whether the community senses transforming power in it. We do not discuss if we prefer, agree with or understand it, but only whether we sense it rings true. The group speaks on it until no new responses or ideas come forward.

Record the statements or parts of statements affirmed by the community in the community's book. Then ask if it is true for anyone else or for us as a whole community. Do every individual or companion group statement one by one before proceeding to community statements to settle disputes or seek direction. Last, discuss how to tend to sufferings for conscience' sake, meet needs and share prosperity.

Settle into silence to open. Practice letting go of one's strains and stresses and sensing life teeming within and around you, the goodness and capability of each person present and your love for life. Feel alive and valuable. Nothing anyone can say or do can make life any more valuable than it is right now. Sense yourself fall away and sense life's infinite and eternal power. In this place, listen for direction for yourself or society at large. If an insight or direction comes do not speak, but allow it to work within you. If you sense it applies to others or the group, then speak.

Read and speak. Read a simple truth that arose, whether tiny or profound, that your companions affirmed. Resist strategies, plans, shoulds or lists. Bring forward statements of what you have found you need to have or let go of to stay aware of transforming power in your life; what you have learned from experimenting with your daily life; how transforming power has shaped and guided your life; or any practices or directions you have found necessary to preserve peace among us. Read the statement and share your best sense of what rings true. Resist impulses to exaggerate, elevate or infuse emotion for persuasion's sake. Facts may not express the weight of feelings or consequences, but describe the facts, feelings and consequences independent of each other.

Listen. As a person speaks, others practice listening from the heart with relaxed, non-anxious attention, confident in the speaker's goodness and capabilities. Discernment improves the more we know the people and topic. So listen in a quiet, generous, open, patient manner. Do not rush to conclusions. Listen plainly to where the words come from. Let insights or feedback arise from within you. Allow them to surprise you.

Restate. After any clarifications, ask someone to restate the main point to check their perception with the speaker. To bring a statement to the group and hear it read back can dislodge new insight that may take us in a new direction. Without discussion, the person or companion group may realize they need to work on it more. Do not indulge in discussion. If that is enough to continue to work, then accept that they will give it more attention and bring it back later if relevant. If they feel ready to proceed, then ask for feedback.

Offer feedback. When we follow an inward guide to make decisions, we rely on silence and feedback to protect us from the pitfalls of egotism or distress. So we must learn to offer and receive feedback well. Notice that many people have had painful experiences of damaging group judgment. We have little positive experience in giving or receiving feedback. So offer gentle, generative feedback not to judge the speaker, but to share your sense as information for the speaker's use.

The experience of feedback does not resemble our image. To talk about it often increases distress, so dive in and practice, but go slowly, gently. Do several demonstrations before allowing small groups to practice. And remind new groups to take the work seriously.

Offer feedback only if the speaker asks for it. If someone requests feedback, ask yourself, "Do I sense the life and transforming power in their statement? Do I sense it rings true in the speaker?" Speak of what you sense, not whether the person is right or wrong. Name your sense of the presence and movement of transforming power and let go of everything else, no matter how much it hooks you into wanting to respond. At this moment, respond to this one question only: "Do I sense the life and transforming power in their statement?"

Keep it simple and speak for yourself. Do not embellish to manage distresses or fears or speculate on other's emotions. Respect others to speak for themselves and tend their own emotions. Offer what part of the statement you sense rings true, then respect the person to accept it or not as they see fit.

When receiving feedback, take a deep breath and say, "Thank you." Rigidity signals distress, which stems from past personal pain or injustice, not current offenses. Ask for a moment to discharge emotions or to make a note to attend to them later. Then consider the feedback. What if it were true? Let any truth change you, no matter how small or large.

Offer and receive feedback as information, without qualification, defense, persuasion or coddling. Let the information sink in without wrestling with it. If a statement resonates with others in the group, the person should give it more attention before bringing it back to the group.

Record what the group affirms. Record the portions of the statement that the group affirms in a community book with the names of the people who brought that statement forward to the group. Only after that ask, "Is it true for anyone else?" If so, add their names. If true for everyone in the group, record it as a community statement. Do not interpret, improve or change the words. Record only what the group affirms, not the whole discussion. This practice produces a written record of compelling questions, encouragements, insights and practices affirmed by the group, offering guidance for individuals in the community.

Record group decisions. Record what the group affirms. If unanimous, record the sense of unity. When two or three themes or tracks emerge, ask if they resonate. If you sense discord, look for where it comes from, learn from it and seek a deeper unity. If no consensus of conscience emerges, get better acquainted before seeking the source of disharmony or the way forward. If you sense accord, then record the unity or the resonant directions to support each one in concert. Life takes many paths, not a single position. So group decisions may point to a single path or several paths headed in the same direction. Reread the community book of record to remember the guidance and explore its implications for our lives.

Settle into silence to close. End with silence. Appreciate each person, the group and the gift of life.

Attend to Individuals, Community and Society

People of love and conscience test their discernment with one another and seek a consensus of conscience. We each open to guidance in our own unique, organic way and pace. As we experiment with love and conscience within ourselves we gain confidence and conviction. As we exchange feedback, we learn from and change one another. A consensus of conscience emerges from this practice. Short cuts do not get us there.

The community comes to trust discernment over an image, desire, compromise or grand plans. As we align our private and public lives with reality, we reduce stress and increase both results and our joy in life. This then increases our skill and preparation for seeking guidance and settling disputes among us. Seeking consensus without the personal transformation bears no resemblance to engaging in this whole ecology of practice.

Offer feedback to individuals before attending to community concerns. Personal transformation and mutual testing of discernment, transforms individuals and communities, which then transforms how we seek direction and settle disputes. So we experiment with conscience in daily life and exchange feedback first, then seek direction and settle disputes as a community. An individual's statement may inspire a community to action. Take up these implications, then seek collective direction. Be prompt in responding to and settling disputes. Do not let them linger. We may suffer or prosper from actions we take for love and conscience' sake. Historic literature includes examples and resources for addressing the challenges of suffering in people's movements, but far fewer for addressing the challenges once prosperity results from our success. Prosperity, not suffering, often leads to the demise of conscientious people's movements.

As we experiment together, we come to respect each other's abilities to meet life challenges wherever love and conscience lead. We stand by each other in times of suffering when we were part of affirming their path. The terrain of love and conscience may be rugged. It can cause unearned suffering or spectacular prosperity. Either one can distract us from the love and conscience that led to it. A culture of peace requires that we stand by both those who suffer for conscience' sake and those who prosper from it. We cannot rescue each other from the consequences of our actions, but we can offer solidarity along the way. To meet the challenges of prosperity, we agree to commit to use what we need and share the rest. This makes "need" and how to "share" public conversations.

Each time you go through these steps, beware of rigidity and certainty. The closer we come to truth, the more we need to be flexible, curious and open. Sometimes discernment takes a sudden turn in a different direction. Do not fear you were wrong in the past or have become inconsistent or unreliable today. Be honest and genuine.

As companions test individuals' discernment, we cultivate a culture of peace in our affinity group. As communities test companion groups' discernment, we cultivate a culture of peace as a community. As regional and global societies test communities' discernment, we cultivate a culture of peace as a society. As groups, communities and societies document the results of discernment, they offer guidance back to individuals in a self-referential, regenerative cycle of social life that animates a culture of peace.

When this ecology of feedback becomes integrated into our culture, unified insight and action demand much less discussion or effort. Manfred Halpern (2009) points out:

"Our task is not to capture the state, but to build linked communities that can substitute for the bureaucratic, hierarchic powers that be. That will take time, but surely not as many centuries as it took to develop the nation-state. Affinity groups constitute the most basic and most pervasive social tissue of a transforming society. People in small groups help each other most concretely, face to face, with sympathy and understanding to go through the experience of breaking and recreating to enrich each other's lives. They interconnect with other such groups to constitute the nuclei of what we can and need to do together."

An existing community, social or religious group may experiment with this ecology of tools, practices and activities. As we integrate these into our own unique lives and communities, we support each other to:

1. Experiment with transforming power and integrity in daily life.

2. Live into the justice, joy and liberty of conscience in a community.

3. Express and document in public record a culture of peace.

These practices shed our old selves to uncover our core selves. We become shaped and guided by transforming power through compassion, kindness, humility, forgiveness, gentleness and patience, and most of all through love, truth telling and integrity. Novices take awkward steps and make mistakes, but repetition builds familiarity, skill and fluidity. Take small steps together to cultivate a culture of peace.

"Step by Step"

This traditional folk song came from a 19th century mine workers' union document. It captures the persistence of communities of conscience. [Music by Waldemar Hille, sung by Pete Seeger, 1964.]

Step by step the longest march,

can be won, can be won.

Many stones can form an arch,

singly none, singly none.

And by union what we will,

can be accomplished still.

Drops of water turn a mill,

singly none, singly none.

Act on conscience, in joy!

Part IV

~

CREATE CULTURE

Engaging Peaceful Society

Loving people, who practice peace and nonviolence in daily life,
engage in conscientious, discerning communities, and
create cultures of peace for the future well-being of life.

~

We stand together against any form of violence—
prejudice, exploitation, incarceration or war.
Without peace and safe haven, nothing else matters.

~

Chapter 14

⁓

Create

Cultures of Peace

We have identified minimal sets of practices that transform ourselves with love and transform social order with conscience, setting a foundation for a culture of peace. Culture then forms through creative responses to life's challenges. When we feel loved, capable and secure, we cultivate and express collective intelligence and creativity for everyone's welfare. When we feel unloved, incapable and insecure, we act out of rigid distress patterns, leveraging power through deceit, humiliation, cruelty and violence.

People of love and conscience invest in a healthy, creative public culture. We do not believe governance or economy requires violence, corruption, deceit, theft or subjugation. The measure of a culture is in its treatment of women, children and the less advantaged.

Anyone placed in a violent setting long enough shows historic, rigid patterns of trauma and oppression, not cultural creativity. We do not regard these as "culture." War survivors do not choose to be deceitful, untrustworthy, greedy culture. Colonial survivors do not choose to be subservient, submissive, corrupt culture. And oppressors do not choose to be arrogant, dispassionate, controlling culture. These rigid patterns follow universal patterns of collective distress. They inhibit the richness of creative, flexible, cultural responses. They destroy cultural wealth that proliferated before the war, occupation or oppression.

We are learning to name these patterns, which receives an odd mixture of palpable relief and grimacing guilt. On the one hand, people say, "You mean we're not just bad people?" On the other, they wince, "Oops, you caught me!" Naming collective rigid patterns can release their hold on people. This opens a momentary opportunity to change long-standing societal patterns. To make these changes still requires extensive practice.

To my surprise, communities with long histories of violence are quick to embrace this insight. If the group shares a genuine wish for peace and identifies a societal rigid pattern, the simple act of naming it may rob it of power. They welcome explanations of intergenerational trauma and how punishment reenacts the pain and suffering. When they learn to notice, name and discharge individual and collective distress patterns, they can bring good thinking and creativity to establishing a culture of peace.

This chapter offers guidance in four crucial arenas. We speak up for nonviolence and peace. Then, we visit with strangers even enemies, invest in living wealth and express love and conscience to transmit around the world and into the future.

Speak Up for Peace

The preemptive killing in war accumulates wealth to a few, it does not create or protect. As I absorb this truth, I stand up for peace and realize any form of state-sanctioned violence should be illegal.

~

The people of love and conscience find our protection in preserving peace with each other and the Earth, not in violence or war.

~

Peace does not avoid risk, but neither do wars. We do not find security in preemptive violence, intimidation, humiliation or their profiteering. Still, we face threats, but we respond to them through genuine diplomacy, development, justice, law and consequences.

By 2001, the Berlin Wall had come down and the Soviet Block dismantled. The attacks of 9/11 appalled the world. If the U.S. had treated these attacks as a crime, we would have united the world and strengthened international law. But corporate interests moved fast. The U.S. invaded Iraq, even though the perpetrators were Saudi. The government transferred 40 billion U.S. dollars into the hands of a few contractors and created a new array of global enemies to secure a steady flow of public military funds.

War is not only unconscionable, war is deceitful. We cannot justify war as a necessary evil because today war is unnecessary, and therefore immoral. Human violence and destructiveness do not make us safer and in no way compare to the loving, generous, regenerative power of life. As Paul K. Chappell pointed out (Goodman, 2011):

"In the twenty first century war actually makes us less secure. The United States has military bases in about 150 countries; we spend more on war than the rest of the world combined; we have the most powerful military in human history; and we're some of the most terrified people on the planet. War and military occupation haven't made us more secure. They've made us more hated ...."

Many authors support this conclusion with comprehensive works on the decline of warfare (Goldstein, 2011), real steps to end war (Swanson, 2011; Hathaway & Shapiro, 2017) and effectiveness of nonviolent action (Sharp, 1980; Chenoweth, 2011). Explore the Global Nonviolent Action Database and A Force More Powerful on the internet.

To manage the onslaught of issues and information, people shut out collective concerns as a matter of habit. We may or may not work for justice, development, education or relief, as we so choose. But every social activity relies on the freedom of peaceful safe haven. So every one of us shares a responsibility to stand up for peace.

～

We stand together against any form of violence—
prejudice, exploitation, incarceration or war.
Without peace and safe haven, nothing else matters.

～

Safe haven is a primary human need and civic responsibility. This is as natural and essential as a single glass of water, a fresh breath of air or a healthy organic meal. This amazing, beautiful planet needs everyone to stand up for peace.

Destruction occurs in an instant, but creativity can take a lifetime. Weed out prejudice and violence with diligence and discipline. Shift aspirations from rigid and exploitative to creative and expressive powers. As human beings, we are one people on one plot of land, Earth. Enemy-making does not protect us. It endangers the whole planet. We have a responsibility to claim public cultures of peace as the public norm through cooperation and noncooperation guided by love and conscience.

In 1848, members of the Seneca Falls Convention wrote in the Declaration of Sentiments, "Whenever any form of government becomes destructive …, it is the right of those who suffer from it to refuse allegiance to it …." We accept this right as an obligation. Civil disobedience does not threaten society, it protects society.

To call to end war may sound as absurd today as the call to end slavery sounded in its time. We outlawed slavery because it was wrong. Declaring slavery illegal did not end slavery, it made it unacceptable in public life around the globe. While many communities experience violence and deceit as more normal than peace and honesty, families, tribes, religions and communities everywhere teach peace and honesty. Humans inherently recognize them as necessary for a healthy, sustainable society.

An Imam in a formerly closed, militant Sumatran village of refugees was driven by war into a harsh mountainous plateau. He once asked me what I promised to whom so I could come to visit them. I laughed. "Oh no, nothing!" I hesitated, "Well, one thing. I promised I would visit with people who believed peace was possible. And that we would use our best mutual discernment to take steps to preserve peace."

We sat in silence. It was consistent with what he knew of me and our interactions. His decision was firm. He trusted me.

I said, "You and I know it's not that easy. I can only agree with what I can to explain to thousands of people who support me. And they must concur that it's right. You, too, answer to thousands of people. We cannot just do whatever we want. And our decisions must lead to good results."

He smiled, he knew this well.

Before he had only spoken through his lieutenants, but from then on, he spoke directly to me. He received friends traveling with me in his home and introduced us to his family. Our conversations became candid. This was a new experience for a revered religious leader in a guarded, suspicious, war-torn community. He shared genuine concerns and tested solutions. I did so in return. Both of his daughters taught at the preschool we started. He changed as a husband, father and grandfather, and as a top-ranking spiritual advisor and community leader.

He spoke out against violence in a territory rife with jihadist recruitment, "I understand that the U.S. has been terrorized by many terrorists who act in the name of Islam. But it's important I tell you that Islam teaches no one to become a terrorist. They just use the name of Islam. We as Muslims ourselves don't recognize them as Muslims. Islam teaches jihad, that's true. But not jihad that murders people or destroys buildings. Jihad meaning to call people who don't know the natural laws of God to come to know. If they don't want to become Muslims that is their right."

The local village head looked at him terrified, "You'll get yourself killed talking like that!" But truth became the currency he trusted. His personal transformation taught thousands of people in his community and in the region by example. To take responsibility for our culture, we take responsibility for our own actions. We call others to take right action and expect right action as the standard in public life.

We do not normalize violence or deceit or laugh anxiously at jokes about them, or internalize false myths designed to mislead. Speak up for love, conscience and peace. Expect yourself and your families, communities and society to follow the common agreements. Document and share your experiences. What would life be like if we expect this of ourselves and shared our experiences with each other?

Care for and Get to Know Strangers

Oppressors often know nothing of the people they oppress while oppressed people know everything of their oppressors. A lack of interest or curiosity in people or groups often signifies a prejudice against them. Interest and curiosity can break cycles of oppression, cultivate empathy and support compassionate justice. When we interact with people different from ourselves, we discover what's universal. Inversely, confidence in the universal releases us to appreciate and respect differences.

Isaac Penington (1660) warned not to mistake similarity or uniformity for unity. Our similarities do not unite us and our differences do not divide us. It's our judgments about the differences that break the peace and unity. To discover the universal Spirit of Life amidst the differences forms the true ground of love and unity. Reaching beyond differences to personal connections with strangers, even those we consider enemies, can be daunting, but can lead to great insight and healing.

After spending a weekend with a group traveling with Friends Peace Teams, a Javanese refugee exclaimed, "You'll never know how much we've changed. Before you came, we thought of nothing but revenge. If anyone had told me it could be different, I would have looked them in the eye and told them 'You don't know. You have never walked in my shoes.' But now our lives are so different, and so much better. We never think of revenge."

Peace requires the freedom to travel, assemble and speak. When brainstorming "safety," people recovering from war often call out "freedom to travel" first. Yet people with such freedoms seldom think of them. We can learn from and share with others because of these freedoms, and their power can end wars. Travel led to the insights and activities in this book. Assembling prevents violence, isolation and exploitation everywhere. Speaking allows people to document and share what we learn.

When we travel, we take responsibility for interacting with whole communities and sharing their news with our communities back home. These interactions guide and test discernment. They also spread the financial and ecological costs of travel. Everyone who is able should either travel for peace or support someone who does. Isolated, forgotten people return to violence. Hospitality with your neighbors weaves the fabric of global peace. Governments outlaw assembly in war zones because people gathered with confidence and conviction are more powerful than war or oppression. Beware of visiting that comes from the distress of needing to:

- *Earn a sense of value.* When we lose touch with the value of life, including our own, then visiting can reinforce a sense of worthlessness.

- *Rescue others from oppression.* When we use our competence on others to avoid our role in oppression, then visiting can reinforce oppression.

- *Appease a sense of guilt.* When we feel guilty about our life or choices, then visiting can distract us from making difficult, necessary changes.

- *Numb oneself through busy-ness.* When we cannot stand our own feelings, then visiting can further exhaust and numb us.

- *Mask control of others.* When we lack a sense of efficacy and self-control, then visiting can become an effort to control others.

- *Play God oneself.* When we lose confidence in life, then visiting often turns into an effort to exert oneself as a supreme leader.

For people of love and conscience, our motivation to visit matters. We test ourselves and one another to make sure our visiting comes from a need to:

- *Listen to love and conscience.* When we stop and listen, then visiting can instruct and guide us with new ideas and insights.

- *Experience the transforming power of friendship.* When we open to others, then visiting can become empowering.

- *Be available.* When our house and relationships are in order, then visiting makes our time, energy, knowledge and skill available to others.

- *Distribute life's gifts.* When we have what we need, then visiting allows us to share the rest with others.

- *Liberate us from privilege.* When we give up aspirations for unfair and unnecessary power, then visiting gives us access to mutual discernment.

- *Build security through peaceful, caring relationships.* When we realize that peace requires everyone, then visiting allows us to invest in connections and security through goodwill and generosity.

Visiting tests our understandings of mutuality and balance in relationships. We agree to hold ourselves to tests of equality, simplicity and integrity as we visit. We can preserve peace if we bring all our skills to bear. Get to know "the other." Open to friendship and understand the common humanity, expectations and agreements necessary for healthy relationships. Affirm, care for safety, communicate, empathize, cooperate and resist. Discharge emotion, practice resiliency, connect and build confidence and conviction. Value and tend our relationships and open to the unexpected. Listen to others and change based on what we hear. We come to know ourselves better once we know others. Not only does the comparison reveal our commonalities and differences, we fill in the details of each other's stories and make connections.

I stood in a 16-foot flood of murky water from erosion caused by palm oil plantations alongside workers who made two dollars a day or less. They had lost their homes and crops to the flooding. So I know the real costs in people's lives of purchasing cheap, processed food made with palm oil in a U.S. grocery store. Getting to know strangers in ways that challenge misconceptions helps to inform us and contradict our prejudices. Then we can seek sources of misinformation and distress within ourselves to discharge, heal and change. We can take responsibility to rethink what we thought we knew and become curious again.

I often extend invitations for our activities to people I know the least, even people I hesitate to welcome. Look for ways to reach out to farmers, professors, teenagers, senior citizens, prison guards, formerly incarcerated citizens, state troopers, artists, AA members, refugees, activists and health workers of every political party, religion, class, race and age. To develop friendships with people very different from ourselves takes investment. We practice expressing ourselves in loving, honest ways as hosts, guests, cultural workers, teachers, counselors, lawyers, artists, musicians, authors, storytellers or citizens.

Invest in Living Wealth

A culture of peace shifts our perception of wealth to the living wealth of the natural world. My father, Dean Hoover, imprinted on me an immediate awareness of this living wealth. He related directly to people and the natural world with great joy and delight. He told us what he called a new, old story. The story tells how water flows through all life, including our own. We can tell the same story of carbon, albeit at a slower rate.

A New Old Story of One Glass of Water

A single glass of water has more molecules of water than there are glasses of water in the entire world. These molecules are constantly mixing. So when I pour a glass of water out it mixes with the rest of the water in the world quite quickly. At which point, molecules from that glass will be in every other glass of water in the world. So, this glass of water has water that has done everything water has ever done:

• Gone through every plant, animal and person who ever lived.

• Gone down every river, through every factory, power plant and home.

• Been in every inch of every ocean.

Human bodies are over 80 percent water, making people flickering flames of water and rock dancing on the Earth.   ~ *Dean Hoover*

As water, air and carbon flow through every being, the condition of each one of us affects the rest of life. Poisons and pollution anywhere travel across the planet. War and violence anywhere return home over generations. Human beings are too interdependent to be enemies. All living beings share common needs and resources on one common amazing, beautiful planet.

Jean-François Noubel expressed this in a Vow of Wealth (2009):

"I decide to welcome and embrace all the wealth that springs around me, in its material and immaterial forms ... I will invent and master every tool, technology and practice that allows the strict application of this vow, in the context of our epoch and culture."

This reflects a society structured in accord with life's pure, natural existence. Manfred Halpern (2009) described the importance of this:

"Our biosphere, reaching from the depths of the earth and oceans to the outer reaches of the atmosphere, is the physical environment and interaction we share with all other living and inert entities on the earth. We can ignore it, or relate to only fragments of it, or try to dominate it. But our very capacity to breathe, to eat, to have room for being—to live—depends more and more upon our recognizing our responsibilities as partners within this ecology."

Peace depends on creating social structures that treat the natural world with dignity and respect as well as other people.

Arthur Brock's presentation "New Economy, New Wealth" (Prezi. com, 2009) presents an expanded understanding of living wealth. Currencies can represent a variety of values. Monetary currencies represent transactional wealth of parts and products. They ignore systems' properties, performances, interrelationships, evolutionary capacities and the natural materials and processes on which they rely. This living wealth comes to us free in many forms: time, health, talent, relationships, knowledge, capabilities, natural materials, joy, peace and beauty. Human honesty, maturity, integrity, sincerity and love nurture and create more wealth. We exchange these for money, which serves as a proxy for these genuine gifts. We may then use the money in their service or disservice. The former makes us healthy and whole; the latter makes us parasitic and toxic.

This living wealth resides in the simplicity of direct relationships with other people and the natural world. In relationships we give up exclusive control, and trust develops as genuine relationships fulfill needs in ways we never expected. Healthy relationships simplify life and draw our attention towards direct knowledge through living experiences.

Trauma sets in when we become overwhelmed by a sense that needs outstrip resources, and we freeze. But when our attention focuses on the living wealth, teeming within and around us, we realize life's transforming power and grace outstrip any human need. We do not become overwhelmed. The richness of life itself encourages and enlivens us, regardless of the challenges we face.

Commercial culture creates the illusion that financial wealth has ultimate power. We inflate technological value because of its effectiveness in accumulating money. Mediated, commercial relationships disembody the parts and products and turn our attention towards the objects, robbing us of relationships, knowledge and skill. This obscures reliance on living wealth and our love for life with full confidence and conviction, which leads to fear of the natural world and each other. We no longer build trusting relationships with nature and the other human beings inhabiting the Earth.

The Bible teaches distrust of greed as dangerous to the soul. A camel may only go through the "needle-gate" when unladen (Matthew 19:24). Notice, the "love of money" not money itself leads to the root of all evil (1 Timothy 6:7-11). A love for the power claimed to one's person through accumulated financial wealth displaces a love for the power experienced through relationships with others in the rich diversity of life.

When we realize that wealth resides in living relationships, money serves as a proxy for the regenerative gifts of life and we use money in the service of these living relationships. Prudent use of financial wealth in the service of life facilitates, even determines, just and ecologically sustainable social development. Only when we disembody money from its source, it accumulates to itself becoming socially and ecologically erosive.

Toward a Right Relationship with Finance (Haines, et al., 2016) notes how "much of the wealth in the country is not serving the common good." They explain further:

"Those of us who are experiencing hardship may feel ashamed of struggling with debt, seeing it as a personal failing. Feeling isolated and inadequate, we may not speak up. Those of us who are trying to manage savings in an ethically sensitive way may feel uncertain about how best to do it, and uneasy about having opportunities that seem unavailable to others. Feeling separated and insecure, we may not speak out. This entanglement and dependency constrains our imagination and saps our ability to consider and actively work toward alternatives. As we face the implications of continuing in the same direction, we are challenged to imagine new possibilities. We need to develop some very different ways of organizing our economy, and an exit strategy from the current one. The first requires an enormous exercise of the imagination, and lots of experimentation with different forms on a local scale. The second requires both an understanding of the systems that will need to be redesigned and a withdrawal of our loyalties from the old system."

Oddly enough, few people's movements or traditions offer guidance to navigate prosperity once love and conscience prosper. Along with agreements and guidance for struggles for justice, we need agreements and guidance for investments for protecting living wealth, not depleting it. This

Vow of Wealth

I decide to welcome and embrace all the wealth that springs around me, in its material and immaterial forms.

I welcome wealth as what brings us closer to the manifestation of truth, goodness and beauty.

I welcome wealth as life giving life, and life evolving life, for the great alliance between matter and light.

I commit to build meaningful, generative agreements that lead to harmonious and joyful relationships with my human brothers and sisters and with other living beings.

I commit to offer others what they need for the fulfillment of their life.

I commit to welcome what others offer me for the fulfillment of my life.

I commit to nakedness and vulnerability, and to welcome my incompleteness, so I can open myself to receiving from others.

I commit to welcome others' nakedness and vulnerability, and to welcome their incompleteness. There I find the joy of proposing my gifts.

I will not support whatever keeps living beings separated from Wealth.

I will not support ideologies and acts that degrade abundance into artificial scarcity, for that triggers greed and war.

But rather than fighting against these ideologies and acts, I will tap into the infinite creativity that birth gave us. I will become an artist, I will co-create with my fellow brothers and sisters, and new paths will reveal. The future will not come from my reaction, it will come from my creation. Future manifests pure art, it springs up from my presence to the present.

I will invent and master every tool, technology and practice that allows the strict application of this vow, in the context of our epoch and culture.

~ Jean-François Noubel

guidance comes as we allow love and conscience to direct how we spend our time, talents and money. Hence we notice what we need to stay alert to transforming power.

For example, stop consuming corporate media. Do not let corporate interests brainwash your mind, choose what you think or think about. We stop purchasing the same products from the same stores and thus accumulating wealth to the few. Otherwise, wealth accumulates to the mega-rich and robs the entire human species of the resources to live.

Stuckey (1988) from the Monteverde community in Costa Rica suggested establishing replacement over extraction pricing. Today companies base prices on the cost of extraction and they take whatever they want. If we required companies to replace or restore the natural resources they use, destructive, degenerative products would become unaffordable and restorative, regenerative products available.

People of love and conscience discuss what we need, where to get it and how to share the excess with others. We practice speaking to one another, which prepares us to speak in public. Widespread public expression of conviction counteracts gaslighting, a real danger for truth tellers.

Gaslighting. Public manipulation, denial, misdirection or lying to destabilize and delegitimize specific persons or groups of people who speak the truth.

Gaslighting disorients those who experience it and the public. To shift public perception, we must dismantle our admiration for privilege and speak out. Then, we can withdraw support to the public behaviors and structures that protect the abuse of power with impunity and demand new ones.

Express Love and Conscience

Global citizens unite as we transform personal life with love and community life with conscience. But our transformation alone does not create a peaceful society. Investing in living wealth, we must call one another to create cultures of peace. Transformed people and communities let down our guard and expose ourselves to create and document peaceful cultures, a risky business of seeking creative solutions to our human challenges.

When we experiment with conscience in our lives, we recognize things for what they are regardless of how they appear. People ask, "What do you think? Is this right or not?" They often listen because we become reliable witnesses to how transforming power exists and works in the world.

Call on Each Other
to create compassionate, just cultures of peace.

Cultivate Expression
How does my life speak to others?
With whom do I share my suffering and prosperity?
Do I bear witness to insights and practices discovered?
Do I break false, immoral laws and enter objections in public record?

How does my life speak to others? As Edison noted about genius, we experience with peace: it requires one percent inspiration and 99 percent perspiration. To allow the inward life to shape our outward forms, embodying inspiration takes more discipline and courage than one might imagine. Do you sense the sun descending in the evening sky to the horizon? Or do you sense a massive planet under you rolling away from the sun at 1,675 kilometers or just over a thousand miles per hour? Even if you know this fact, do you experience it (Swimme, 1994)? Can you see a star-filled night below you and sense gravity pulling you in to a spinning Earth? Can you stop seeing enemies and see human beings with challenges and joys sharing one planet? It takes a deliberate effort to embody a fact to allow it to alters our worldview.

But embodying insight leads to further insight. As Quaker Caroline Fox attested (1841), "Live up to the light thou hast, and more will be granted thee." We cannot see where a loving, conscientious life will lead, but if we apply the insights gained, we continue to receive more. Whether gradual or abrupt, social progress builds on decades even centuries of experimentation in ordinary lives. When the fabric of our lives possesses what we express, our message is compelling. We too can play our part in the historic trajectory by documenting our efforts for peaceful, nonviolent governance. As we express insights and practices for feedback in discernment, we prepare ourselves for the demanding task of expressing what we discover in the public record.

With whom do I share my suffering and prosperity? Peace and nonviolence does not protect us from suffering. People who struggle for cultures of peace often face undeserved suffering. We stand by each other during times of suffering. We cannot rescue each other, but can stay present wherever love and conscience lead. We look into our persecutors' eyes and wish they could experience the liberty and joy we do. Until you have walked this path, it's difficult to grasp.

Prosperity can sometimes prove more daunting than the suffering. Sustained prosperity leads to hoarding and greed, and eventually to theft and looting. Looters claim credit, overshadowing the culture that produced the prosperity in the first place. We enjoy questioning our own and each other's integrity.

Nanik in Central Java commented, "Friends Peace Teams invites us to learn what is real. To notice how simplicity is actually operating, to the point that what we consume is a matter of simplicity, something that needs serious attention." This practice has led her on an amazing journey at Peace Place Training Center and School in Pati, Central Java.

Once we use what we need, how do we share our prosperity? Help often does not help. Our motives for reaching out matter. Useful sharing occurs within the context of companionship, not when we see others as objects of our "help."

We do not fix one another, but are present to one another. We do not offer answers, but nurture relationships based on trust and forgiveness. We do not take over, but lend a hand and lighten a load. The art of learning how and when to share (or not) takes time, honesty, practice and feedback. Learning ways to share wealth poses a great challenge today.

Do I bear witness to insights and practices discovered? Witnessing serves a few purposes:

1. *Initially, bearing witness changes oneself.* The discipline of expression shapes insight and allows for feedback and maturity.

2. *Eventually, bearing witness creates culture.* The visibility of expression makes unique solutions to human challenges available.

3. *Finally, bearing witness sustains peace.* The public record allows culture to spread to new locations and new generations.

We express experiences, insights and practices in a variety of media such as pamphlets, books, performances, exhibits, concerts, arts and crafts. The visibility allows us to exchange feedback and seek direction for us as a people. Then we extend the results into the curriculum, journalism, peace accords, laws, contracts, protocols and court testimony to guide other individuals in society.

In Aceh, after the war (1976-2005) and the tsunami (2004), personal documentation was an important part of recovery. Those who have documentation of ourselves and our ancestry have a hard time imagining life without it. We have birth certificates, yearbooks, transcripts, licenses, photographs and stories from friends and neighbors. Some people lost their entire families, communities and documentation. There was no record of their existence anywhere. I gained a new appreciation for Frances Harwood's point that "… sharing stories builds a sense of community. It triggers, informs, and gives the psyche the strength, the courage and the connection to take action in the world." Stories, art and literature are as important as food and water to a culture of peace. Thomas McEvilley noted, "The (art) exhibition … is a ritual attempt to bond a community around a self-definition." As we seek to create loving, conscientious communities, we need to engage in art, theatre, discourse and gatherings. These rely on practices of writing, composing, creating, publishing, distributing, disseminating, performing, traveling and speaking.

The convenience and reliability of commercialism and hours spent on electronic screens usurp a creative public life. We must value creative people and creative works. Community sing along, theatre and other cultural events can include everyone, but we need writers, artists, musicians and other creators to invest talent, skill and practice. As Jens Braun points out, until we have music and songs we are not a movement.

Until you have lived in an uneducated, uninformed, lawless, unjust civil society, you cannot imagine its harshness. Citizens must engage in local government, public schools, public news and broadcasting as well as law, justice and enforcement to ensure it reflects peaceful, nonviolent methods. The practices and insights of love and conscience apply in every occupation, but art, education, media and law play a central role. People do as we are trained, so we must codify the practices of peace into the curriculum, journalism, peace accords, laws, contracts, protocols and court testimony.

Curriculum determines what universal skills we pass on and if we develop creative thought, decision-making and action. Paul Chappell began a movement for peace literacy. He views peace not only as a goal, but as a skill set taught and transmitted in ways that integrate well-being into personal, social and political life. For a culture of peace to take root, we embed universal practices and creative expression into a curriculum from infancy through adulthood.

The media determine what information people receive and how they make sense of it. A handful of global, mega-rich individuals control information today, and design that information to accumulate wealth. In the meantime, we lose access to and sight of the needs and creativity of cultures of peace. We come to realize how much we need people of love and conscience to generate media.

Peace accords, laws and contracts along with their enforcement codify insight and guidance for society. When the laws and contracts fail us, we enter our position into court testimony. Whether or not we prevail, our testimony to the world becomes public record. Government regulations, organizational procedures and professional guidelines establish protocols. As citizens, we adhere to these agreements, but we also object to those that no longer support us and insist on new ones.

Do I publicly break rules, regulations or laws that are wrong? We abide by the law to preserve peace. Art, media and law codify moral direction for a people and should document what rings true. Falsehoods (recognizing corporations as persons or corporate charters as contracts) or immorality (allowing war or torture), codified into law, corrupt the written record and destroy a culture of peace. When this occurs, citizens must resist. If negotiation or lobbying fails to repeal such a law, then we have a moral imperative to violate such laws and enter our conscientious or religious objection into public record. This makes moral stands available and visible for viewing by any member of the community.

We must invest in peaceful cultures and speak up for peace and the living wealth of people, communities and the natural world. Then document the questions and guidance we find for ourselves to spread the culture of peace around the world and bear witness to love and conscience in public life.

"If I Had a Hammer"

The Acehnese loved to hear the song, *If I Had a Hammer*, by Lee Hays and Pete Seeger (Ludlow Music, Inc., 1949), probably because, after thirty years of war, the powerful symbols in the song speak to them about overcoming oppression and violence—the hammer as a symbol of manual labor, the bell as a symbol of calling the community to one's aid and the song as a symbol of enduring love and care.

> *Well I got a hammer, and I got a bell,*
> *and I got a song to sing, all over this land.*
> *It's the hammer of Justice. It's the bell of Freedom.*
> *It's the song about Love between my brothers and my sisters,*
> *all over this land.*

Create culture, in joy!

Yes, peace is present …

and possible for us …

when we ….

love life and practice peace;

act on conscience and practice discernment;

and create culture and practice expression

of love and conscience.

~

Simplicity does not abdicate power
through austerity or denial, but
derives power through direct relationships
with people and the natural world.

~

Chapter 15

~

Step Up

An old Cherokee man said to his son, "A fight is going on inside me. It's a terrible fight between two wolves. One is evil, the other is good."

The grandson asked, "Which wolf will win?"

The man replied, "The one I feed."

He paused, then added, "The same fight is going on inside you and inside every other person, too."

The Cherokee Nation (FirstPeople.us) encourages us to:

- Not feed anger, envy, sorrow, regret, greed, arrogance, self-pity, guilt, resentment, inferiority, lies, false pride, superiority or ego.
- Feed joy, peace, love, hope, serenity, humility, kindness, benevolence, empathy, generosity, truth, compassion and faith.

Through daily practice, we come to know the inner nature of things and stand up to greed and deception. Other people come to trust the validity of our word. As we step up, we need to do so on the realistic, strong foundation of personal experience. As we experiment we find that things are not always as they appear.

Historic Steps

During a time of great persecution of in England, many Quakers migrated to the United States in search of a society to live in accord with their conscience. William Penn published *The Great Case of the Liberty of Conscience once more briefly debated and defended to the Supreme Authority of England* (1670). He wrote:

"Toleration has not been more the cry of some than persecution hath been the practice of others … (Relief from our cruel sufferings) has been often promised us, and we as earnestly have expected the performance; but to this time we labor under the unspeakable pressure of nasty prisons, and daily confiscation of our goods, to the apparent ruin of entire families."

They sought a society where they could live in accord with their conscience. I marvel at their faith and insight that love and conscience could govern well, and at their tenacity to suffer imprisonment and apparent ruin of their entire families for that faith. They could look into their persecutors' eyes and say, "I wish you could know the liberty and joy I experience."

Two hundred years later, women and men gathered at the Women's Rights Convention in Seneca Falls, New York. They wrote the Declaration of Sentiments (1848) using the Declaration of Independence as a guide:

"Whenever any form of government becomes destructive, … it is the right of those who suffer from it to refuse allegiance to it … Prudence, indeed, will dictate that governments long established should not be changed for light and transient causes; and accordingly all experience hath shown that mankind are more disposed to suffer, while evils are sufferable, than to right themselves by abolishing the forms to which they are accustomed. … it is their duty to throw off such government, and to provide new guards for their future security."

Inspired by the movement to abolish slavery, Lucretia Mott and Elizabeth Cady Stanton organized this first-ever Women's Rights Convention. They had met at the 1840 World Anti-Slavery Convention in London and worked with Frederick Douglass on equal rights for everyone. In 1865, the United States ratified the Thirteenth Amendment to the Constitution, stating:

> "Neither slavery nor involuntary servitude, except as a punishment for crime whereof the party shall have been duly convicted, shall exist within the United States, or any place subject to their jurisdiction."

Today we are disappointed they accepted slavery in any form. Rather than ridding public life of slavery, acceptance of slavery as a punishment for crime set the stage for the unconscionable mass incarceration of African-Americans. These movements worked towards a culture of peace and documented their efforts in public record. Their confidence and conviction in the transforming power of life, moved them to action. They acted out of a deep sense of faith and of responsibility for their part in society.

In the next century, massive nonviolent people's movements arose to resist abuse of power and oppression. Gandhi's great Salt March in 1930 challenged British colonial rule in India. Martin Luther King's Montgomery bus boycott in 1965 challenged U.S. racial segregation in the U.S.. They offered guidance on how to live loving, conscientious lives and to resist destructive, oppressive abuse of power. They felt a moral obligation to take part in public life and a social responsibility for the outcome.

Over the centuries, people have supported peaceful and just societies. Citizens have led good, hard-working lives through daily diligence. We have cried out for prudent, wise governance to protect ourselves against abuse. Civil rights leader Bob Moses refers to this as an "earned insurgency." We earn the right to stand up against oppression and injustice by: 1) risking real suffering ourselves in the movement, 2) getting knocked down and standing back up again, 3) speaking with moral authority to the powers and 4) calling on people out of concern for humanity (Moses, 2014).

The fire of discipline temper our movements. Participants risk stepping out of the familiar and doing the uncertain. We embody the experience of transforming their lives as we call on others to join us in changing our social agreements and patterns.

Ordinary people led these extraordinary movements. They faced the powers, but they believed truth would have its way. People took a stand in every century. Social improvements are progressive, but are not a given.

Social progress culminates from the number of people who choose the self-discipline to live in accord with love and conscience.

Our time is now. Take a stand on behalf of humanity for our century.

In my lifetime, people have enjoyed the prosperity reaped from historic movements, but no longer remember those formative experiences. Nothing parallels the contemporary daze of consumerism coupled with the control of computer technology and corporate impunity.

Many of us find ourselves paralyzed or unable to grasp the speed, magnitude and dynamics of contemporary violence and oppression or how to extricate ourselves from it. We become complacent and lose touch with the need for insurgency against maleficent oppressive forces. Or we become outraged and lose touch with the need to earn our insurgency. Or we may swing between complacency and outrage.

Lack of experiential, embodied knowledge from disciplined, personal and social transformation causes us either to retreat to small private lives or to strike out against perceived perpetrators. We face an increasing magnitude of corporate greed, religious and political violence and environmental destruction. People lose trust in the nonviolent power of love and conscience and exaggerate the power of violence and rage.

We need to take the next bold step forward for humanity to preserve life on the Earth. We need to experience confidence and conviction in the regenerative, transforming power of life and speak out against the degenerative, deforming power of violence. In 1978 I lived on Pine Ridge Reservation and saw the brutality of the U.S. government and local tribal police towards their own people. Special Weapons And Tactics (SWAT) called native children out of school to watch them run up and down the school building walls on ropes. Then they told the children to go home and tell your parents that if they tried to fight, they would lose. Silo Blackcrow was one of the few living, full-blood Lakota men. He bore rights to the treaties signed by Crazy Horse. The U.S. signed 99-year leases for much of Montana, Nevada and the Dakotas. By U.S. law those territories should have reverted to his control on behalf of the Lakota people. But instead, military helicopters landed at his log cabin. Soldiers ran and rolled on the ground pointing their guns at the house. One man came forward to tell him not go into town to pray for the American Indian Movement (AIM).

In 1980, I saw the U.S. military support Korean General Chun Do Huan after the massacre of civilians at Gwangju, Korea. I provided care to the first people tortured by U.S. sensory-deprivation methods. I watched Koreans' hearts broken when the U.S. supported an illegitimate military dictator over a legitimate elected official when given the chance.

In 2001, U.S. president, Bill Clinton, did not pardon Native American activist Leonard Peltier. FBI agents have testified in court that they fabricated the ballistics and paid off witnesses to convict him because "one of 'them' must pay." He has served a life sentence for official U.S. racism.

In the same year, the United Nations Conference against Racism, Discrimination, Xenophobia and Related Intolerances proposed a resolution to recognize the Trans-Atlantic Slave Trade as a crime against humanity. I cried as U.S., European and Canadian representatives walked out in opposition to this resolution.

I married a man afflicted by multigenerational trauma from the brutality of the U.S.-orchestrated *coup d'état* in Indonesia in 1965. At five years old, he walked out of his preschool to people shooting each other and cars on fire in the streets. When our first daughter turned five, he flew into blind rages. Neither of us understood why or knew how to respond. This atrocity perpetrated by the U.S. well out of sight of American people came back to destroy my family. I have experienced these unfathomable violations of people near and dear. They were not news stories that passed in and out of my awareness. They were my life experiences from my teen years onward.

Now, colonization is on the rise. Colonization is the act of settling in, establishing control and appropriating a territory and its people for one's own use. Today corporations not nations settle into our neighborhoods, take control and appropriate our every activity for their gain. They consider each person wearing their logo to be their marketing force. We work for and buy from corporations and indenture ourselves through debt from them to access their advertised dreams. People end up doing what corporations, not love and conscience, dictate. Corporations take control of law and make it inaccessible to citizens. Citizens no longer invest in constitutions, contracts, covenants and laws to codify our cultural insights and practices.

The time has come for our next historic step to stand up and call for a culture of peace. Make war and public-sanctioned violence illegal. Protest the forced payment of war taxes, refuse to pay war taxes or pay into escrow for the U.S. government once it honors your right to conscientious objection to war. The Nineteenth Amendment retains the rights exercised by the people to the people. And under state law of that time, many conscientious people refused to pay remunerations for armaments or war.

Require integrity and respect for human rights and dignity of life. Refuse to buy from corporations formed on legalized falsehoods and greed. Reduce, reuse, recycle and buy from sources nearest to you. Write contracts for what you expect from your producers and suppliers. Care where the products you buy come from. Find your voice and speak up. Create a society in which you are proud and delighted to live.

Simple Steps

Paul Krafel's *The Upward Spiral* (2008), a slow-moving, gorgeous homemade video, shifted my sense of the power of life. He shows how rainwater accumulates in torrents of run-off. The full force of its power becomes visible as it gashes into the hillsides and erodes the ground to a dusty brown. Any human effort to slow the water or mitigate its destructive power is futile. But Krafel studies where the water pools at the top of the hill before it runs off. He cuts small channels in the hilltop with a hand trowel. Then, when it rains, he goes out to direct the run-off into the small, dispersing channels away from the gullies.

As it rains, the viewer watches the gullies fill in and soften. As the rainwater soaks across the hillside, trees, grasses, flowers, birds and butterflies come back. The full force of the water's power is no longer destructive, it's regenerative. The same volume of water is erosive and destructive even thrilling when accumulated but nurturing and regenerative even soothing when distributed.

An image of the erosive power of torrents of accumulated wealth struck me. I saw how to bring the rich diversity of loving, conscientious communities come back to life on the Earth. We need to take action at the headwaters. We must stop buying the same products from the same companies in the same stores that accumulate wealth into fewer and fewer hands. Spread the wealth to others including those working on the land and producing products and culture. Fund this commitment with time, attention, love and money.

Pledge of Love and Conscience

- Value and enjoy life's intelligent, loving, zestful, capable nature.
- Stay aware of and alert to life's power, beauty and joy.
- Attend to and care for the inward life of love, wisdom and health.
- Release pain and distress, re-evaluate life choices, develop capabilities.
- Experiment with conscience in daily life by action, decision and word.
- Test discernment in silence, integrity and its source, history and fruits.
- Test discernment with companions, community and neighbors.
- Meet everyone's basic needs with generosity, love and conscience.
- Reach out to others, enjoy and explore commonalities and differences.
- Liberate from prejudice and privilege, interrupt cycles of oppression.
- Express experience and experiments with life in the public record.

We invite everyone to commit to peace and nonviolence and exercise the disciplines that these commitments require.

Experiment with love and conscience in daily life. Invest in documenting and expressing the results. Join us in pledging to do so nonviolently and experience the fruits of the justice, joy and liberty that come from societies of love and conscience!

Take simple and historic steps for a new, compelling nonviolent people's movement, borne from the daily diligence of lives grounded in the transforming power of life, love and conscience. Cry out for the end of public-sanctioned violence and earn our right to insurgency.

Pledge of Nonviolence

- Recognize the interconnection of life, and the inescapable congruence between means and ends.
- Learn how nonviolent struggles achieve just causes.
- Refrain from violence in deed, word and thought.
- Oppose systems, not people; win over, do not coerce.
- Abstain from abusive language, threatening gestures and intoxicants.
- Dismantle the unjust and establish the just.
- Keep decorum and self-control and think before reacting.
- Counter violence, without resorting to violence.
- Learn the history, theory and future promise of nonviolence.
- Minimize exposure to commercial media, violence and consumerism.

~ Abbreviated from MettaCenter.org

A movement of love and conscience leads in directions we never imagined nor would have gone by virtue of a strategy or plan. This road map of activities prepares us, but love and conscience only gives us enough guidance for the next step. If you're willing to take it, in private and public life, more insight will follow.

Appendices

~

I.   Volunteer Opportunities

II.   Glossary

III. Learning Activities

IV.   Cooperative Games

V.   Index of Practices and Activities

VI.   References

VII. Quotes

VIII. About the Author

Appendix I

~

Volunteer Opportunities

We recommend and participate in voluntary networks, such as:

- *Local communities of conscience,* set up your own local groups, arrange training and sign the Declaration Against Paying for War (*ConscienceStudio.com*).

- *Power of Goodness* collects illustrated stories of how nonviolence and reconciliation worked, or has inspired others to work for peace (*Power-of-Goodness.info*).

- *Friends Peace Teams in Asia West Pacific,* develop long-term relationships with communities dedicated to peace building, healing and reconciliation (*FriendsPeaceTeams.org*).

- *Conscience & Peace Tax International* directs taxes away from preparation for war towards peace building (*nwtrcc.org or cpti.ws*).

- *Alternatives to Violence Project* practices nonviolence in our lives, homes and communities and facilitates workshops in prisons, schools and communities (*AVP.International*).

- *Re-evaluation Counseling* exchanges counseling to liberate ourselves from experiences of distress and oppression (*RC.org*).

- *12-Step Programs* admit we have no control over addiction, recognize a higher power, examine errors with a sponsor, make amends, learn to live anew and help others (*AA.org*).

- *All Kinds of Play* engages in original, authentic, creative play with people of all ages from young children to seniors (*Playcentre.org.nz*).

Please let us know of others who support societies of love and conscience.

Appendix II

~

Glossary

Affirmation: An accurate statement that identifies and articulates specific authentic goodness and capabilities of a person, place or thing, in a manner that values, upholds, supports, uplifts, encourages, strengthens and defends.

Community of Practice: A group of people, conscious of living together in a shared habitat who share a common practice, in this case living in accord with the transforming power of life.

Companion: A person who exchanges regular good attention with another to cultivate love and conscience, experiment with transforming power in daily life and exchange feedback for discernment.

Confidence: To trust life's transforming power, including one's own goodness, capabilities and faculties of love and conscience, convinced of its unchanging validity and reliability confirmed through personal experience and experimentation.

Conscience: An inner knowledge of right and wrong with an inward drive to do what is right.

Consensus: A convergence of judgment that leads to a sense of accord, unity and solidarity in sentiment, belief, feeling and action.

Conviction: An experience of life's transforming power beyond our own ego, understanding or control accessible when we feel inadequate, fail or become the perpetrator.

Core Self: An experience of one's whole, authentic being, which is good, capable, free of distress and constant, yet can mature with awareness, knowledge and experience.

Culture of Peace: Unique ways we cultivate collective intelligence, capabilities and creativity to respond to the needs and challenges of life in friendly, harmonious, relaxed, nonanxious relationships legally ordered in ways that transmit around the world and into the future.

Developmental Play: Joyful, creative, voluntary, engaging activities to practice and experiment with behaviors and interactions without dread of consequences, strengthening our goodness and capabilities. Through play we generate new uses of resources, ideas, products and purposes and experience intelligence, imagination, growth, adaptation and maturity.

Discernment: The human ability to comprehend the inner nature and relationships of things, especially when obscure, that leads to keen insight and judgment.

Discharge: Physical release of emotion and bodily tension caused by experiences of hurt or pain. Relaxed, nonanxious attention encourages emotional discharge when not interrupted, inhibited or interfered with by sympathy or rebuke.

Distress: Extreme physical or emotional strain that arises when current events restimulate painful memories, interrupting our usual functioning, flexibility and adaptability.

Ecology of Practice: Interdependent practices using their own outputs as inputs in self-referential cycles to generate a specific social environment: individuals shape communities, which shape society, which offers guidance back to individuals.

Equality: Recognition of the unconditional gift of life and equivalent value and dignity of everyone that calls for their fair, just and equal treatment, rights and opportunities to develop inherent capabilities.

Equity: Fair treatment of individuals that accounts for unjust historic and current inequalities and imbalances of power to rectify injustice and restore balance of power.

Experiment: To try out, test and demonstrate relying on transforming power to shape the manner of our lives and guide our decisions and actions that lead to thorough, fundamental, unanticipated changes in our private and public lives.

Friendship: A familiar, direct relationship among two or more people, whether similar or very different from one another, who share loving attention, feelings of goodwill and mutual trust and support.

Gaslighting: Public manipulation, denial, misdirection or lying to destabilize and delegitimize specific persons or groups of people who speak the truth.

Humility: An experience of being brought down to one's core self, grounded in the absolute, incomparable, equal value of every life that leads to a wholehearted, authentic, unpretentious, unassuming manner.

Implications: Conclusions or consequences drawn from an insight that restore integrity.

Integrity: Consistency among beliefs, words, actions and reality: 1) accurate and reliable, 2) authentic and genuine, 3) fruitful and valid.

Internalized Oppression: To believe false denigrating, derogatory messages of oneself. Without an alternate explanation for one's subservient condition, one may subjugate, denigrate or sabotage oneself, people close or similar to oneself or members of one's own group.

Liberation: Freedom from restrictions to thought or behavior, such as war, slavery, incarceration, oppression, exploitation, occupation, domination or rigid social convention by another.

Liberty: Ability to speak and act in accord with one's heart and conscience, free from oppressive restrictions imposed by an authority on one's way of life, behavior, or political or religious views and from the control of others, fate or necessity.

Liberty of Conscience: A freedom and joy experienced when one acts in accord with one's conscience, lifting the distresses of guilt and shame.

Living Wealth: Natural gifts of life such as time, health, talent, conscience, love, beauty, relationships, knowledge, skills, capabilities and natural materials that maintain our strength, promote our well-being and allow human beings to survive and flourish.

Love: An open, tender affection for and sense of the preciousness of another, while free to take leave without ill judgment or retribution.

Nonviolence: Removal of or resistance to a damaging force, humiliation or intimidation and redirection towards peaceful means, often for social benefit.

Oppression: Inhumane and unjust treatment, control, exploitation or invalidation of others that forms distress patterns in individuals and groups either to: 1) give in and be defeated, as if accepting or agreeing to it; 2) become the perpetrator, turning on others, especially younger, weaker people, to escape the role of victim; or 3) become a martyr or rescuer confining others to the roles of victim and perpetrator, maintaining access to privilege by ignoring it.

Peace: Loving, harmonious, relaxed, non-anxious relationships with a sense of tranquility, sincerity and well-being legally ordered free from intentional violence, hostility or war.

Perfect: A state of being fully genuine, as in "perfectly oneself," or of being complete, as in a "perfect whole."

Practice: To perform activities that exercise particular skills to gain or maintain proficiency. To learn from the contrast between experience and what was intended to adjust what we imagine, expect and believe.

Prejudice: A negative, hostile or unfair opinion of another person that causes injury or damage. Prejudice instills social distress patterns that reinforce prejudice, such as bias, bigotry, partiality, intolerance, discrimination, inequality and inequity based on race, sex, age, ability, class or caste.

Preserve Peace: To keep the peace already present and inherent in life by practicing nonviolence, healing human distress patterns and relying on the intrinsic power and generosity of life, not building or making peace of human design.

Principled Friendships: Loving, trusting, supportive relationships among people, who hold each other to universal principles of peace and nonviolence in private and public life.

Privilege: Use of unfair and unnecessary power over others without liability or obligation to others, often afforded legal impunity.

Public Life: A person's open, visible, day-to-day interactions with ordinary adults in a community and attention to community affairs and governance.

Public Record: Documents and information open, available and visible that may be viewed by any member of the community, especially pertaining to the behavior, agreements and governance of the people.

Reconciliation: Restoration of friendly, harmonious relations often through finding common ground or sense of common humanity.

Reconnection: Personal contact that mends a broken bond with another person, type of people, situation, activity or other aspect of life and reestablishes communication, relationship and affinity.

Remembering: Calling to mind an experience with full mental awareness without reliving or reenacting its emotional intensity and being able to interpret its full meaning for one's life and identity.

Resiliency: The ability to withstand, adapt, recover or bounce back relatively quickly and well from difficult or potentially traumatizing situations.

Safety: Establishment of personal stability, inner strength, genuine self-care, emotional regulation and effective self-management, free from addiction, self-harm or injury by others.

Secondary Trauma: A mental state of disorganization that occurs after one hears firsthand accounts of or witnesses traumatic events or cares for traumatized people instilling deep patterns of emotional distress.

Simplicity: Organization of life based on unencumbered, unmediated, direct relationships among people and with the natural world.

Sovereignty of the Natural Person: The supreme power or authority that resides in the people who organize government and entrust the power to govern to it.

Transformation: A thorough, fundamental change in form or appearance through the natural processes of growth and development.

Transforming Power: The palpable living, generative, healing movement of life that changes individuals and situations for the better.

Trauma: A perceived threat that overwhelms usual functioning or adaptability with a sense of terror or helplessness, constricting attention to self-preservation. A mental state of collapse and disorganization that occurs when one cannot resist or flee a perceived threat instilling deep patterns of emotional distress.

Turning Point: A moment when violence feels eminent, but we choose to open to and rely on the creative transforming power of life rather than the destructive power of might, which transforms us, others and our situation for the better.

Violence: Intentional threat or act to hurt, humiliate, denigrate, exploit, damage or kill someone or something, often for personal or political gain.

Visit: To spend time with a person or place for the purpose of mutual interest, goodwill, care and concern.

Appendix III

~

Learning Activities

Play Station Examples

1. Clay and tools (for 4-6 people)

2. Finger paint (2-4)

3. Oobleck (2-4)

4. Water with liquid soap and whisks (2)

5. Newspaper for crushing, ripping, making balls (4)

6. Pencils, crayons, pastels for drawing (4-6)

7. Watercolor, ink and pencil for painting (3-6)

8. 250-unit set of blocks (2)

9. Two sets of Tinkertoys ™ or 1,000 LEGO ™ pieces (4)

10. One package of Set ™ Game (4)

11. Two kick balls and three to six juggling balls (4-6)

12. Beads and strings (2-4)

13. A box of sidewalk chalk (4)

14. 6-12 story books and pillows (2-4)

15. Gardening area and tools (2-4)

16. Cloth and sewing supplies and patterns for simple items (2-4)

17. Repair center, supplies and items needing repair (2-4)

These activities in 17 play stations offer 49-72 places to play. When divided by three people equals enough places for 16 - 24 people to play. See Appendix IV for more activities and materials.

Outdoors Materials

Swings, see-saws, merry-go-rounds, slides and equipment for basketball, soccer, volley ball, ping-pong, badminton, shuffle board, swimming …

Dress-Up Materials

Stove, pans, cooking utensils, small basins, plastic food, plates, spoons, cups, sponges, wipes, shelves, brushes, clothespins, ropes, beds, pillows, blankets, fabrics, mats, hats, capes, clothes, slippers, shoes, sandals, dolls with doll beds, clothes, baby powder, etc and materials for a study desk, gardening, carpentry, sports, crafts, store ...

Additional Play Materials

Sand and/or water tables with plastic animals, dolls, traffic signs, small cars, bark, twigs, grasses, flowers

Hand puppets, dolls and accessories

Paper (large and small)

Pens, pencils, crayons, erasers

Stapler, scissors, tape, rubber cement

Paints with large and small brushes

Water colors with smaller brushes

Toy cars and trucks

Buckets, shovels, hoes, spades, scoops

Mugs, bowls, spoons, bottles of proportional sizes

Balls, of all sorts

Measuring cups, funnels, sieves

Items for sorting and sequencing

Hand pumps, bubbles

Toothbrushes, scrub brushes, sponges

Play dough, puzzles

Construction, gardening, cooking and cleaning supplies

Beads, strings, sewing machines, needles, thread, tweezers

And so much more ...

Many references and resources for excellent learning activities for supporting human development exist.

Appendix IV

~

Cooperative Games

Group Games Standing Everyone Active

Body Percussion. Everyone taps their own body in a rhythm.

Floor Pat. Kneeling on the floor, place your palms down on the floor alternating your hands with those of the two people to each side. Starting with one hand, tap the floor one hand at a time around the circle. Tapping twice reverses the direction.

Hokey Pokey. Sing, "Put your [right hand] in, put your [right hand] out, put your [right hand] in and you shake it all about. You do the Hokey Pokey and you turn yourself around. That's what it's all about! Yeah!" Repeat varying the body part on each round.

Knee Clap. Sitting in a circle with everyone's knees close to one another, everyone at the same time pats both of their own knees twice, then pats one knee to their right and their own right knee twice, then pats one knee to the left and their own left knee twice, then pats both of their own knees twice, then claps their hands, then clicks their fingers with both hands, then everyone raises their hands and feet in the air together and cries, "Wee!"

Morning Stretch. Everyone leads a stretch in turn, while others copy.

My Bonnie. Sing, "My Bonnie lies over the ocean, my Bonnie lies over the sea, my Bonnie lies over the ocean, oh bring back my Bonnie to me. Bring back, bring back, oh bring back my Bonnie to me, to me. Bring back, bring back, oh bring back my Bonnie to me, to me." On every "B" sound, change your position from standing to sitting or vice versa.

Picking Grapes. Everyone stands up, reaches as high as they can to pick grapes, then drops forward at the waist to pick up grapes that dropped.

Rhythm Clap. Everyone in a circle closes their eyes and begins to clap. No more instruction is needed, just give it time to find its own rhythm.

Group Games Sitting

Count 1 - 10. Invite the group to count, one at a time, from one to ten, with no two people speaking at the same time. When two or more people speak at the same time, start again.

Purple Stew. Pointing to one person, sing together: "Hi there _(say their name)_, how do you do?! Fancy meeting you in a purple stew. We're making a purple stew, whip, whip, whip. We're making a purple stew, whip, whip, whip. With purple potatoes and purple tomatoes and YOU in a purple stew." Point to the next person and repeat around the circle.

Unfolding Story. Start a sentence or an idea of a story and let the next person continue, going around the circle several times.

Wake Up in the Forest. Each person selects a forest animal. Go around the circle and have each person name the animal and make the sound. Then, all together, crouch down and begin making the sound softly, increasing the sound as everyone stands.

You're Amazing. Look to the person to your right and say, "You're amazing, because you __ (add a statement that is incredulous, such as "You served a gourmet meal at the summit of Mount Everest")__." The person replies either, "Yes, that's true, I'm amazing because __(repeating the statement exactly)__." or "No, I'm not amazing because of that, but I am amazing because __(make a statement that is amazing and true about oneself)__." Continue around the circle.

Zip, Zap, Boing. Turn your head to the right and say Zip. The person to the right repeats Zip until goes all the way around the circle. Then turn your head to the left and say Zap and that gets passed around the circle. Then show how to look at the sender of either Zip or Zap and without turning your head say Boing to the sender, which reverses the direction around the circle. You may limit each person to three Boings, if necessary. Play Zip, Zap, Boing for awhile. Once the group has the hang of it, look at someone across the circle and say Kerpluie, which sends the lead to someone across the circle, who may say Zip to the right, Zap to the left, Boing to the sender or Kerpluie across the circle.

Group Games: Passing an Activity

Elephant, Bird, Palm Tree. Stand in a circle with one person in the center. The center person points to one person and says "Elephant", "Bird" or "Palm Tree". The person pointed to and the people to their right and left act it out. Elephant: center person makes a trunk and side people form large round ears with their arms. Bird: The center person makes a beak with two hands and the side people raise their arms outward and wave them like wings. Palm Tree: The center person raises their two arms above their head and the side people raise their arms over their heads and wave them high like palm fronds. The center persons continues to point to people and name one of the three until someone makes an error. That person then comes to the center. People make up new ones such as skunk, outhouse, jello or washing machine.

Pass the Face, Dance or Song. Standing in a circle pass a face, dance or song. One person starts and the group copies, then the next person changes it to a different face, song or dance as you go around the circle.

Pass the Hacky Sack or Hot Potato. Standing in a circle kick a Hacky Sack or pass a ball as a hot potato from one person to the next.

Pass the Pulse. Standing in a circle, holding hands, squeeze the hand to your right, passing the pulse around the circle. To reverse squeeze twice.

Pass the Putty. Standing in a circle, hold an imaginary ball of putty in your hands, pantomime working the putty into a gift to hand to the person on your right. The next person repeats around the circle.

Pattern Ball. Standing in a circle, everyone holds up one hand. Toss a ball to someone across the circle, who in turn tosses it to someone across the circle. After receiving the ball, take your hand down until everyone has gotten the ball. Remember who you received the ball from and who you tossed it to. Repeat the pattern adding up to half the number of balls as there are people in the circle. Stop and reverse the pattern. Repeat the pattern with one unusual object going in the reverse.

Whatcha Doin'? In a circle, one person pantomimes an activity. The person to their right says, "Whatcha doin?" The person pantomiming responds with an activity they are NOT doing, and the person asking has to pantomime the activity the person said, not what they are doing. The next person asks, "Whatcha doin'?" and it repeats around the circle.

Group Games Moving

Big Wind Blows. Ask everyone to sit in chairs or stand in a circle. One person stands in the center. The person in the center begins by saying, "The big wind blows for everyone who ..." saying one thing that is true about themselves and that helps others get to know them. Everyone for whom that is true changes places, not returning to their original place or shifting one to the right or left, but going across the circle. Five or more rounds mixes people. When finished ask people to stay in their new seats. Ask them to sit in a new seat each time they return to the circle. Notice how doing this affects the sense of community.

Blanket Game. The group breaks into two, and each half hides behind one side of a blanket held up between the two groups. Each group has one person come forward and sit in front, facing the blanket. On a count of three, drop the blanket and the two facing the blanket race to say the other person's name (can use affirmation name). When one person says the other's name, have them stand and introduce themselves to each other so the whole group can hear. Whichever one said the other person's name first gets that person for their group. Play long enough and everyone ends up on one side!

Bump Tag. Find a pair and link elbows. Two people do not link elbows; one chases the other. The person being chased can be safe by linking elbows with someone. When they do so, the person on the other end of the linked pair becomes the person chased. When a free person gets tapped, the roles reverse and they chase the other person.

Back to Back. Tell everyone to stand back to back with one odd person out. The person out calls out another instruction for people to follow, such as front to front, nose to nose, elbow to elbow, and so on. When people switch to a new partner, the caller joins in leaving a new person out who becomes the next caller.

Car and Driver. In pairs, one person stands behind the other with their hands on the front person's shoulders. The front person is the car and closes their eyes. They are then steered by the driver in the back. (The car will have a better experience if they don't peak!) The person in the back, the driver, directs the movement of the car by walking with their hands on their shoulders. The car and driver will have better experiences if they try to build trust.

Clapping Hot/Cold. Someone leaves the room. The group selects an object. When the person returns, the group claps louder as the person gets closer to the object and softer as the person gets farther away until the person identifies it. People take turns leaving and returning to the room to guess the object.

Crocs and Frogs. Place half sheets of newspaper on the ground to represent lily pads. One person will start and stop clapping, singing or playing music. Another person is the crocodile, and everyone else are frogs. When the sound starts, the frogs swim around. They are not allowed on the lily pads. When the sound stops, the frogs hop on the lily pads. Any frog not on a lily pad or any part of a foot on the ground (off a lily pad), may be captured by a crocodile and then becomes a crocodile. After the music starts again, lift some newsprint off the ground, reducing the available number and size of the lily pads.

Equidistant. Everyone stands in a circle. Silently, without anyone else knowing, each person selects two other people. Ask everyone to raise their hand after they have made their selection. Once every hand is raised, say "Go". Everyone has to move so they are equidistant from the two people they selected. You may reflect on this game.

Here I Sit. Sitting in a circle with one empty seat, a person from either side of the empty seat can move into it and say, "Here I sit." The person beside them moves into the newly emptied seat and says, "In this chair." The person beside them moves into the newly emptied seat and says, "With my friend, __" and then names someone in the circle. Invite them to name the person whose name is hardest for them, or they need to ask their name. That person moves to the empty seat and then repeat the sequence with the seat they vacate.

Houses and Tenants. Two people face each other holding hands over their heads acting as "houses," with a third person in between them acting as a "tenant," and one odd person out. If the odd person out calls out "Houses," the tenants stand still while the houses let go and form new houses over a tenant. If the odd person out calls "Tenants," the houses stand still while the tenants find a new house. If the odd person out calls "Earthquake", both houses and tenants move and change places in any role. The odd person joins in. A new person becomes the odd person.

Howdy, Howdy, Howdy. Sitting in a circle, one person goes around the circle, until they tap one person, who gets up and goes the opposite way around the circle. When the two meet, they face each other, shake hands and say, "Howdy, howdy, howdy." Then they proceed in the same direction they were going originally. Whoever reaches the empty seat first sits down and the other person goes around the circle again and taps someone new.

Human Pretzel. Standing in a circle, everyone makes a fist with their right hand, then reaches across the circle with their left hand to take another fist (right hand), then they hold hands and try to untie the knot without letting go of each others' hands.

Jail Break. Everyone links arms in pairs. Each pair gets a number and stands in a "safe" location in the room. But one pair stands in the center. This pair is not safe, they are "in jail." The center pair calls out three or more numbers and the pairs who hear their number run to find a new safe location. The pair without a "safe" location ends up in jail in the center. They then call out three or more numbers, and so forth. After three or so rounds, tell the group that the pair in jail may also call out Jail Break, then every pair has to run to find a new safe location.

Line Up. Line up in accord with your birthdays without speaking.

Limbo Sticks. Find a lightweight, straight stick (or roll a sheet of flip chart paper on the diagonal) for each group of six people. Two lines of three people each standing facing one another with their index fingers pointing out in front of them alternating their fingers with the person facing them. Hold the stick above their fingers saying, "Everyone's fingers must touch the stick, while the group lowers the stick to the floor." Reflect on this game. The sensation of the mind thinking one thing while the body does something else gives a visceral feeling of how good intentions are not enough. Actions and intentions do not always match. In communities of privilege, the performance anxiety can be so high that the people cannot focus on the experience.

Machine. One person takes a position, repeatedly making a movement and a sound. One by one people add to the person before them with a movement and a sound until everyone has joined the machine.

Ms. Mumbly. Standing in a circle, one person says to the person on their right, "Have you seen Ms. Mumbly?" They reply, "No, but I'll ask my neighbor." The two are not allowed to smile or show their teeth. Then go around the circle.

Pruee. Everyone closes their eyes. Designate one person to be the Pruee, who must stand still, silently. The others walk around the room with their hands out saying "Pruee, pruee." When they meet someone who is silent, they link arms with that person and become part of the Pruee, standing still and silent, until everyone has joined and is silent.

Slo Mo Tag. Each person has a chair or location in the room. One person leaves their seat, tags someone else and tries to return to their original seat before being tagged. If they get back to their seat, then they the new person tags someone else and tries to return to their own original seat. If they get tagged before getting to their seat, the roles reverse and they chase the other person. But do this in slow motion.

Sun and Umbrella. Everyone stands in a circle. Silently, without anyone else knowing, ask each person to select two other people, one to be their sun and one to be their umbrella, and then raise their hands once they have made their selection. Once everyone has raised their hands, say, "Go." Everyone changes their position to keep their umbrella between them and their sun. Once the pattern is established (grouping up, lining up, or running in circles), freeze the group and point out the overall pattern. Come back to the large circle and repeat this three times. Reflect on this game. Notice that these group patterns often get interpreted as "conflict" in a community, but actually are created by the interpersonal dynamics when group members sit with or speak to some people more than others.

Group Songs

Dear Friends. Dear friends, dear friends. Let me tell you how I feel. You have given me such treasures. I love you so.

Let It Go. Let it go, let it out, let it all unravel. Let it free, so it can be, a path on which to travel.

Be Like a Bird. Be like a bird, who halting in her flight, on a limb too slight, feels it give way beneath her, yet sings, sings, knowing she has wings, yet sings, sings, knowing she has wings.

Step-by-Step. Step by step the longest march, can be done, can be done. Many stones can form an arch, singly none, singly none. And in union what we will, can be accomplished still, drops of water turn a mill, singly none, singly none.

Weave, Weave. Weave, weave, weave us together, weave us together in harmony and love.

See also Friendly Classroom for a Small Planet (1977, Priscilla Prutzman, et al and 1998, CCRC) and other cooperative game resources.

Appendix V

~

Personal Practices and Group Activities

Personal Practices

Welcome Each New Day	37
Make Friends	65
Greet People	65
Affirm Self, Others and Life	71
Learn from Mistakes	74
Ask for Permission to Share Other's Stories	74
Ask: Is it Needed? How Can I Share?	77
Adhere to Agreements	79
Ground Oneself in the Present	89
Keep a Log or Journal	102
Plan for Love	102
Plan for Conscience	103
Plan Self-Care Based in Self-Knowledge	113
Use Positive Words	122
Formulate Affirmative Statements	123
Listen Well to Everyone	124
Form Questions	124
Plain Listening	126
Plain Speaking	128
Balance Speaking and Listening	129
Ask: How Does This Affect Me and Others?	132
Choose Who to Finance or Boycott	138
Sit in Silence, Alone and With Others	142
Express Emotion	145
Take Time to Heal	145

Seek the Source of Emotion	146
Do Not Take Other's Emotions Personally	146
Notice and Soften Rigidity	147
Relax the Floor of the Abdomen	153
Learn from and Reintegrate Parts	165
Track Awareness	187
Ask What I Need to Have or to Let Go Of	193
Be Available and Prepared	193
Haudenosaunee Thanksgiving	194
Advice to Self	204
Write Insights and Ask for Feedback	214
Notice the Group as a Real, Living Entity	216
Write a Personal Commitment to Community	216
Write a Personal Commitment to Liberation	234
Test Discernment	250

Group Activities

Expectations for a Culture of Peace	58
Road Map for a Culture of Peace	60
Affirmation Names	66
Big Wind Blows	67
Agreements to Practice	68
Good Listening	69
Read My Face	70
Affirmation in Pairs	71
Core Self	87
Good Companions	90
Stories of Violence	92
Stories of Nonviolence	95
Transforming Power	96
Mandala Interviews	97
Role Plays	99
Personal Commitment	101
Whisper Circle	103
Empty Chair	104

Stand on a Line	*110*
Companion Group Sessions	*114*
Form Ongoing Companion Groups	*116*
Concentric Circles	*126*
I-Messages	*129*
Empathy	*133*
A Problem I Face Right Now Is	*133*
Broken Squares	*135*
Paper Tear	*137*
Stress, Distress and Reactions	*148*
Stories of Trauma	*150*
Speak Up	*154*
Memorial Sculptures	*155*
River of Life	*156*
Cooperative Games	*167*
Play Sessions	*168*
Characteristics	*171*
Greetings	*173*
Clean Up and Classify	*173*
Gathering for Silence	*187*
Gathering for Sharing	*189*
Step into the Circle	*190*
Transforming Power in Hard Times	*191*
List Questions and Encouragements	*193*
Breakthrough	*220*
Call Out Core Selves	*228*
Labels	*229*
Liberation from Oppression	*233*
Concentric Circles on Privilege	*234*
Companion Group on Prejudice and Privilege	*234*
Speak Out	*240*
Picture Sharing	*247*
Fishbowl Feedback	*254*
Companion Group Feedback	*255*
Gathering for Discernment	*259*

Appendix VI

⁓

References

A Force More Powerful (taken March 2018). Documentary series of http://www.aforcemorepowerful.org

Angeles Arrien (1993). The four-fold way: Walking the paths of the warrior, teacher, healer, and visionary. New York: Harper Collins Publishers.

Ashton-Warner, Sylvia (1963). Teacher. New York: A Touchstone Book, Simon and Schuster.

Bell, Tim; Ian H. Witten and Mike Fellows with Sam Jarman (2015). *Computer Science Unplugged!* Online at http://csunplugged.org/books/

Braun, Jens (2010). Safety Fourth. Spark Vol. 41, No. 2. New York: New York Yearly Meeting.

Brock, Arthur (2009). New economy, new wealth. https://prezi.com/xmzld_-wayho/new-economy-new-wealth/

Chenoweth, Erica and Maria Stephan (2011). Why civil resistance works: The strategic logic of nonviolent conflict. New York, NY: Columbia University Press.

Chappell, Paul K. (2013). The art of waging peace: A strategic approach to improving our lives and the world. Westport, CT: Prospecta Press.

Chappell, Paul K. (2012). The end of war: How waging peace can save humanity, our planet, and our future. Norwalk, CT: Easton Press.

Cherokee (taken 2013). Two wolves: A Cherokee legend. http://www.FirstPeople.us/FP-Html-Legends/TwoWolves-Cherokee.html

Connolly, Paul and Jacqueline Hayden (2007). From conflict to peacebuilding: The power of early childhood initiatives. Redmond, WA: World Forum Foundation.

Cooper, Wilmer (1991). The testimony of integrity in the Religious Society of Friends. Wallingford, PA: Pendle Hill Pamphlet #296.

Edwards, Corinne (1995). Love waits on welcome: … and other miracles. Kalamazoo, MI: Steven J. Nash Publishing.

Feldenkrais, Moshe (2009). Awareness through movement: easy-to-do health exercises to improve your posture, vision, imagination, and personal awareness. New York: Harper Collins.

Fellows, Mike (Taken April 2017). Quote taken from https://en.wikipedia. org/wiki/Michael_Fellows#cite_note-15

Figley, Charles R., Ed. (2002). Brief treatments for the traumatized: a project of the Green Cross Foundation. Westport, CT: Greenwood Press.

Fromberg, D. P., Editor (1990). Play issues in early childhood education. Appeared in Continuing issues in early childhood education by C. Seedfeldt (pp. 223-243). Columbus, OH: Merrill.

Fromm, Erich (1947). Man for himself: An inquiry into the psychology of ethics. New York: Rinehart & Company.

Fromm, Erich (1981). On disobedience and other essays. New York: Harper & Row.

Fromm, Erich (2014). Erich Fromm and the conscience. Taken January 2017 http://www.heathwoodpress.com/wp-content/uploads/2014/01/ fromm-conscience.pdf

Gentry, J. Eric (2002). Compassion fatigue: the crucible of transformation. The Journal of Trauma Practice. The Haworth Maltreatment and Trauma Press; The Haworth Press, Inc. Vol. 1, No. 3/4, pp. 37-61.

Gentry, J. Eric (taken January 2017). Private Professional Consultation Materials, from www.compassionunlimited.com

Global Nonviolent Action Database (taken March 2018). See https:// nvdatabase.swarthmore.edu

Goldstein, Joshua S. 2011. Winning the War on War: The Decline of Armed Conflict Worldwide. New York, NY: A Plume Book of Penguin Books.

Goodman, Leslee (April 2011). Fighting with another purpose: veteran Paul Chappell on the need to end war. The Sun Magazine, Issue 424.

Grossman, Dave (2009). On killing: The psychological cost of learning to kill in war and society. New York, NY: Back Bay Books/Little, Brown and Company.

Haines, Pamela (Ed.) with Ed Dreby, David Kane and Charles Blanchard (2016). Toward a right relationship with finance: debt, interest, growth, and security. Quaker Institute for the Future, Focus Book 9.

Halpern, Manfred (1987). Choosing between ways of life and death and between forms of democracy: An archetypal analysis. Alternatives XII, pp. 5-35.

Halpern, Manfred; David Abalos, Editor (2009). Transforming the personal, political, historic and sacred in theory and practice. Scranton, PA: University of Scranton Press.

Halpern, Manfred (Taken January 2017) Quotes on Facebook.com/manfredhalpern Posted by Joshua Halpern on January 28, 2014.

Hathaway, Oona and Scott Shapiro (2017). The Internationalists: How a Radical Plan to Outlaw War Remade the World. New York, NY: Simon and Schuster.

Herman, Judith (2015). Trauma and recovery: The aftermath of violence—from domestic abuse to political terror. New York, NY: Basic Books.

Holmes, Tom (2011). Parts work: An illustrated guide to your inner life. Winged Heart Press: Kalamazoo, MI.

Hoover, Nadine (July 2006). Money as a Proxy for the Gifts of Spirit. Philadelphia, PA: Friends Journal.

Jackins, Harvey (1962). Fundamentals of co-counseling manual,

Johnson, David (2013). A Quaker prayer life. Inner Light Books: San Francisco, CA.

Juilliard v. Greenman (1884). 110 U.S. 421.

Katz, Lilian; Edwards, C.; Gandini, L.; Forman, G., Editors (1993). The hundred languages of children: The Reggio Emilia approach to early childhood education. Norwood, NJ: Ablex Publishing Corporation.

Krafel, Paul (2008). The upward spiral. Video project of HOPE (Hands On Phenomenal Ecology). Cottonwood, CA: Chrysalis Charter School.

Leach, Penelope (2013). Your baby and child. New York: A. A. Knopf.

Levine, Peter (1997). Waking the tiger. Berkeley, CA: North Atlantic Books.

Levine, Peter A. (2005). Healing trauma. Sounds True, Inc.; Boulder, CO.

Lindner, Evelin (2012). A dignity economy: Economy which serves human dignity and preserves our planet. Lake Oswego, OR: World Dignity University Press.

Ma'anit, Adam (Nov. 1, 2007). The guilt complex. New Internationalist Magazine, Issue 406. http://newint.org/features/special/2007/11/01/special_feature/#sthash.fm4ot14W.dpuf

Montessori, Maria (1914). Dr. Montessori's own handbook. Brooklyn, NY: Frederick A. Stokes Company. A public domain book.

Moses, Bob (January 26, 2014). An earned insurgency: Bob Moses on reality asserts itself. Interview transcript. Washington, DC: The Real News Network.

Maliguzzi, Loris (taken January 2017). 100 languages, from www.childrenfirstschool.org Italy: Reggio Emilia Preschools

Morris, Ruth (1998). Penal abolition: a practical manual on penal abolition. Toronto, ON: Canadian Scholars' Press Inc.

Noubel, Jean-François (2009; taken January 2017). Vow of Wealth, from http://noubel.com/vow/

Parten, Mildred (1929). An analysis of social participation, leadership, and other factors in preschool play groups. Doctoral dissertation at the University of Minnesota.

Penn, William (1670). Great case of liberty of conscience once more briefly debated and defended. Rare Reprints. Whitefish, MT: Kessinger Publishing.

Piaget, Jean (1972). Some aspects of operations. Appeared in: Play and development: A symposium with contributions by Jean Piaget, Peter H. Wolff and Others, edited by Maria W. Piers. New York: W. W. Norton & Company.

Prutzman, Priscilla et al (1998). Friendly Classroom for a small planet. Nyack, NY: Children's Creative Response to Conflict.

Schaaf, Gregory with a Foreword by Jake Swamp (2004). The U.S. Constitution and the Great Law of Peace: A Comparison of Two Founding Documents. Santa Fe, NM: Center for Indigenous Arts & Cultures Press.

Sharp, Gene (1980). Making the abolition of war a realistic goal. Cambridge, MA: The Albert Einstein Institute.

Sheeran, Michael (1996). Beyond majority rule: Voteless decisions in the Religious Society of Friends. Philadelphia, PA: Philadelphia Yearly Meeting of Religious Society of Friends.

Smith, Gar (2017). The War and Environment Reader. Charlottesville, VA: Just World Books.

Stuckey, Joseph (1988). Kicking the subsidized habit. San Diego, CA: National University.

Swanson, David (2016). War is a lie. Second Edition. Charlottesville, VA: Just World Books.

Swanson, David (2011). When the world outlawed war. Charlottesville, VA: eBookIt.com

Swimme, Brian and Thomas Berry (1994). The universe story: From the primordial flaring forth to the Ecozoic era—A celebration of the unfolding of the cosmos. San Francisco, CA: Harper Collins.

van der Kolk, Bessel A. (2014). The body keeps the score: brain, mind and body in the healing of trauma. New York: Penguin Books.

van der Kolk, Bessel A. and Alexander C. McFarlane and Lars Weisaeth (2006). Trauma stress: The effects of overwhelming experience on mind, body, and society. The Guilford Press: New York and London.

Williamson, Marianne (1992). A return to love: Reflections on the principles of a course in miracles. New York: Harper Collins. Chapter 7, Section 3, pp. 190-191.

Women's Rights Convention at Seneca Falls (1848). Declaration of sentiments. Seneca Falls, NY on July 19-20, 1848.

Woolman, John (1774). A plea for the poor. New York: Collection of the New York Public Library.

Woolman, John; Phillips P. Moulton Ed. (1971). The journal and major essays of John Woolman (1720-1772). Richmond, IN: Friends United Press.

Vygotsky, L. S. and Michael Cole with the President and Fellows of Harvard College (1978). Mind in society: The development of higher psychological processes. Cambridge, MA: Harvard University Press.

Appendix VII

~

Quotes

War is an unnecessary evil. We know how to create cultures of peace.

*To love those called enemies and become friends,
so begins the work of peace.*

Love is the first motion. ~ John Woolman, 1720 - 1772

*We preserve peace by living in accord
with life's transforming power.*

*We have one commitment:
to practice opening to and relying on life's transforming power
to guide our private and public lives.*

*With humility, shortcomings lead to conviction and compassion.
Without humility, shortcomings lead to humiliation and violence.*

*When adults playfully explore our worlds, especially with young children,
we can heal and learn in ways that create cultures of peace.*

*Aware of life's regenerative resources that exceed human need,
we face our human condition without freezing,
open to transforming power.*

*We can create peaceful, healthy, sustainable societies with the
liberty to act in accord with love and conscience and
the justice to hold one another to standards of fairness.*

*To reclaim discernment as a foundation for social organization
offers one of the greatest challenges and promises of our time.*

As long as we can stop and stay open to external feedback,
we can trust our inner sense of right action.

The people of love and conscience
find our protection in preserving peace,
not in making war, with each other and the Earth.

We stand together against any form of violence
—prejudice, exploitation, incarceration or war.
Without peace and safe haven, nothing else matters.

A full experience of life's transforming power balances strength with
kindness, integrity with love and justice with compassion.

Love without truth deceives; truth without love hurts.
Truth doesn't triumph, truth guides and prospers.
Love doesn't win, love persists and endures.

Simplicity does not abdicate power
through austerity or denial, but
derives power through direct relationships
with people and the natural world.

Cultures of peace require the hard work of
vigilant, public resistance to the dynamics of oppression.

I expect to pass through this world but once;
any good thing therefore I can do,
or any kindness that I can show to
any fellow creature, let me do it now;
let me not defer or neglect it,
for I shall not pass this way again."
~ Stephen Grellet, Quaker c. 1800

Appendix VIII

~

About the Author

Nadine Clare Hoover is a conscientious objector to war and advocate for peace, with the Earth and with each other. She has lived in the United States and Indonesia since 1980. Nadine offers training and publications through Conscience Studio, coordinates Friends Peace Teams in Asia West Pacific, a Quaker network of worldwide peace workers, and directs the Power of Goodness, a global story pool on nonviolence and reconciliation. She also counsels war tax resisters through the National War Tax Resistance Coordinating Council.

Growing up among Quakers on a farm in western New York State gave her a holistic, resourceful approach to life. In the 1970s she attended many peace rallies, work camps, trainings and retreats. Nadine graduated from George School in 1978 and began a lifelong journey as a Re-evaluation co-counselor and Alternatives to Violence Project (AVP) facilitator.

A graduate of Friends World College, Nadine lived on Pine Ridge Reservation in South Dakota. Then she moved to Japan, South Korea and Indonesia researching the effects of economic world systems on social formation. She married an Indonesian and had two children, Fenna and Sarah Mandolang. Nadine completed a doctoral degree from Florida State University in International Development and Education in 1988 and for two decades consulted with the State of Florida, USAID, UNDP, Asia Development Bank, World Bank and Indonesian Ministries of Education and Religious Affairs. After establishing Al-Falah School in Jakarta, she served as the lead consultant to establish the Indonesian Directorate of Early Childhood Education.

Nadine served as Secretary of Southeastern Yearly Meeting, managed the Friends General Conference Bookstore and is a recorded Quaker minister with New York Yearly Meeting. From 2000 to 2007, she supported Peace Brigades International in Indonesia, and Friends Peace Teams in Asia West Pacific since then. Fluent in Indonesian, Nadine brings together people from various Southeast Asian tribes and religions, both victims and perpetrators, who are often from rough, militant communities, to work towards recovery, reconciliation and peace.

In this grassroots peace work, she has identified an ecology of practices that have helped people recover from extreme violence and preserve cultures of peace. She designs, publishes and facilitates trainings on empowerment, resiliency, play, conscience, liberation and discernment. The workshops use experiential, skill-building activities, not lectures. She accepts a wide range of ages and backgrounds, from teens to adults, and adapts for children and toddlers. Participants report significant personal and social transformations in a wide variety of settings, from preschool to college, communities to refugee camps. Nadine works to make state-sanctioned violence illegal, remove falsehoods from the law, and create cultures of peace.

ConscienceStudio.com and CourageousGifts.com
Power-of-Goodness.info and FriendsPeaceTeams.org
AVP.International, RC.org, Quaker.org
NWTRCC.org, centeronconscience.org

CPSIA information can be obtained
at www.ICGtesting.com
Printed in the USA
FFHW02n0912251018
48925503-53162FF

9 780982 849224